Agent-Based Social Systems
Volume 1

Series Editor: Hiroshi Deguchi, Yokohama, Japan

ABSS — Agent-Based Social Systems

This series is intended to further the creation of the science of agent-based social systems, a field that is establishing itself as a transdisciplinary and cross-cultural science. The series will cover a broad spectrum of sciences, such as social systems theory, sociology, business administration, management information science, organization science, computational mathematical organization theory, economics, evolutionary economics, international political science, jurisprudence, policy science, socioinformation studies, cognitive science, artificial intelligence, complex adaptive systems theory, philosophy of science, and other related disciplines.

The series will provide a systematic study of the various new cross-cultural arenas of the human sciences. Such an approach has been successfully tried several times in the history of the modern sciences of humanities and systems and has helped to create such important conceptual frameworks and theories as cybernetics, synergetics, general systems theory, cognitive science, and complex adaptive systems.

We want to create a conceptual framework and design theory for socioeconomic systems of the twenty-first century in a cross-cultural and transdisciplinary context. For this purpose we plan to take an agent-based approach. Developed over the last decade, agent-based modeling is a new trend within the social sciences and is a child of the modern sciences of humanities and systems. In this series the term "agent-based" is used across a broad spectrum that includes not only the classical usage of the normative and rational agent but also an interpretive and subjective agent. We seek the antinomy of the macro and micro, subjective and rational, functional and structural, bottom-up and top-down, global and local, and structure and agency within the social sciences. Agent-based modeling includes both sides of these opposites. "Agent" is our grounding for modeling; simulation, theory, and real-world grounding are also required.

As an approach, agent-based simulation is an important tool for the new experimental fields of the social sciences; it can be used to provide explanations and decision support for real-world problems, and its theories include both conceptual and mathematical ones. A conceptual approach is vital for creating new frameworks of the worldview, and the mathematical approach is essential to clarify the logical structure of any new framework or model. Exploration of several different ways of real-world grounding is required for this approach. Other issues to be considered in the series include the systems design of this century's global and local socioeconomic systems.

T. Terano, H. Kita, T. Kaneda,
K. Arai, H. Deguchi (Eds.)

Agent-Based Simulation: From Modeling Methodologies to Real-World Applications

Post-Proceedings of the Third International Workshop on Agent-Based Approaches in Economic and Social Complex Systems 2004

With 121 Figures

Springer

Takao Terano, Ph.D.
Professor, Interdisciplinary Graduate School of Science and Engineering
Tokyo Institute of Technology
4259 Nagatsuta-cho, Midori-ku, Yokohama 226-8502, Japan

Hajime Kita, Dr. Eng.
Professor, Academic Center for Computing and Media Studies
Kyoto University
Yoshida-Nihonmatsu-cho, Sakyo-ku, Kyoto 606-8501, Japan

Toshiyuki Kaneda, Dr.Eng.
Associate Professor, Graduate School of Engineering
Nagoya Institute of Technology
Gokiso, Showa-ku, Nagoya 466-8555, Japan

Kiyoshi Arai, Dr. Eng.
Professor, Faculty of Social Systems Science
Chiba Institute of Technology
2-17-1 Tsudanuma, Narashino, Chiba 275-0016, Japan

Hiroshi Deguchi, Ph.D.
Professor, Interdisciplinary Graduate School of Science and Engineering
Tokyo Institute of Technology
4259 Nagatsuta-cho, Midori-ku, Yokohama 226-8502, Japan

Library of Congress Control Number: 2005929336

ISSN 1861-0803
ISBN 4-431-26592-9 Springer-Verlag Tokyo Berlin Heidelberg New York

Springer is a part of Springer Science+Business Media
springeronline.com

Printed in Japan

Typesetting: Camera-ready by the editors and authors
Printing and binding: Hicom, Japan

Printed on acid-free paper
Series number: 7188

Preface

An agent-based approach to computer simulation of economic and social systems provides social sciences with tools for experimental research. In a series of workshops on Agent-Based Approaches in Economic and Social Complex Systems (AESCS), groundbreaking studies of complex economic and social phenomena using computational approaches are being presented and discussed. This volume contains papers selected from presentations at the AESCS'04, which was held at Kyoto University, Japan, May 27-29, 2004. The workshop was the third in a series of Pacific Rim activities in interdisciplinary areas of social and computational sciences, the first and the second workshops having been held in Shimane, Japan, May 21-22, 2001, and Tokyo, Japan, August 16, 2002, respectively.

The objective of AESCS workshops is to foster the formation of an active multidisciplinary community on multiagent computational economics, organizational science, social dynamics, and complex adaptive systems. AESCS brings together researchers and practitioners from diverse fields, such as computer science, economics, physics, sociology, psychology, and complex system theory, in order to understand emergent and collective phenomena in economic, organizational, and social systems. AESCS also provides an opportunity for discussion of the effectiveness and limitations of computational models and methods in social sciences.

The third AESCS workshop focused on the importance of computational models and software for simulation, their combination with gaming simulation played by humans, usage of agent-based gaming simulation in education, and applications to practical problems. We also had two invited talks and two organized sessions. The first invited talk was "Crisis Management Simulation in Digital Cities," by Professor Toru Ishida, Kyoto University, and the second was "Making a Thin Market Intentionally: A Challenge of the U-MART Project," by Professor Yoshinori Shiozawa, Osaka City University. Organized sessions were "Education/Gaming," organized by Kiyoshi Arai and Toshiyuki Kaneda, and "U-Mart: An Artificial Market Testbed," organized by Hajime Kita.

The chapters of this book originated as papers selected from those presented at AESCS'04. In the workshop, 39 papers contributed from 11 countries were presented, and from them, we selected 21 papers for the post-proceedings. All papers were reviewed by at least two peer reviewers, and reviewers' comments were carefully considered by the program committee members for fairness and consistency in the selection process.

The selected papers are divided into the following topics.

As methodological contributions, Tanuma et al., Ashburn et al., and Callahan discuss computational models and modeling methodologies. Treatment of dilemmas and cooperation, which is also an important fundamental issue in the agent-based approach, are discussed by Yamashita et al., Yamamoto et al., and Marchiori and Warglien. Combination of agent-based approaches and gaming simulation, a promising study topic, is discussed by Mizuta and Yamagata, Taniguchi et al., and Suematsu et al.

Agent-based approaches are applicable to various social problems. Contributions by Takahashi and Goto, Suganuma et al., and Meyer et al. are applications of these approaches to organizational issues. Application to markets and other issues in economics is discussed by Chen and Huang, Takahashi et al., Koyama et al., Andrews et al., Heppenstall et al., and Kaihara and Fujii. Further, contributions by Comfort et al., Kaneda et al., and Zaima are applications to public management issues such as disaster, transportation, and environment.

Publication of this volume is partly supported by the 21st-Century COE Program "Creation of Agent-Based Social Systems Sciences (ABSSS)" of the Tokyo Institute of Technology. We also acknowledge the support and encouragement of many people who helped us to hold the workshop and prepare this volume. We also thank Prof. Akira Namatame of the National Defense Academy, Prof. Hiroyuki Matsui of Kyoto University, Ms. Yayoi Mizuno of the Nagoya Institute of Technology, and Dr. Yusuke Koyama of the Tokyo Institute of Technology for their assistance in managing the workshop, and Mr. Akikuni Sato and Ms. Asami Kawakami of Kyoto University for their help in typesetting the volume. In addition, we thank the staff of Springer-Verlag, Tokyo, for their assistance in publishing this volume. We hope that those who are interested in recent progress in agent-based simulation in the social sciences will find the book attractive and useful.

Takao Terano AESCS'04 General Chair
Hajime Kita Co-Organizer
Toshiyuki Kaneda Co-Organizer
Kiyoshi Arai Co-Organizer
Hiroshi Deguchi Publication Chair

Conference Committee

Workshop Chair

Takao Terano, Tokyo Institute of Technology, Japan

Workshop Organizers

Hajime Kita, Kyoto University, Japan
Toshiyuki Kaneda, Nagoya Institute of Technology, Japan
Kiyoshi Arai, Chiba Institute of Technology, Japan

Program Committee

Robert Axtell, Brookings Institution, U.S.A.
Shu-Heng Chen, National Chengchi University, Taiwan, ROC
Sung-Bae Cho, Yonsei University, Korea
Claudio Cioffi-Revilla, George Mason University, U.S.A.
Yoshi Fujiwara, ATR Network Informatics Laboratories, Japan
Toshiya Kaihara, Kobe University, Japan
Thomas Lux, Kiel University, Germany
Hideyuki Mizuta, IBM JAPAN, Japan
Yoshiteru Nakamori, JAIST, Japan
Akira Namatame, National Defense Academy, Japan
Keiji Suzuki, Future University-Hakodate, Japan
Keiki Takadama, Tokyo Institute of Technology, Japan
Shingo Takahashi, Waseda University, Japan
David W. K. Yeung, Hong Kong Baptist University and St. Petersburg State University, China
Makoto Yokoo, Kyushu University, Japan

Publication Chair

Hiroshi Deguchi, Tokyo Institute of Technology, Japan

Contents

SOARS: Spot Oriented Agent Role Simulator – Design and Implementation

Hideki Tanuma[1], Hiroshi Deguchi[2] and Tetsuo Shimizu[1]

[1]Institute of Medical Science, University of Tokyo, 4-6-1 Shirokane-dai, Minato-ku, Tokyo 108-8639, Japan
[2]Department of Computational Intelligence and Systems Science, Tokyo Institute of Technology, 4259 Nagatsuta-cho, Midori-ku, Yokohama, Kanagawa 226-8503, Japan

Summary. In this paper we present the design of an agent-based simulation language called SOARS (Spot Oriented Agent Role Simulator). SOARS is designed to describe agent activities according to roles within social and organizational structures. Role taking processes can be described in our language. SOARS is also designed according to the theory of agent-based dynamic systems. Decomposition of multi-agent interaction is one of the most important characteristics of our framework. The notion of spot and stage gives spacial and temporal decomposition of interaction among agents. We apply our multi-agent framework to policy analysis of emerging virus protection in the case of SARS.

In the latter part of the paper, we explain the implementation of the SOARS simulation platform. The simulation engine and related built-in functional objects are implemented in Java language. An application user can describe the agent-based simulation model only by writing script in SOARS script language without knowledge of Java classes. If needed, the user can customize the function of SOARS by implementing additional Java classes. The easiest way to customize is to develop special functional objects, and the SOARS platform will be the interface between such customized objects.

Key Words. Spot, Agent-Based Social Systems Science, SARS, SOARS, Agent-Based Dynamic System

1 Introduction

We often use simulation analysis in agent-based modeling. These days Ascape[1] by The Brookings Institution and Repast[2] by the University of Chicago and Argonne National Laboratory are becoming popular. In the history of agent-based modeling, Swarm by the Santa Fe research institute has been very influential.

---

[1] http://www.brook.edu/es/dynamics/models/ascape/default.htm

[2] http://repast.sourceforge.net/

Repast is called the social science version of Swarm. In Japan, MAS (Multi-Agent Simulator)[3] has been developed under the influence of Swarm for educational purposes. Repast, Ascape and MAS are descendants of Swarm which has been developed nor for social sciences but for cellar-type simulation.

In this paper we introduce a new type of modeling framework for the agent-based dynamic system (ABDS) and develop an agent-based simulation language called SOARS (Spot Oriented Action Role Simulator).

SOARS has been developed for infection protection against SARS in hospitals. In hospitals, there are large numbers of agents: doctors, nurses, patients, radiographers, inspectors, office workers and volunteers, who move about among many spots.

We have developed a framework for agent-based modeling not only for simulation but also for theoretical analysis of agent-based dynamic systems. We especially focus on parallel and sequential decomposition of multi-agent processes. Lisp has provided a primitive language for AI. In the same way, we try to provide a primitive language for agent-based modeling depending on the agent-based dynamic systems theory now being developed.

2 Basic Design of SOARS

(1) Three Layer Modeling Framework

SOARS is a modeling framework with three layers. On the bottom layer SOARS is written in Java. We use Java for programming the extension of SOARS, called information objects or resolvers under the regulated interface. On the middle layer of SOARS we provide an original scripting language to describe role behavior of agents. On the top layer of SOARS we provide a model builder with GUI for developing a SOARS application model. A power user can use Java for extending the model components of SOARS. On the bottom layer we can add various types of new functions on agents and spots of SOARS as objects or resolvers by programming in Java. On the middle layer the SOARS scripting language is provided for modeling agent roles. On the top layer the GUI-based model builder helps a user who has enough domain knowledge but lacks appropriate programming skill.

(2) Static Structure of SOARS: Agent, Spot, Resolver, State object

In SOARS we introduce several notions for modeling an agent-based dynamic system; they are the agent, the spot, the resolver, information and the physical object.

---

[3] http://www2.kke.co.jp/mas_e/MASCommunity1.html

The spot is an abstract notion of a localized field or a place where agents interact with each other. Agents move among spots. Each spot and agent has a state that is described by equipped objects. Spots are used to represent not only a concrete physical place but also an abstract place for interaction such as a committee. In the following example we use concrete spots in a hospital, such as a consultation room or a hospital ward. A spot is equipped with a state object that is called an information object or a physical object. A spot is also equipped with a special type of object called a resolver. A resolver on a spot describes an interaction among agents.

In the following example of a hospital infection model, a group of agents consists of office staff, cashier staff, reception staff, nurse, doctor, examiner, visitor, and patient. A group of spots inside a hospital consists of locker room, office, medical office, reception, examination waiting area, examination room, nurses' station, consultation waiting area, consultation room, ward, cashier, and mortuary. Spots which exist outside a hospital are home, business office and school.

(3) Dynamical Structure of SOARS: Step, Stage, Phase, Turn

Scheduling of SOARS is given as follows.

```
Step k start
  Stage i start
        Agent Phase start
              Agent turn j start
                    1) General rule execution
                    2) Active Rule execution
                    3) Self Resolution: if necessary
              Agent turn j end
              Agent turn j+1 start,..., Agent turn j+1 end
        Agent Phase end
        Resolver Phase start
              Resolver turn j start
                    Resolution: calculation of interaction
              Resolver turn j end
              Resolver turn j+1 start,..., Resolver turn j+1 end
        Resolver Phase end
  Stage i end
  Stage i+1 start ,...., Stage i+1 end
Step k end
```

At the turn of each agent on agent phase, the rules of the role of an agent and self resolver are executed turn by turn. In each resolver turn the program of resolver is executed turn by turn and the result s are returned to requested agents and spots. The process is shown in Fig. 1.

Step is a basic time unit of a discrete time dynamic system. A step is divided into several stages. Each stage represents a typical interaction or activity among agents and spots in a given dynamic system. Each stage is divided into two phases called agent phase and resolver phase. In the agent phase, agent rules are executed at each agent turn. In the resolver phase a resolver on a spot calculates the interaction among agents and spots.

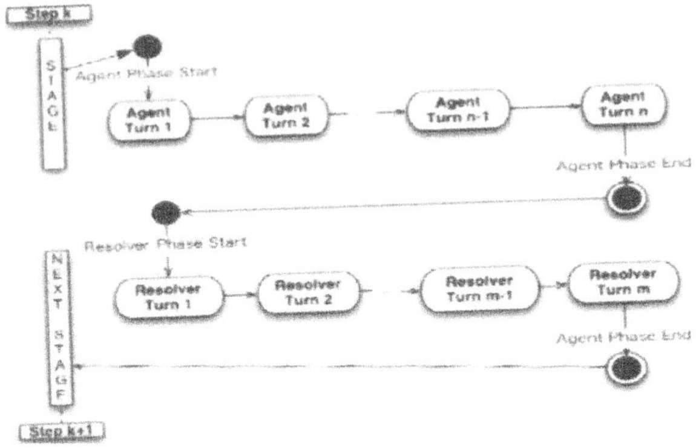

Fig. 1. Structure of Stage

(4) ABDS: Structure of Agent-Based Dynamic System (ABDS)

An agent-based dynamic system (ABDS) is a dynamic system which is an extension of the classic model of dynamic systems such as the distributed parameter system or the lumped parameter system. In ABDS we formulate moving agents and objects of the field expressed by a set of spots.

Let Sate_Space be a state space for an ABDS, Stage_Type be a set of stage type, Agent_Set be a set of agents, Spot_Set be a set of spots respectively. Let num_agent = |Agent_Set| and num_spot =|Spot_Set|. Agent_ID and Spot_ID denote index set as {1,..., num_agent} and {1,..., num_spot} respectively.

Let Fa be a set of one to one function from Agent_ID to Agent_ID. Let Fs be a set of one to one function from Spot_ID to Spot_ID as follows.

Fa={ f | f:Agent_ID->Agent_ID and f is a one to one function }

Fs={ g | f:Spot_ID->Spot_ID and f is a one to one function }

OPA[i]j :Sate_Space --> Sate_Space denotes a state transition operator at agent turn j on agent phase of stage i. OPA[i] = Π {OPA[i]j | j $\in$ Agent_ID } denotes a state transition operator at agent turn j of stage i, which is generated as a cartesian product of OPA[i]j. In the same way OPS[i]j :Sate_Space --> Sate_Space denotes a state transition operator at resolver turn j on resolver phase of stage i.

OP[i]= Π { OPS[i]]j | j $\in$ Spot_ID }.

Then total state transition operator at stage i is defined as $OP[i]=OP[i]\times OPA[i]$. We assume the following commutative condition for transition operators OP[i] and OPA[i] at any stage as follows.

(1) $\forall i\in Stage\_Type\ \forall x\in Sate\_Space\ \forall f, g\in Fa$

$\Pi\{OPA[i]f(j)\mid j\in Agent\_ID\}(x)=\Pi\{OPA[i]g(j)\mid j\in Agent\_ID\}(x)$.

(2) $\forall i\in Stage\_Type\ \forall x\in Sate\_Space\ \forall f, g\in Fs$

$\Pi\{OPS[i]f(j)\mid j\in Spot\_ID\}(x)=\Pi\{OPS[i]g(j)\mid j\in Spot\_ID\}(x)$.

Where f and g mean permutation of agent index and spot index.

Then the following commutative property holds.

$\forall i\in Stage\_Type\ \forall x\in Sate\_Space\ \forall f, g\in Fa\ \forall u, v\in Fs$

$\Pi\{OPS[i]u(j)\mid j\in Spot\_ID\}\times\Pi\{OPA[i]f(j)\mid j\in Agent\_ID\}(x)$

$=\Pi\{OPS[i]v(j)\mid j\in Spot\_ID\ (x)\times\Pi\{OPA[i]g(j)\mid j\in Agent\_ID\}(x)$.

In our ABDS we assume the commutative condition for transition operators. If the transition operators satisfy the commutative condition then the result of state transition dose is not affected by the execution turn of agents and resolver at each stage.

(5) Interaction Decomposition

We distinguish the following three types of interaction in ABDS.

1) Inter agents Interaction
2) Interaction between agents and spots
3) Inter spots Interaction

Inter agents interaction should be mediated by a certain resolver on a spot in our modeling framework. Interaction between agents and spots is basic in our framework. The interaction is described by rules of agents or resolvers of spots. Properties of agents and spots change after the interaction.

If we are interested in the propagation process among state quantities of a field, inter spots interaction is required. For describing inter spot interaction we have to introduce a neighborhood model of spots and a two stage interaction model.

For example a two dimensional field interaction is modeled by a distributed parameter dynamic system. It can be approximated by a two dimensional lattice structure of spots. A lattice structure of spots can be constructed by assuming a suitable neighborhood model and interaction among neighborhood spots. In the same way, a network type interaction among spots is modeled by a lumped parameter dynamic system that can be modeled by a network type neighborhood model and interaction among spots.

In agent-based dynamics many agents and spots interact with each other. The interaction decomposition is important for modeling agent-based dynamics. We distinguish two types of decomposition. The one is temporal decomposition of interaction. The other is the spacial decomposition of interaction. The spacial decomposition is done by our spots structure. The commutative condition for transition operators guarantees the execution turn does not affect the result in each agent turn and resolver turn.

To satisfy the commutative condition for transition operators we introduce a two stage model for inter spots interaction. In the resolver phase of the first stage, each resolver notices the state of the spot in relation to the neighborhood spots. In the second stage, each resolver calculates its change. Then, propagation of the state of spot can be executed without being affected by a calculation turn. A step is divided into several stages depending on the ABDS model, as is shown in the previous two stage model. The stage model is very important for temporal decomposition of interaction. We investigate the stage model in the concrete ABDS modeling as follows.

3 Infection Model in a Hospital and City

In a hospital, many agents such as staff and patients move and interact at many spots. The hospital is forced to take prompt measures in the case of an emerging virus infection like SARS. There are many organizational measures for virus protection. We have to distinguish the effective measures of high cost performance. We present a prototype model of a SARS virus infection with a hospital organization model and a simple city model.

(1) Spot Structure

1) Hospital Model: Hospital consists of the following spots; Locker room, Office, Medical office, Reception, Examination waiting area, Examination room, Nurses' station, Consultation waiting area, Consultation room, Ward, Cashier, Mortuary.
2) Home: Agents go back home after finishing their work in hospital or to an office or to school.
3) Business Office: Adult agents who are not hospital staff or patients work in a business office in the daytime.
4) School: Students go to school in the daytime. Fig. 2 and 3 show patient and doctor view of the hospital respectively.

(2) Role Structure

Rules of agents are described as roles of agents. In our hospital model the following roles are introduced: office staff, cashier staff, reception staff, nurse, doctor, examiner, visitor, and patient.

(3) Stage Structure

We introduce the following stage structure.
1) Role Taking stage: An agent takes and changes his role at a suitable situation.

2) Moving stage: An agent moves from spot to spot depending on his role.
3) Infection stage: Spot contamination from infected agents and agent infection from contaminated spot and infected agents are treated in this stage.
4) Measure stage: In our prototype model we only compare "no policy model" with "trace and isolation without vaccination policy" where SARS carrier's contacts are traced and isolated.
5) Business Stage: Results of examination and consultation are reported and treated.
6) Data collection stage: At this stage simulation data are collected.
7) Progression stage: State transition of infection and contamination level is treated.

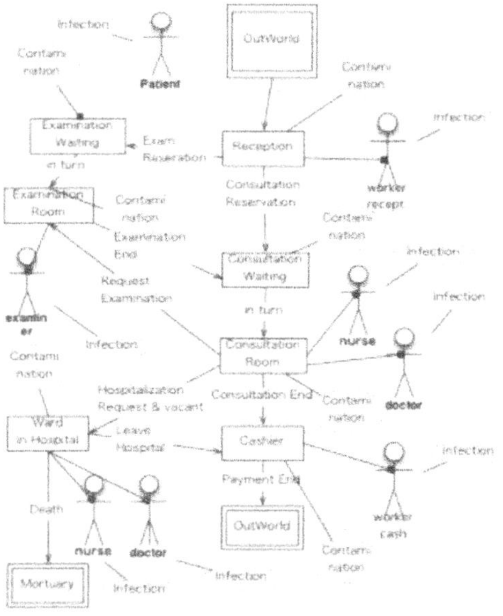

Fig. 2. Patient View of Hospital

(4) Infection Resolution Process

At the infection stage an agent notifies his infection level at the spot where he is staying at his turn of the agent phase. The resolver calculates contamination level of the spot and infection level of agents at resolver turn of the infection stage.

(5) Model Assumption

We assume 800 agents consisting of 200 families in our model. One family consists of two adults and two students. In hospital there are six doctors, six nurses, one examiner, one office staff, one cashier staff and one reception staff. Other adults work in offices. Infection and contamination will happen at the hospital, at the office and at home. We assume an organizational structure only in hospital. Each agent acts depending on the rules of the role.

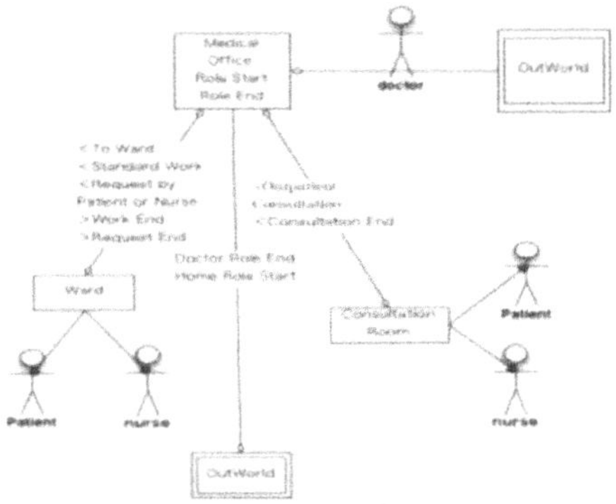

Fig. 3. Doctor View of Hospital

(6) Measures to prevent infection

There are several types of measures to prevent infection.

1) Sterilization of spots: Sterilization is a basic measure against infection. We can add level property of sterilization, which affects contamination probability.

2) Infection protection for agents: Protection level property can be added to doctor, nurse, examiner and office staff of the hospital, which affects infection probability. The level property can be added to any agents for public health protection policy.

3) Isolation policy for agents who had been in close contact with the SARS patient: Trace and isolation are very effective, even if there is no vaccination. This has been pointed out by Epstein [Epstein 2002]. In our model, the trace and isolation policy is very powerful in preventing infection. We introduced a trace and home isolation policy. We simulate a 3-day 100% isolation case where people who have contacted SARS patients over the past three days are traced and 100% captured and ordered to remain isolated at home. Family members are also isolated for 14 days. If imperfect virus inspection is available then we can evaluate the effect of the isolation after imperfect virus inspection by simulation.

4) Gatekeeper policy: A gatekeeper policy is a very important measure to prevent infection. In hospital or at airports, a fever check is a basic gatekeeper measure.

(7) Simulation Scenario

In this prototype modeling we only compare the no policy case with the trace and home isolation case. The result is shown as follows. Figure 3.3 shows the no policy case. In this case all agents are infected and recovered agents have immunity. Figure 3.4 shows the trace and home isolation policy case. The policy is effective. Infection is controlled and the number of recovered agents with immunity is less than a hundred.

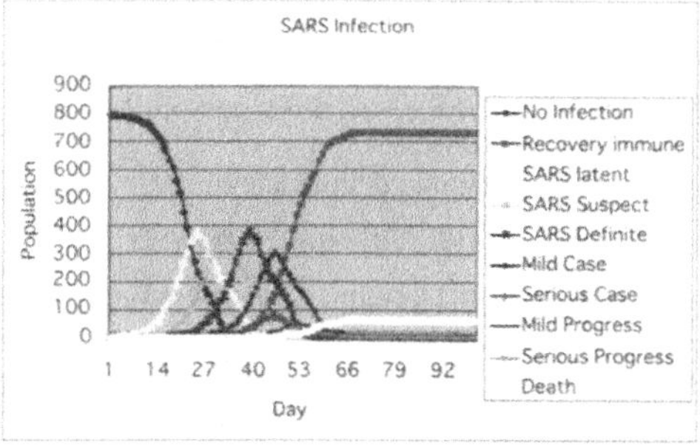

Fig. 4. No Policy Case

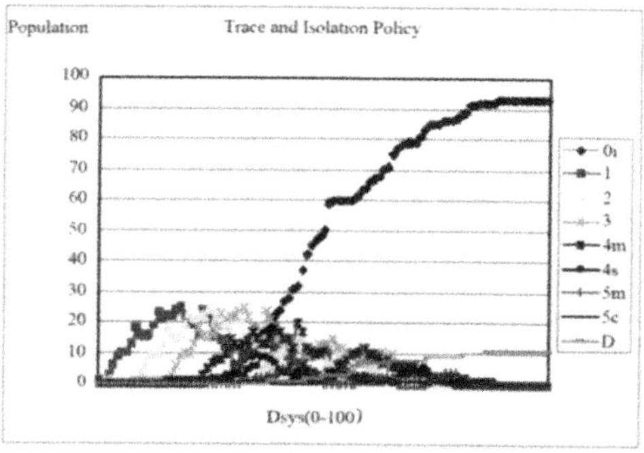

Fig. 5. Pursuit and Isolation Policy Case

5 Implementation of Simulation Platform

In the SOARS environment, the application users write the simulation model in a spreadsheet based script language, and can use some additional functional objects implemented in Java classes if needed. The simulation engine is also implemented in Java language, and skilled users can easily expand the function of the SOARS library by implementing subclasses.

(1) SOARS Library

The SOARS library is implemented in Java language and composed of the following packages and the belonging classes.

env package – the simulation model components and the engine classes
main package – the simulation entry main function classes
role package – the role related classes implementing the rule methods
script package – the script parser and the command formula parser classes
time package – the simulation time model classes
util package – the functional objects and the related interfaces
view package – the Swing GUI components and the logging output classes

Usually the SOARS library is served as an executable JAR file which starts up the main GUI console. The application users can specify the class path URL in the SOARS scripts, and then the additional functional objects are dynamically loaded by the SOARS engine.

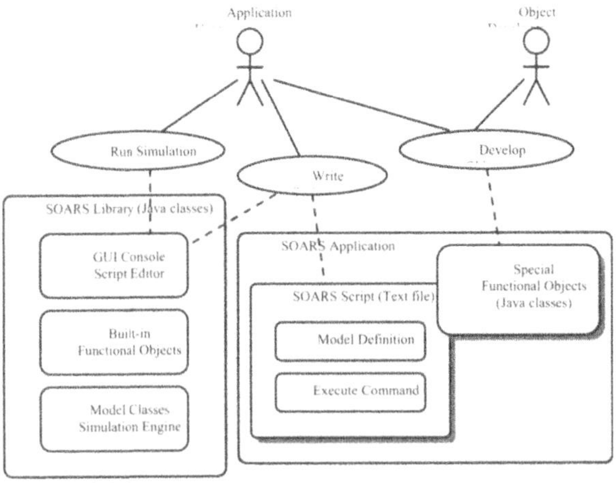

Fig. 6. System Overview of SOARS Platform and Related Use Cases

(2) Structure of SOARS Script Language

The SOARS script language consists of the following parts;

Model definition – the definition of the simulation model elements,
Execution command – the description of the running parameters,
Other information – some additional information e.g. class path URL.

The script language has spreadsheet-based format and is saved as a tab-separated text file. The basic unit of the script is a group of row lines separated by some blank lines called 'paragraph'. For example, the following paragraph defines three spots named 'Home', 'School', and 'Office'.

spot
Home
School
Office

The first row of each paragraph specifies the paragraph method. In the above case, the keyword 'spot' specifies the spot definition paragraph method and the following rows are passed as the method parameter. Deep into the Java implementation, the paragraph method named 'spot' is implemented as the function which has the following signature and is actually invoked using the Java reflection.

```
public void spot(Iterator paragraph);
```

The definition of the agents and the rules needs many parameters and applying only the paragraph method is insufficient. So, the special paragraph method 'itemData' leads to the secondary unit of the script language called 'item'. For example, the following paragraph defines five agents named 'Worker1', 'Worker2', 'Student1', 'Student2', and 'Student3'.

itemData			
agentNumber	agentName	agentCommand	agentCreate
2	Worker	<Office>moveTo	
3	Student	<School>moveTo	

The second row of the 'itemData' paragraph specifies the extra script methods called 'item method'. All contents of the third row or below are passed as the parameters of the item method of same column. In the case, the item methods have the following signatures in the Java implementation.

```
public void agentNumber(String item);
public void agentName(String item);
public void agentCommand(String item);
public void agentCreate(String item);
```

The standard script methods are implemented in the following Java class inheritance chain.

```
class script.ScriptParser;
```

This class implements the Java reflection mechanism.

```
class env.ObjectLoader extends script.ScriptParser;
```
This class implements the model definition methods.
```
class main.MainGUI extends env.ObjectLoader;
```
This class implements the execution command methods.

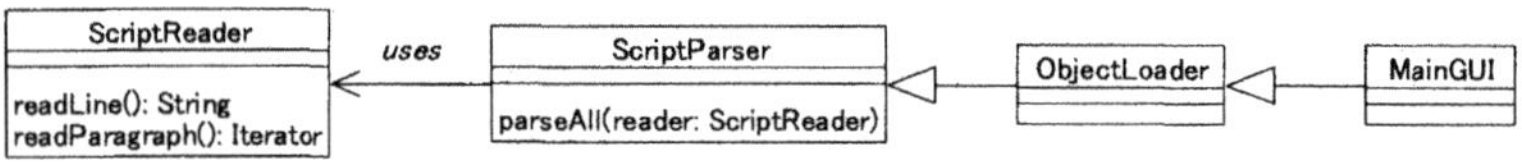

Fig. 7. Script Method Related Implementation Classes

(3) Description of Rule Action Formula

In the agent definition paragraph, the item method 'agentCommand' gets the initialization command formula as a parameter string. For the previous example, the command formula '<Office>moveTo' means that the agents move to the spot named 'Office' at first. Also, the item method 'ruleCondition' takes the rule condition formula and the method 'ruleCommand' takes the rule command formula. Each action rule of the agents is expressed as some condition formulae and a command formula and then form an if-then rule action formula.

The fundamental component of the rule action formula is a rule method. The rule methods are implemented in the subclasses of role.Role and invoked by the Java reflection. The standard rule methods implemented in the class role.RoleStructure are the following:

String property related – keyword, set, is, get, put,
Functional object related – askEquip, setEquip, isEquip, getEquip, putEquip, printEquip,
Role related – activateRole, setRole, isRole,
Time related – setTime, isTime,
Spot related – moveTo, isSpot,
Debug tracing related – trace, traceOff,
Other utilities – TRUE, FALSE, doSelfResolution.

In the rule action formula, the rule method is sometimes decorated with a string parameter and some operational prefixes. For example, the method moveTo needs a spot designation prefix operator written in angle brackets like this: <School>moveTo. The spot designation operator adds the Spot object parameter in the Java implementation. The previous formula invokes the Java method which has the following method signature.

```
public void moveTo(Spot spot);
```

Some rule methods take a string parameter suffix. The method 'keyword' defines the agent's string property keyword. For example, the rule action formula 'keyword FLAG' invokes the Java method below.

```
keyword("FLAG");
```

Also, the composition of the prefix operator and the string parameter makes different context. The rule action formula '<School>keyword FLAG' defines the string property keyword 'FLAG' of the spot named 'School'. This formula invokes the Java method which has the following signature.

```
public void keyword(Spot spot, String parameter);
```

A rule method which returns a boolean value is called 'rule condition method'. In the standard rule methods, the following rule condition methods are defined.

```
is, askEquip, isEquip, isRole, isTime, isSpot, trace,
traceOff, TRUE, FALSE
```

The rule condition methods can be used as a parameter of the 'ruleCondition' item method. For example, the formula '<Office>isSpot' means whether the agent is at the spot 'Office' or not. The condition methods can also be composed by some binary operators to make more complex formula. For example, the next formula describes the rule actions that if the agent is at the spot 'Office' or the spot 'School', then move to the spot 'Home'. We call such a composed formula 'command formula', and call the formula which returns a boolean value 'condition formula'.

```
<Office>isSpot || <School>isSpot ? <Home>moveTo
```

The parsing process of the rule action formula is implemented in the Java abstract class script.CommandParser. The abstract methods of parsing command and condition terms are implemented in the classes role.RuleCommandParser and util.AskCommandParser. The former class interprets the spot designation prefix and the latter does not. The rule action formula is converted to the Condition class instance by the parser classes and wrapped in the Rule class instance with a debugging information string. These Rule instances are stored in the RoleType class instance, and then executed by the SOARS simulation engine.

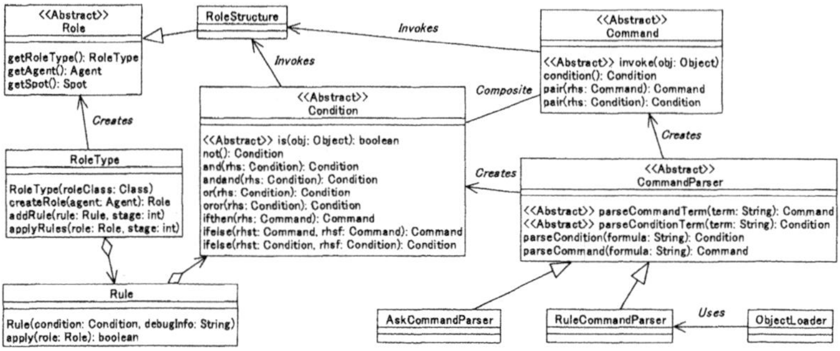

Fig. 8. Rule Action Formula Related Implementation Classes

(4) Simulation Model Objects and Functional Objects

The SOARS simulation model is mainly composed of the following elements;

Agent – the subject of the rule action,
Spot – the place where the agents move to,
Role type – the kind of agent rule action pattern,
Stage – the action sequence slot which the simulation time step is divided into,
Rule – the agent action command set described in if-then formula.

Each agent and spot has two types of attributes. One is literal information called 'property' which is a dictionary-like data structure formed of 'key=value' string to string mappings. This information can be used as the rule action branching flags and the logging variables. Another is object information called 'equipment' which is also a dictionary-like data structure, but formed of 'key=object', and the object can be any Java class instance. The functional objects can be stored in the equipment, and usually these objects implement some interfaces to communicate with the SOARS script language. These attributes are stored in the instance of the common subclass env.EquippedObject of the agent class env.Agent and the spot class env.Spot.

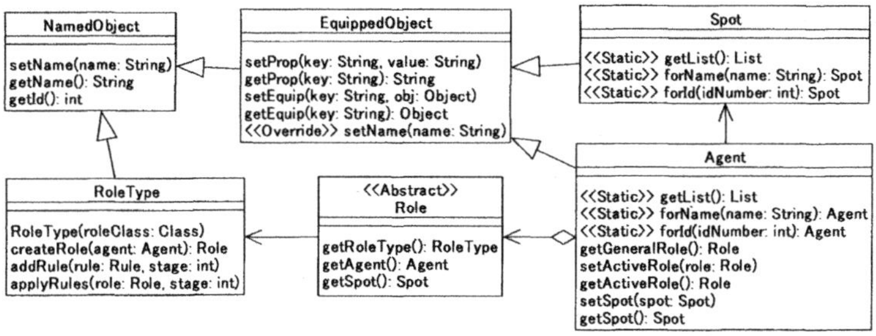

Fig. 9. Simulation Model Implementation Classes

6 Conclusion

We have developed a new type of agent-based simulation language called SOARS which depends on the concept of agent-based dynamic systems. Agent-based modeling is becoming more important for evidence-based policy making. Agent-based simulation will provide traceability of the evidence for economic, social and organizational planning. ABM is becoming a core of developing agent-based social systems sciences. Classic agent-based simulation tools are strongly affected by cellar type simulation. We insist that new ABM tools should be based on a new dynamic systems concept for agent-based modeling. We have developed both the theory of an agent-based dynamic system and a spot oriented agent role simulator in our SOARS project. The SOARS project is an open project. If you are interested in SOARS language please contact deguchi@dis.titech.ac.jp. Updated information on SOARS can be found at <http://degulab.cs.dis.titech.ac.jp/soars/index.html>.

References

[Deguchi 2004] H. Deguchi, Economics as an Agent Based Complex System, SpringerVerlag, 2004

[Epstein 2002] Joshua M. Epstein, Derek A. T. Cummings, Shubha Chakravarty, Ramesh M. Singa, and Donald S. Burke, "Toward a Containment Strategy for Smallpox Bioterror: An Individual-Based Computational Approach" Center on Social and Economic Dynamics Working Paper, No. 31, Brookings Institution, December 2002

Interactive inversion of agent-based models

Trent Ashburn[1], Eric Bonabeau[1], Ihsan Ecemis[1]

[1]Icosystem Corporation, 10 Fawcett St., Cambridge, MA 01238, US, eric@icosystem.com, http://www.icosystem.com

Summary. A financial market example illustrates how Interactive Evolutionary Computation (IEC) can be used for agent-based model inversion. The example shows that IEC can be used to discover a model that reproduces synthetic data generated with a very simple model.

Key words. interactive evolutionary computation, agent-based modeling, inverse modeling, financial markets.

1 Introduction

There have been a number of attempts over the last decade to model financial markets with agent-based modeling (ABM) (Palmer *et al.*, 1994; Arthur *et al.*, 1997; Caldarelli *et al.*, 1997; Levy *et al.*, 2000; Lux & Marchesi, 1999; Mantegna & Stanley, 1999; Bonabeau, 2002; LeBaron, 2001). In ABM, systems are modeled as collections of autonomous decision-making entities, called agents. Each agent individually assesses its situation and makes decisions based upon a set of rules. Agents may execute various behaviors appropriate for the system they represent –for example, buying or selling. Repetitive interactions between agents are a feature of ABM, which relies on the power of computers to explore dynamics out of the reach of pure mathematical methods (Epstein & Axtell, 1996). The power of ABM lies in their ability (1) to let the modeler describe behavior in very natural terms and (2) to capture emergent phenomena. A financial market seems to be a natural fit for ABM. The dynamics of the stock market results from the behavior of many interacting agents, leading to emergent phenomena that are best understood using a bottom-up, ABM approach. While ABM is useful in producing market-like aggregate-level patterns from individual-level rules, the main issue in financial markets ABM is calibration and validation: how can one evaluate the quality of a model, from both a structural perspective (for example, how sound is the model?) and from an econometric perspective (for example, how well does that model reproduce the data quantitatively?). In practice calibration and validation of financial markets ABM are often neglected. One reason is that the use of purely numerical scoring methods to evaluate data fit and guide the search for explanatory models constrains the search path so dramatically that no good fitting model is found or the best fit is generated by a low-plausibility model. In many situations the fitness function for a model cannot be practically formulated mathematically. This problem can be overcome if one can allow more subjective factors to guide the search for "good" models, enabling ABM users to integrate financial economics expertise into their models. In other fields, such as in the geosciences, calibration and validation are called inversion, or system identification. Boschetti & Moresi (2000; Wijns *et al.*, 2003) have proposed to replace the numerical evaluation of data fit by a subjective evaluation. A technique originally developed to generate "interesting" images and pieces of art (Dawkins, 1987; Sims, 1991, 1992, 1993; Banzhaf, 1997) is used to perform model inversion by integrating subjective knowledge into the evaluation process. The technique (see Takagi, 2001 for a review) is a directed search evolutionary algorithm which requires human input to evaluate the fitness of a pattern (here, the fitness might be how well the model reproduces the data *qualitatively*) and uses common evolutionary operators such as mutation and crossover (Goldberg, 1989; Forrest, 1993) to breed the individual-level rules that produced the fittest collective-level patterns. Interactive evolutionary computation (IEC), as this technique is known, combines computational search with human evaluation (Takagi, 2001). In this paper we present an application of IEC to financial markets ABM inversion. One simple example is given to illustrate how IEC can be used to discover the parameters of an agent-based model of a financial market from aggregate observations. The user operates a visualization tool to navigate a parameter space using genetic operators. Parameter values define traders and their trading strategies which, in turn, generate a synthetic price history. The user's goal is to find a combination of parameter values that can reproduce a target price history. The experiment uses a simple model to generate a synthetic target price history.

2 The agent-based market model

A simple model of a financial market is used in the experiment. Each model simulation includes its own order management and clearing mechanism (an order book), traders operating trading strategies, a market maker posting orders on the book which are matched with traders' orders, and a price history. At the end of each time step, after all trading and market-making, the arithmetic mean of the best bid and best ask is appended to a simulation's price history.

The book. The book matches orders in a continuous double-sided auction. It holds and clears both limit orders and market orders, where clearing is the action of matching a bid with a same-priced ask and removing these from the book. Same-priced limit orders are matched with other limit orders or market orders. In the process of clearing, the size (number of shares) of each matched order is reduced by the amount of the smaller-size order. Orders with size zero are removed from the book. Upon order submission, the book immediately clears any and all clearable orders. Orders are characterized as follows: (i) Bid:

an offer to buy; (ii) Ask: an offer to sell; (iii) Best bid: the highest bid; (iv) Best ask: the lowest ask; (v) Limit order: a bid or ask at a specific price or better; (vi) Market order: an offer to buy at the best ask or sell at the best bid.

Traders. In each time step, traders take turns trading according to their strategies. Traders trade once per time step, each trader submits only market orders, and traders' strategies (described in each experiment) are based upon a set of initial conditions and the price history of the stock. After each trader trades, the market maker trades.

Market maker. To ensure liquidity in the market, there is one market maker in each simulation, tightening the spread and maintaining order depth. The *spread* is the difference between the best bid and the best ask. When a trader trades, bids or asks are often cleared from the book, which widens the spread in a particular direction. *Spread tightening* is the action of the market maker adding bids if the trader had bought, or adding asks if the trader had sold, until the spread is a specific dollar amount. In our experiments, the market maker separates all its orders in $1 increments, and attempts to maintain a spread of $1. *Order depth* refers to the number of uniquely-priced bids and asks that the market maintains on the book. This buffers trading and must be of a sufficient depth to handle all trading; several hundred orders typically suffice in our experiments.

3 Interactive evolution

The IEC search method employs a genetic algorithm and a graphical user interface to facilitate the user acting as the fitness function. A small initial population of agent based models is generated with random parameter values. The resulting price histories are generated by running the models, and then shown to the human observer. The observer selects interesting patterns according to whatever objective and subjective criteria the observer may be using to visually compare candidates with the target. These selections are considered the fittest individuals of the generation. The user configures a set of genetic operators - elitism, mutation, and crossover – which are used to produce a new generation of models from the user-selected "fittest" individuals in the previous generation (Goldberg, 1989; Forrest, 1993). The new generation is then simulated and the resulting price histories are again presented to the observer. This procedure is iterated until interesting patterns emerge from the search that more closely match the target. Over multiple generations the population may converge toward the target.

3.1 User interface

The user interface (Figure 1) is a critical component of the method, which depends crucially upon the user's ability to evaluate visualizations of the candidate solutions (Takagi, 2001). Obviously this method can only work if the population

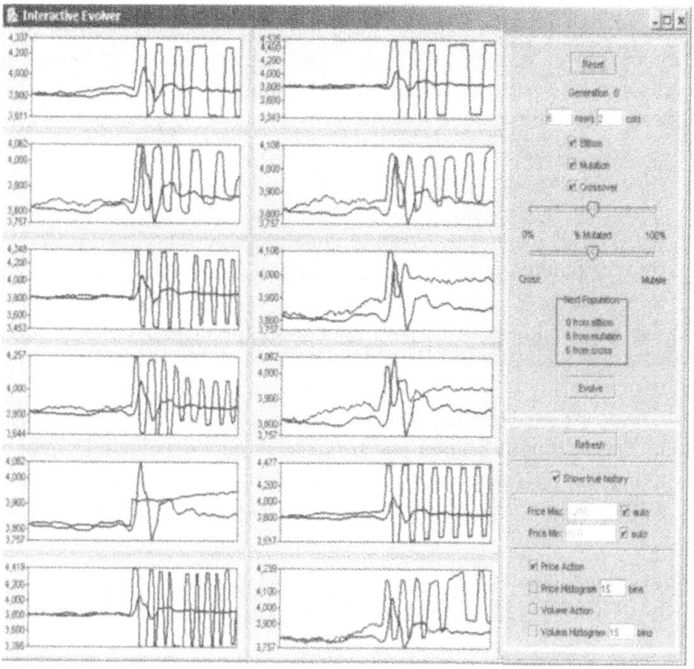

Fig. 1. User interface

size is kept small and if interesting patterns emerge after a reasonably small number of generations. The user interface shows the price histories of each candidate model in the left window, each overlaid on top of the target price history. On the right are two controls panels: (1) the main IEC control panel configures the size of the left-hand visualization grid, toggles genetic operators, controls the chance that a gene is mutated, and controls the proportion of crossover versus mutation; the evolve button produces the next generation; (2) the second control panel controls model drawing.

3.2 Evolutionary algorithm

Each model simulation and its price history can be considered a phenotype; the genotype codes for a set of trading strategies and their parameters used in the simulation. The parameters of these strategies vary across genotype, and it is the composition of these genotypes that we are interactively evolving. The genotype of a model has genes that are numbers – initially random numbers. Each number codes for a specific aspect of the set of traders (how many of each kind of trader, parameters of each strategy) and has bounds specific to the aspect it codes for. For example, a gene that codes for the number of traders might be bounded between 10 and 100. Candidates are either selected or not, and non-selected candidates are discarded. The user may turn on and off each of three genetic operators to produce next generation members - elitism, mutation, and crossover. Elitism is applied first; then crossover and mutation are performed on randomly chosen selected members to produce remaining members. The number of new members produced by crossover versus the number produced by mutation is a proportion chosen by the user.

- *Elitism* – Selected candidates are copied to the new generation.
- *Mutation* – The user controls the chance that each gene is mutated - between 0% and 100%. As the mutation algorithm iterates through each gene, a random number between 0.0 and 1.0 is chosen. If that number is less than the mutation percentage (expressed as a decimal, 50% is 0.50), that gene is mutated to a new value with the bounds of that variable. The specific algorithms used for mutation are described with each experiment.
- *Crossover* – Double-point crossover chooses crossover points in a uniform random fashion and produces a new candidate by recombining two parent genotypes from among the selected candidates. The specific algorithms used for crossover are described with each experiment.

4 Experiment

In this model, during each time step, a trader can buy, sell, or do nothing. Each trader can only sell as much as the trader has bought. Each genotype, including the target genotype, contains six initially-random real-number values that code for price thresholds for three traders, which trigger buying and selling (Figure 2). Each trader has two thresholds – an upper and a lower, bounded between $90 and $110.

Position	**Genes**	**Codes for**
1	101	Trader 1 upper threshold
2	95	Trader 1 lower threshold
3	99	Trader 2 upper threshold
4	93	Trader 2 lower threshold
5	107	Trader 3 upper threshold
6	99	Trader 3 lower threshold

Fig. 2. Genotype representation.

Each trader's trading strategy works as follows:

- If $p \leq L$, switch to *buy mode:* buy one stock each time step at market price.
- If $p \geq U$, switch to *sell mode:* sell one stock each time step at market price

where p is the most recent price in the price history, L is the trader's lower threshold, and U is the trader's upper threshold.

Reflected in Figure 3, this strategy often produces wave-like patterns in the price history.

The market marker's initial best bid is \$100 the best ask is \$101, and all the market maker's orders are limit orders of size 1. Each simulation is run for 20 time steps and the user reviews 12 candidates in each generation.

We found it possible, using IEC, to reach an exact visual match with the target over an average of 6 generations in 10 trials (the target being the stock price time series). The fewest number of generations to reach the target, on average, was achieved by mutating the population of candidate genotypes until thresholds were discovered that matched thresholds present in the target, even though these thresholds did not necessarily occur in the same candidate genotype. Then, crossover is employed to recombine the proper thresholds until the matching combination is discovered.

Figure 4 shows a typical sequence of evolution steps with interactions. The user navigates the space of models by using his intuition to decide which solution has the desired qualitative features. In this particular situation, with a synthetic time series generated by a simple model, a perfect match can be reached. In other situations, for example with real data, a perfect match is not always possible.

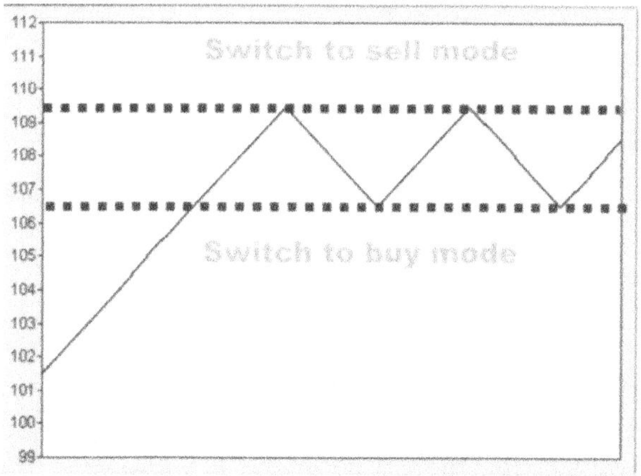

Fig. 3. An example of the price action resulting from one trader using the threshold-based strategy. Thresholds are shown as dotted lines.

4 Modularity and comparison with GA

One of the first questions one may ask about the example described in the previous sections is, "why can't a straight genetic algorithm (or an optimization method) come up with similar results in a short amount of time?" The answer is not trivial. In fact, it is worth testing. In order to apply a GA with an automated rather than user-defined fitness function, one has to define one such fitness function.

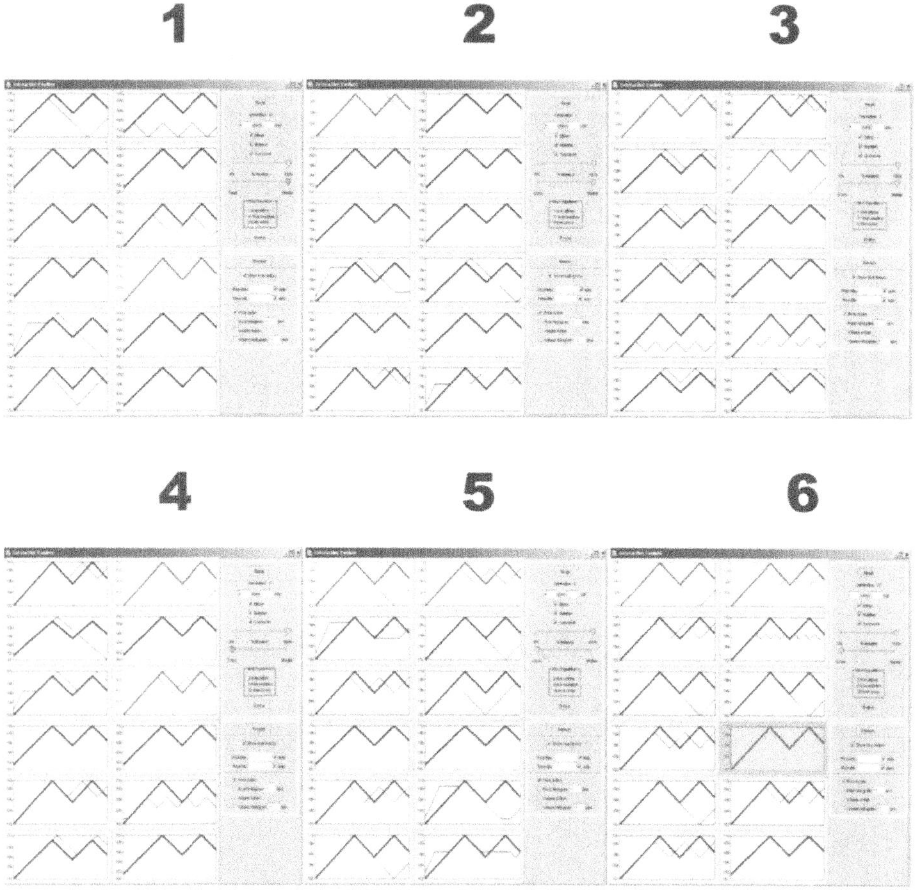

Fig. 4. Example sequence of evolutionary interaction steps. In each display the target time series is represented by a bold line and the solution is represented by a lighter line. Solutions highlighted in yellow are selected for the next generation. The solution highlighted in green is a perfect match.

The easiest and most natural one here is simply the inverse of a fitting error function

$$E=\left(N^{-1}\sum_{t=0}^{N}\left(p_t-a_t\right)^2\right)^{1/2},$$

where p_t and a_t represent the model-predicted and actual price at time t, respectively. A simple GA was used, where the probability to be selected for each mutation or crossover operation is proportional to $1/(E+0.0001)$. Each generation consisted of 12 genotypes with 2 elites surviving to the next generation. 5 genotypes are created through mutation and 5 genotypes through crossover, 2 genotypes are randomly generated. The system was tested with 30 random initial conditions. Figure 5 shows a comparison between IE and the GA. Figure 5a shows the results of this experiment in terms of the number of cases which could find the solution after a given number of generations, while Figure 5b shows the error E as a function of generation number. GA and IE reach the solution in 8.7 and 10.9 generations, respectively, therefore the GA performs slightly better.

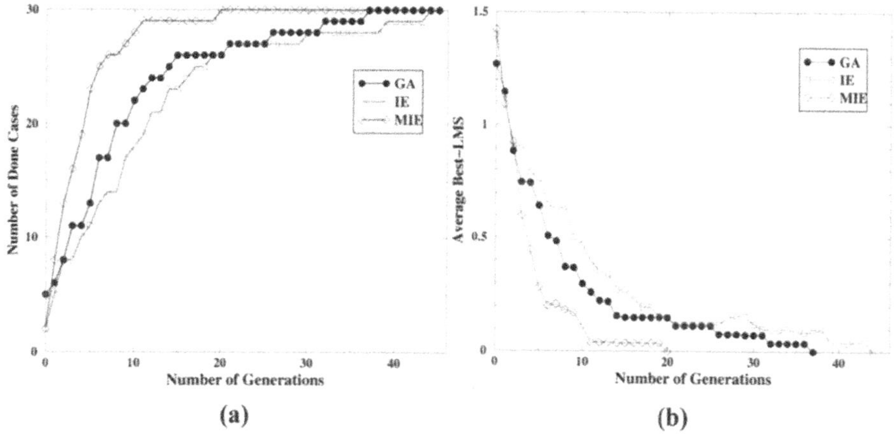

Fig. 5a, b. Example sequence of evolutionary interaction steps. In each display the target time series is represented by a bold line and the solution is represented by a lighter line. Solutions highlighted in yellow are selected for the next generation. The solution highlighted in green is a perfect match.

Another interesting aspect of IEC is the fact that users using IEC often find parts of a solution they like and end up selecting solutions that have such interesting parts. Because they are not given the opportunity to select only part of a solution, they have to select an entire solution. We tested the effectiveness of a modularity-based selection strategy. To introduce modularity in a way that is relevant to the user, we divided each phenotype (basically a time series) into 5 temporal modules of equal size (see Figure 6). The user can select any number of modules from as many phenotypes as he wants. The system was tested with 30 random initial conditions as above. It is clear from Figure 5 that Modular IEC (MIEC) outperforms both IEC and the GA, indicating that modularity significantly enhances the user's search capability.

5 Conclusion

We have shown with a simple financial markets example how IEC can be used to perform agent-model inversion. When applied to simple models and reasonably small parameter spaces that have human-interpretable visualizations, IEC as a technique nicely combines human expertise with evolutionary computation and may improve the speed and accuracy of search in the fields of model inversion and model design, particularly when goal evaluation is multi-variate, complex, or qualitative. Although a straight optimization algorithm such as a genetic algorithm (GA) with a least-mean squares objective function does find a solution, IEC enables the user to estimate models without having to define a problem-specific, *ad hoc* objective function. One useful extension to this work consists of using IEC to fit two or more aggregate-level datasets simultaneously, thereby increasing the plausibility of the discovered model. It was also shown that adding modularity to the user selection process greatly enhances the user's ability to find a good solution.

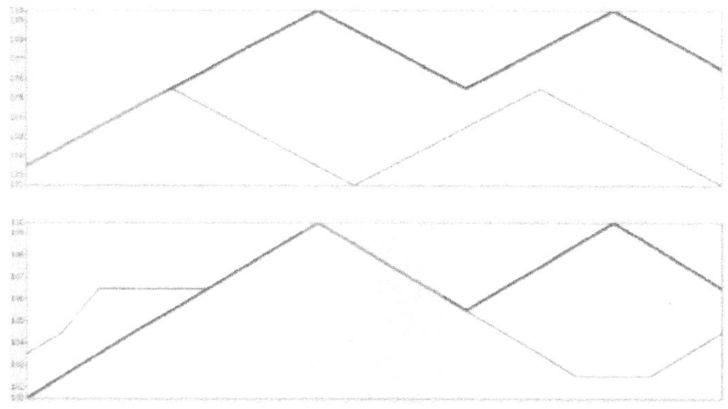

Fig. 6: Example sequence of evolutionary interaction steps. In each display the target time series is represented by a bold line and the solution is represented by a lighter line. Solutions highlighted in yellow are selected for the next generation. The solution highlighted in green is a perfect match.

References

Arthur, W. B., Holland, J. H., LeBaron, B., Palmer, R. G. & Taylor, P. (1997) Asset pricing under endogenous expectations in an artificial stock market, in *The Economy as a*

Complex Evolving System II, eds. Arthur, W. B., Durlauf, S. & Lane, D. (Santa Fe Institute Studies in the Sciences of Complexity, Proceedings Volume XXVII, Addison-Wesley, Reading, MA).

Ball, P. (2002) Stock market shock explained. Physicists model recent trading frenzy. Nature Science Update, http://www.nature.com/nsu/020923/020923-18.html

Banzhaf, W. (1997) Interactive evoution. In: Handbook of Evolutionary Computation (T. Baeck, D. Fogel, and Z. Michalewicz, eds), Ch. C2.10, pp. 1-5, Oxford University Press.

Bonabeau, E. (2002) Agent-based modeling: methods and techniques for simulating human systems, *Proc. Nat. Acad. Sci. USA* **99**, 7280-7287

Boschetti, F., Moresi, L. 2001. Interactive inversion in geosciences. *Geophysics* 66, 1226-1234.

Caldarelli, G., Marsili, M. & Zhang, Y.-C. (1997) A prototype model of stock exchange. *Europhys. Lett.* **40**, 479-484

Dawkins. R. 1987. *The Blind Watchmaker*. W. W. Norton, New York.

Epstein J. M., Axtell R. L. (1996) *Growing artificial societies: social science from the bottom up* (MIT Press, Cambridge, MA).

Farmer, J.D. (1999) Physicists attempt to scale the ivory towers of finance. *Computing in Science and Engineering* (IEEE), November-December 1999, 26-39.

Forrest, S. 1993. Genetic algorithms: Principles of adaptation applied to computation. *Science* **261**: 872-878.

Goldberg, D. E. 1989. *Genetic Algorithms in Search, Optimization and Machine Learning*, Addison-Wesley Longman Publishing.

LeBaron, B. (2001) A builder's guide to agent-based financial markets. *Quantitative Finance* **1**, 254-261

Levy, M., Levy, H. and Solomon, S. (2000). *Microscopic Simulation of Financial Markets: From Investor Behavior to Market Phenomena*. (Academic Press, San Diego, CA).

Lux, T. & Marchesi, M. (1999). Scaling and criticality in a stochastic multi-agent model of a financial market. *Nature* **397**, 498-500

Mantegna, R. & Stanley, H. E. (1999). An Introduction to Econophysics, Cambridge University Press

Muchnik, L. & Solomon, S. (2003). Statistical mechanics of conventional traders may lead to non-conventional market behavior. *Physica Scripta* **T106**, 41-47.

Palmer, R. G., Arthur, W. B., Holland, J. H., Le Baron, B. & Tayler, P. (1994) Artificial economic life: a simple model of a stock market, *Physica D* **75**, 264-274.

Sims, K. 1991. Artificial evolution for computer graphics. *Computer Graphics* **25**: 319-328.

Sims, K. 1992. Interactive evolution of dynamical systems. Pages 171-178 in: *Towards a Practice of Autonomous Systems: Proceedings of the First European Conference on Artificial Life* (F. J. Varela & P. Bourgine, eds.), MIT Press, Cambridge, MA.

Sims, K. 1993. Interactive evolution of equations for procedural models. *Vis. Comput.* **9**: 446-476.

Takagi, H. 2001. Interactive evolutionary computation: fusion of the capabilities of EC optimization and human evaluation. *Proc. IEEE* **89**: 1275-1296.

Wijns, C., Boschetti, F. & Moresi, L. 2003. Inversion in geology by interactive evolutionary computation. *Journal of Structural Geology*, in print.

Modeling the Exchange of AIDS Prevention and Treatment Strategies in Hong Kong

Richard J. Callahan[1]

[1]Linder & Associates, 90 Park Avenue, Suite 1700, New York, NY 10016 USA

Summary. The following research investigates communication among workers for AIDS-related non-governmental organizations (NGOs) in Hong Kong. The study seeks to learn to what extent full-time and part-time workers for those NGOs applying to the AIDS Trust Fund (ATF) discuss their prevention or treatment programs with their colleagues, and relates this exchange of information to the strategies that the NGOs use to fund and implement their programs. Ethnographic fieldwork contextualizes network models of communication and division of labor derived from quantitative questionnaires with a multidimensional scaling algorithm. Qualitative and quantitative evidence suggests that competition for funding and a cultural preference for hierarchy in Hong Kong discourage the sharing of ideas. Information exchange occurs primarily through strong ties within and between offices, and the Hong Kong Coalition of AIDS Service Organizations (HKCASO) emerges as the chief mechanism for sharing HIV/AIDS prevention strategies among the NGOs in Hong Kong.

Key words. Social network analysis, HIV/AIDS, Hong Kong

Overview

This is a paper about the structure of competition, and how staff members for AIDS-related non-governmental organizations (NGOs) in Hong Kong work towards a common goal of HIV/AIDS prevention and treatment. As the global HIV/AIDS epidemic progresses and countries around the world mobilize resources to reduce the impact of AIDS on their societies, managing and efficiently channeling funds through government and non-government organizations (NGOs) to achieve measurable success constitutes a universal challenge. The purpose of this study is to explore to what extent a structural analysis of the sharing of strategies among HIV-AIDS-related NGOs in Hong Kong yields insight into the organizational culture and the effectiveness of those NGOs in their response to AIDS.

Conducted in summer 2002, this research combines ethnographic fieldwork using participant observation and key informant interviews with a quantitative questionnaire for network analysis, and investigates the extent to which non-government organization (NGO) workers in Hong Kong discuss prevention and treatment strategies with colleagues in their own and other organizations. A multidimensional scaling algorithm models communication among full-time and part-time workers of those NGOs applying to the Hong Kong AIDS Trust Fund (ATF) for funding.

A Comparison with Agent-Based Modeling

This study is based on a general view of the NGO workers as semiotic agents independently devising strategies to fund and implement their prevention and treatment programs within their social and political environment (Joslyn 1999). The algorithms driving this analysis, however, do not treat the NGO workers as agents with a set of rules to govern their interactions, but simply as actors, or nodes in a network. The exchange of prevention and treatment strategies among staff members are modeled as a type of connection between pairs of staff members that varies in strength by the frequency and type of communication. The power of these techniques lies in aggregating information into a sociocentric model of the entire communication network. Coupled with ethnographic research, these models often can explain why agents perceive their environment in the way they do, given their location in the network. By yielding insight into overall network structure, these models constitute reliable benchmarks for initially assigning rules to describe agent behavior and for evaluating the accuracy of agent-based NGO collaboration simulations. In addition, some techniques for determining social distance in the following network models could be applied to agent-based modeling.

This paper continues with a description of the selection of a network boundary, criteria for including individuals in the network study, and relations used to develop network models. The multidimensional scaling algorithm used for the analysis is then discussed, and results of a structural analysis of communication and prevention work among the NGOs are presented. Qualitative data from the key informant interviews contextualizes the network models.

Selection of the Site, Network Boundary, and Relationship to be Modeled

The territorial limits of the Hong Kong Special Administrative Region (SAR) constituted the geographic boundary for this research. Hong Kong has enjoyed a period of both few infections and abundant funding for AIDS prevention and treatment, but an economic downturn since 1997 led AIDS-related NGOs to focus their efforts on "target groups" considered at highest risk for infection. All full-time and part-time staff members for AIDS-related NGOs in Hong Kong were included in the study. NGOs are considered "AIDS-related" if and only if at the time of this research, they were applying to the ATF for funding or had done so in the past. Using self-identification to define an individual's membership in an AIDS-related NGO, this study uses a realist approach to boundary identification (Laumann et al. 1989).

Table 1. AIDS-related NGOs in Hong Kong considered for the study, their sizes and target groups

Organization	Abbreviation for study	Full-time staff	Part-time staff	Target groups
TeenAIDS	TA	2	2	Youth
Hong Kong AIDS Foundation	HKAF	16	0	Youth, Travelers, CSWs*, IDUs*, MSM*, STD clinic visitors
St. John's Cathedral HIV Education Centre	SJ	1	1	Travelers, Women
Action for REACH OUT	AFRO	6	0	CWSs*, IDUs*
Caritas AIDS project	CAR	1	1	Youth, Travelers
Hong Kong Council of Social Service (HKCSS) AIDS Project	HKCSS	1	1	Health workers
Chi Heng Foundation	CH	3	0	MSM
Society for AIDS Care	SAC	10	0	Patients
AIDS Concern	AC	13	11	MSM, Travelers, Youth
Hong Kong Federation of Women's Organizations	HKFWO	**	**	**

*CSW: Commercial Sex Workers. IDU: Intraveneous drug users. MSM: Men who have sex with men.
**: Not included in this study.

A Multidimensional Scaling Algorithm for Network Analysis

The algorithm for this analysis, Data_Without_Variables (DWV), was developed by Dr. Joel Levine at Dartmouth College (Levine et al. 2001). The input is a frequency matrix F in which F_{ij} is the number of observed occurrences of a particular type of relationship directed from actor i to actor j in a network. DWV randomly scatters a set of vertices corresponding to rows and columns in F across an n-dimensional space, where n is defined by the user. DWV calculates the distance between all scattered vertices according to the following equation:

$$d(i,j)=\left[\sum_{k=1}^{\dim}\left|x_{ik}-y_{jk}\right|^{\rho}\right]^{1/\rho} \qquad \text{(Equation 1)}$$

$d(i,j)$ is the distance between points i and j in the Minkowski metric with parameter ρ (Klein 1998; Levine et al 2001). A ρ value of two corresponds to

Euclidean space. ρ is allowed to be any rational number greater than zero, because social distance in a virtual space does not have to be Euclidean, and often network models using non-Euclidean metrics more closely fit the observed data.

DWV then creates a frequency table $\hat{F}$ from the distances between those vertices using Equation 2.

$$\hat{F}_{ij} = ar_i c_j e^{-d_{ij}^p} \qquad \text{(Equation 2)}$$

$\hat{F}_{ij}$ is the product of row and column multipliers r_i and c_j for a particular row or column in the frequency table, a grand multiplier a, and $e^{-d_{ij}^p}$, the negative exponential of the current distance between vertices i and j raised to a power p, which can also be any positive rational number. The value of p affects the degree to which frequencies attenuate as distance from a vertex increases. Once $\hat{F}$ is calculated, the chi-squared errors between the cells in a candidate (observed) frequency table and their corresponding cells in the actual (expected) frequency table entered as input are calculated and summed. A numerical optimization technique using a downhill simplex method (Nelder and Mead 1965) with simulated annealing (Press et al. 1992) finds a minimum value of the error sum.

While models used for this network analysis cannot be guaranteed to be a "best fit," they do fit the data more closely than the millions of other candidate models analyzed by the optimization algorithm. The resulting model has the highest "signal-to-noise" ratio (Berkowitz 1982), and values for ρ and p in the network model with the lowest sum of chi-squared errors yield insight into the underlying relationship among the NGO workers.

Modeling Communication Among the NGOs

Questionnaire respondents were asked, "In the last two weeks, whom did you talk to about prevention, treatment, or program support strategies in Hong Kong?" Respondents gave the first name and the first letter of each alter's last name to maximize confidentiality while still allowing a researcher to know when two respondents named the same individual (Burt 1998). Respondents also stated the method and frequency of communication. Only communication with feedback and within the scope of the respondent's work is included in a network model.

The first of the two models that follow is built from an incidence matrix indicating the presence or absence of communication with feedback between an NGO worker and another person. Colored vertex labels denote respondents, and random numbers replace names for privacy reasons. Due to the fact that the NGO staff members were writing grant proposals and therefore extremely busy, only 26 of the 71 NGO workers completed questionnaires, a 36.6% response rate. Nonetheless, these 26 respondents described interactions with 95 individuals that included feedback, and even partial data about such a group is highly informative.[1]

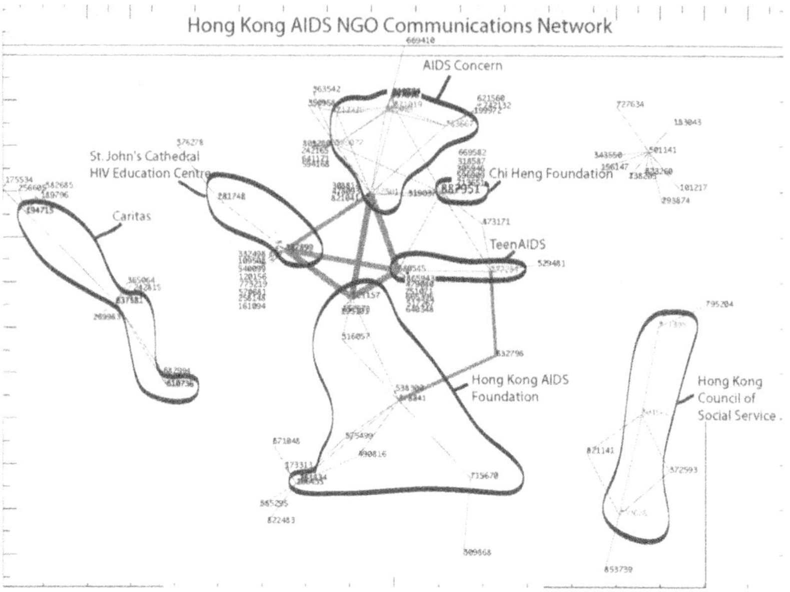

Fig. 1. Hong Kong communication network. ρ =2, p=2, Chi-squared error = 103.106.

The best fit encountered for the model is in Euclidean space with a p value of 2. A distance power of two implies that the expected frequency of interaction between two actors attenuates according to the negative exponential of the square of the distance between them. In other words, the Central Limit Theorem and binomial approximation to the Gaussian distribution model the fundamental processes defining interaction in the network (Levine et al 2001: 13). The values of ρ and p play a greater role in graphs with a large number of cycles, however, as changing the length or direction of an edge connecting exactly one individual to the network does not affect the other vertices. Due to the paucity of cycles in this graph and in the face-to-face communications network that follows, the metric and distance power play a minor role in shaping the above two graphs.

This study was conducted during a competitive time period when the NGOs applied to the ATF for three years of project funding, The most significant finding

---

[1] For a more rigorous discussion of methodology and the Chinese and English versions of the questionnaire, see Callahan (2003).

is the four-clique represented by the thick lines in figure 14.1, denoting a Hong Kong Coalition of AIDS Services (HKCASO) meeting with four NGO leaders in attendance. Absent this clique, St. John's Cathedral HIV Education Centre would be disconnected from the other four NGOs in the center, and only one long bridge would link the Hong Kong AIDS Foundation to the remaining NGOs in the center. For all intents and purposes, HKCASO holds the graph together and plays a vital role in shaping Hong Kong's response to AIDS. Unfortunately, at the time of the study, discussion of prevention strategies at these meetings lacked substance, as the NGO representatives were hesitant even to name their target groups, lest they lose a competitive edge in applying for funding. "One of the biggest problems is trying to get members to show up," remarked one member. Structural equivalence with respect to the funding mechanism led the NGOs to competition that froze meaningful dialogue about implementing effective HIV/AIDS programs (Burt 1992). "Eventually you become the Trust Fund's slave," noted another key informant.

Because few paths exist between pairs of individuals in the above graph, agents may exhibit brokerage behavior, charging others a social commission for access to information from other parts of the network (Marsden 1982). In effect, repeatedly requesting information from an individual without returning the favor creates a *guanxi* (relationship) debt. This hierarchical communication structure confirms one informant's impression that the inter-organizational culture (or environment) is "very top-down...it's about control, control, control and control."

Most NGO workers likely find the disconnectedness of the communication model unsurprising. "We mainly do it alone," commented a member of Caritas, and this perspective makes sense given Caritas' isolation from the rest of the communication network at the time of the study. TeenAIDS, on the other hand, has established itself as an information conduit. Their central role in the network is likely caused by their choice to avoid competition with the other NGOs by not applying to the ATF for funding in September 2002.

In an effort to isolate the effect of strong ties within the communications network, the following model is constructed from a symmetric matrix modeling only face-to-face communication among the NGOs and weighting each edge according to the number of conversations that occurred within a two-week period, such that individuals who spoke more frequently appear closer together.

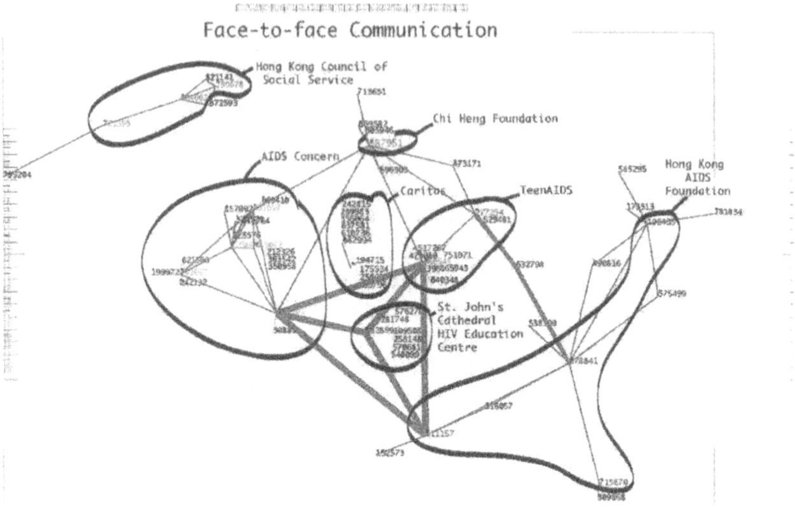

Fig. 2. Face-to-face communication model. ρ =2, p=1, Chi-squared error = 160.673.

This study seems to corroborate other evidence (Bian 1997) that contrary to Granovetter's argument that new information travels through weak ties (1973), bridging social capital in Chinese society instead makes use of strong ties due to China's culture of *guanxi* (cultivating relationships). If face-to-face conversations indicate stronger ties than phone or email conversations, the fact that communication between NGOs occurs in person (figure 2) implies that inter-organizational ties are strong.

Modeling Allocation of NGO Work Towards Vulnerable Groups

One staff member for TeenAIDS posited that the fact that the NGOs have different target groups, not the funding environment, most significantly impacts decision-making. In order for this hypothesis to be investigated, questionnaire respondents were asked about the time they directed towards each target group. To model these preferences and as a test for the robustness of DWV on a graph rich in cycles, responses to this question were converted into a frequency table for input into DWV by assigning to responses weighted edges in a bipartite graph. The respondents comprised one partite set and the other included the general public and all risk groups in Table 1. Table 2 shows minimum chi-squared errors calculated for various values of $\hat{F}$ as input values for ρ and p were varied. Respondents who directed more of their effort towards a particular group received an edge of greater weight.

Table 2. NGO work allocation chi-squared errors for ρ and p parameter combinations.

		Distance power				
		0.5	1	1.5	2	7
Minkowski	0.5	74.1	36.0	29.1	24.4	25.9
Parameter	2	--	25.6	--	38.7	26.2
	4	93.2	31.5	--	36.0	24.3

The second-best fit with a ρ value of 0.5 and a distance power of two demonstrates the robustness of the DWV algorithm in non-Euclidean space and identifies the bipartite structure of the question. As a metric that models actual distance, ρ =.5 has little meaning, since such a metric would violate the triangle inequality for distance. As a theoretical model for social distance, however, it is perfectly valid: the shortest path between two linked nodes is not via the direct connection, but rather includes a third party. In a bipartite graph, the shortest path between two members of a partite set always goes through the other partite set, and so an optimal Minkowski parameter less than one is not unexpected given the structure of the problem.[2]

The fact that a ρ value of 4 and a distance power of seven yields a better fit indicates an underlying structure to the responses more significant than the structure of the question. A high distance power suggests that frequencies attenuate sharply and elements are either members of a group or they are not. The resulting sharply defined groups bear some similarity to network blockmodels put forward by White, Boorman and Breiger (1976).

[2] I am indebted to Dr. Joel Levine for this observation.

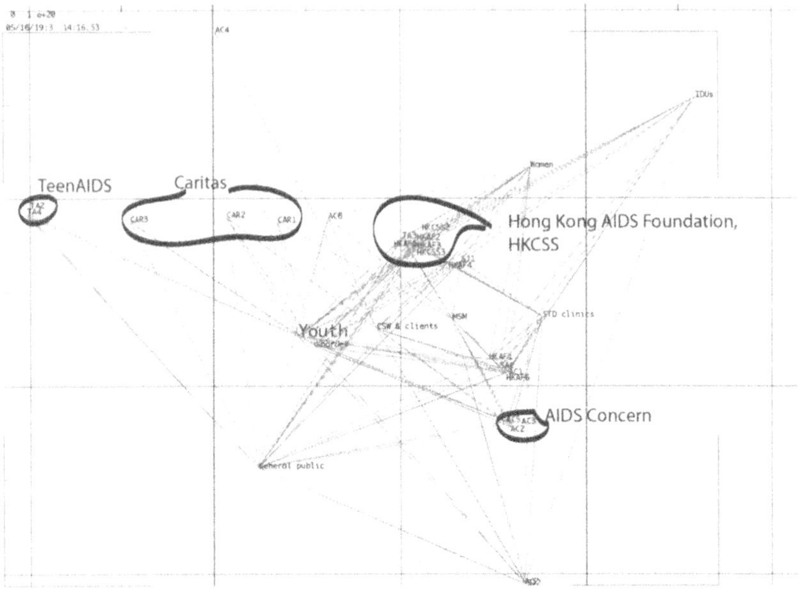

Fig. 3. NGO work allocation. $\rho = 4, p = 7$, chi-squared error = 24.32.

In the end, do the NGOs compete, or do they simply have different target groups? NGO members fall into blockings by organization in Figure 3, corroborating the TeenAIDS staff member's claim that differing target groups give the NGOs distinct identities. Nonetheless, the centrality of the youth category is not surprising because multiple NGOs, unaware of the extent of Caritas's ongoing programs, all sought funding for programs directed towards the ATF's lucrative new youth category. This diagram therefore also corroborates an observed state of competition among the NGOs over "ownership" of target groups. NGOs thus have distinct identities based on differing degrees of focus on the six vulnerable groups, yet they have different targets precisely because they depend on the same funding mechanism. The overall structure is governed by competition.

Conclusion

Sociocentric network models of agent behavior at discrete moments in time may help researchers to design and evaluate agent-based models for simulating and predicting collaboration among NGOs, and may also guide future collaboration among the NGOs themselves. As the HIV/AIDS problem escalates in mainland China, Hong Kong is fortunate to have a diverse and multi-pronged response to HIV/AIDS in place. At the time of this research, no measure of effectiveness consistent from one NGO to the next could be compared to the position of an NGO in a communications network. Policy makers could benefit from standardizing current program evaluation methods, in order to compare the impact of NGO interventions with their network roles. The Hong Kong Coalition of AIDS Service Organizations (HKCASO) is a vital institution for the sharing of strategies for AIDS prevention and care within a social structure that is otherwise extremely hierarchical and competitive. The remarkable lack of strategy sharing among NGOs at the time of the study, coupled with findings from the ethnographic research, suggest that an improved mechanism to encourage greater collaboration among the NGOs would heighten the overall effectiveness of HIV/AIDS prevention efforts in Hong Kong.

References

Berkowitz, S D (1982) An Introduction to Structural Analysis: The Network Approach to Social Research. Toronto: Butterworth & Co.

Bian, Y (1997) "Bringing Strong Ties Back In: Indirect Ties, Network Bridges, and Job Searches in China." American Sociological Review: 62 (3): 366-385

Burt, R (1992) Structural Holes: The Social Structure of Competition. Cambridge: Harvard University Press

_______ (1998) "Project Questionnaire for Graduate School of Business Alumnae Survey: Contacts, Career, and Family." Electronic Document. Retrieved July 2002 from http://gsbwww.uchicago.edu/fac/ronald.burt/research/GSBAS1.pdf

Callahan, R (2003) Modeling the Exchange of AIDS Prevention and Treatment Strategies in Hong Kong. Dissertation, Mathematical Social Sciences, Dartmouth College

Granovetter, M (1973) "The Strength of Weak Ties." American Journal of Sociology 73 (6):1360-1380

Joslyn, C (1999) "Semiotic Agent Models for Simulating Socio-Technical Organizations." Prepared for the DS Project, PSL/NMSU. Electronic Document. Retrieved April 2004 from http://www.c3lanl.gov/~joslyn/nmsu/semagentp.pdf

Klein, A (1998) Textual Analysis Without coding: It Can be Done. Dissertation, Mathematical Social Sciences, Dartmouth College

Laumann, E O, Marsden P V, Prensky D (1989) "The Boundary Specification Problem in Network Analysis," in Freeman, L C, White, D R, and Romney, A K (Eds) Research Methods in Social Network Analysis. Fairfax, VA: George Mason University Press

Levine, J, Klein, A, Mathews, J (2001) "Data Without (Operational) Variables." Journal of Mathematical Sociology 25(3): 225-273

Marsden, P V (1982) "Brokerage Behavior in Restricted Exchange Networks," in Marsden, P V and Lin, N (Eds) Social Structure and Network Analysis. Beverly Hills: Sage Publications

Nelder, J A and Mead, R (1965) "A Simplex Method for Function Minimization." The Computer Journal 7(4): 308-313

Press, W H, Teukolsky, S A, Vetterling, W T, Flannery, B P (1992) Numerical

Recipes in Fortran 77: The Art of Scientific Computing. 2nd edition. Cambridge: Cambridge University Press

White, H, Boorman, S, Breiger, R (1976) "Social Structure from Multiple Networks, I: Blockmodels of Roles and Positions." American Journal of Sociology 81 (1976): 730-780

Effect of Mutual Choice Metanorm in Group Dynamics for Solving Social Dilemmas

Tomohisa Yamashita, Kiyoshi Izumi, Koichi Kurumatani

Information Technology Research Institute
National Institute of Advanced Industrial Science and Technology
2-41-6, Aomi, Koto-ku Tokyo 135-0064, Japan
tomohisa.yamashita@aist.go.jp
kiyoshi@ni.aist.go.jp
k.kurumatani@aist.go.jp

Summary. In this research, we propose group dynamics that enhances the performance of multiagent systems in the Social Dilemmas. As the mechanisms for group formation, mutual choice mechanism for 2-IPD is extended to that for N-IPD. Furthermore, group split based on the metanorm of mutual choice is introduced. As a result of simulations with an evolutionary approach, we confirm the enhancement of the performance of the systems consisting of self-interest agents.

Key words: Social Dilemmas, Norm, Metanorm, Mutual Choice, Group Dynamics

1 Introduction

Recently, multiagent systems have applied more and more frequently as a framework for constructing large distributed systems. Introduction of autonomous collaborating agents gives more flexibility and efficiency to systems. In multiagent systems, usually an agents has only an incomplete information and ability to solve problems in the environment. Therefore, toward the problems that a single agent cannot solve, some agents get together and form a group to collaborate. In a group (a gathering of agents without the assumption of binding agreement), is cooperative behaviors of self-interest agents always promised in multiagent systems? It is difficult to promote cooperative behaviors in the case that an individual agent can always acquire a higher reward by non-cooperative behaviors to the group regardless of other members' behavior although cooperative behaviors of all individual agents for the group maximizes the reward of all members [2]. This situation is generally called the Social Dilemmas, where free-riders who choose non-cooperative behaviors decrease the total reword in the group. In multiagent systems, this problematic situation is often observed in resource distribution and task allocation without central authority. Self-interest agents do not take cooperative behaviors for maximizing the reward of the group because they prefer the individually best outcome to the collectively best outcome. If some mechanisms without central authority prevent free-riders from joining cooperative groups, the total reword in the group can be increased and the performance of the systems can be enhanced. Therefore, group formation, which does not require the existence of central authority, is one of the most important interactions in order to promote cooperation in multiagent systems.

In this paper, in order to realize effective group formation in dilemma situation, we use the mutual choice mechanisms [3] as the basic interaction for group formation, which is the matching mechanism in a multiple 2-person Prisoner's Dilemma (2-PD). The conventional partner choice mechanisms for matching two persons are extended to that for matching N persons, i.e., group formation. As the dilemma situation in each group, an N-person Prisoner's Dilemma (N-PD) is used. Furthermore, we propose a group split rule based on the concept of metanorm [1]. The effect of our proposed group formation on the enhancement of system performance is confirmed through an agent-based simulation with evolutionary approach.

2 Group Formation

In this paper, we propose four kinds of group formations based on unilateral and mutual choice [1]. Group formation in the dilemma situation is modeled as a 2 stage game. The first stage is group formation, where agents choose group members. The groups are determined through group formation, i.e., a population of all agents is partitioned. A group is defined as a subset of the overall agent set. Each agent can join only one group at the same time. The order of decision-making for group formation is set as random. According to this order, the agents make decisions for group formation one by one, and then groups are gradually formed. The second stage is the dilemma game. In the groups consisting of two or more agents, agents play the N-PD with their group members. The result of the N-PD in a group is independent of the agents in other groups. In the groups consisting of a single agent, the agent acquires a fix reward.

2.1 Unilateral choice

In group formation based on unilateral choice, agent i can join group k surely, i.e., group k cannot refuse agent i. Each agent has the alternative of forming a new group or joining an existing group. Agent i chooses one group, and then agent i makes an offer to group k which is most tolerable for agent i. Then,

[1] For more details see Yamashita and Ohuchi[4].

agent i is added to group k. If there is no tolerable group for agent i, agent i makes no offers and forms a new group.

2.2 Mutual choice

In group formation based on mutual choice, the agent making an offer and the group receiving it form a new group only if both mutually agree. Therefore, a group has the alternative of refusing or accepting an offer. After agent i makes an offer to group k (this process is the same as the group formation based on unilateral choice.), group k can decide to refuse or accept agent i by majority vote based on the decision of all members. If the majority of agents in group k agree to accept player i, group k accepts the offer of agent i and then agent i joins group k. If group k refuses agent i, agent i makes an offer to the second most tolerable group. Agent i continues making offers until a group accepts its offer or until all tolerable groups refuse its offer. If agent i is refused by all tolerable groups, agent i forms a new group.

2.3 Group split

A group split rule is proposed based on the concept of metanorm. According to Axelrod [1], if there is a certain norm, a metanorm is that "punish, not only against the violators of the norm, but also against anyone who refuses to punish the defectors." In this model, a norm based on mutual choice is that "don't choose defectors as group members." A metanorm based on mutual choice is that "don't choose, not only defectors, but also anyone who choose defectors as group members." This metanorm realizes group split by dividing one group of agents agreeing the acceptance of an agent (agreeing agents) and the other group of agents opposing (opposing agents). From the point of view of the opposing agents, the agreeing agents violate the metanorm because the agreeing agents choose the agent that opposing agents consider as a defector. In order not to choose the agents who choose defectors as group members, the opposing agents leave from the group.

2.4 Re-offering

By the introduction of the rule of group split, the number of groups including only one agent may increase. Re-offering is proposed to increase the chance to join a group including several agents as soon as possible.

3 Simulation Setup

3.1 Evolutionary approach

In our simulations, a genetic algorithm is applied to evolve the player's strategies. The genetic algorithm is a model of machine learning that derives its behavior from a metaphor of the processes of evolution in nature. The dynamic behavior of agent-based modeling with a genetic algorithm is regarded as a powerful method for modeling social learning.

In implementing the encoding of the chromosomes, the strategy of an individual player is represented by a binary bit string. The two dimensions of a strategy, cooperativeness C_i and vengefulness V_i, are each divided into $2^x - 1$ equal levels, from 0.0 to 1.0. Because $2^x - 1$ levels are represented by x binary bits, a player's strategy needs a total of $2x$ bits: x bits for cooperativeness C_i and x bits for vengefulness V_i.

Each simulation is initialized with a population of all players. Each generation consists of an iteration of group formation and split, and then the Dilemma game. At the beginning of the genetic phase, each player's strategy in a population is assigned a fitness equal to its average payoff given per payoff received. A partner for crossover is selected by means of a tournament selection. Uniform crossover is accomplished between the strategies of a player and a partner to obtain a new strategy for one offspring if the fitness of the partner is better than that of the player in tournament selection.

After that, the strategy of this offspring is subjected to mutation, where each bit is flipped one bit with a certain probability.

3.2 Parameter setting

In this paper, because our purpose is to examine whether group dynamics can promote cooperative behavior of players and enhance the performance of systems, we pay attention to the transition of players' strategies and the average payoff of all players. In order to confirm the effect of the proposed group dynamics, we compare four settings: case 1) only group formation based on unilateral choice, case 2) only group formation based on mutual choice, case 3) group formation based on mutual choice and group split, and case 4) group formation based on mutual choice, group split and re-offering.

It is impossible to keep such a state constant due to the high mutation rate of 0.05. We define the establishment of cooperation as the condition where

Table 1. Common parameters in the simulations of group dynamics.

Number of players	50
Number of generations	5000
Number of group dynamics per generation	200
Coefficient of payoff function a	1.0
Coefficient of payoff function b	0.6
Payoff for lone player $P_{reservation}$	0.1
Initial value of expected cooperation π	1.0
Initial value of Cooperativeness C_i	0.0
Initial value of Vengefulness V_i	0.0
Mutation rate	0.05
Binary bits for C_i and V_i (total bits)	10

Table 2. Number of times cooperation is established in 40 trials of four cases.

case 1	0/40
case 2	4/40
case 3	12/40
case 4	40/40

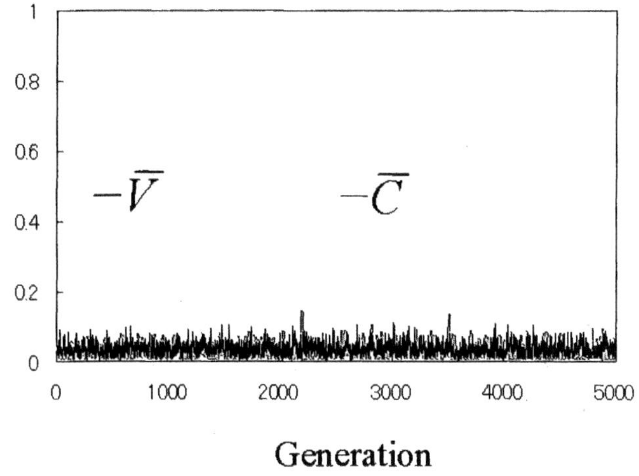

Fig. 1. Example of the failure of the establishment of cooperation in case 1: the transition of the average cooperativeness $\bar{C}$ and vengefulness $\bar{V}$ from 0 to 5,000 generations.

both average cooperativeness of all players ($\overline{C}$) and average vengefulness ($\overline{V}$) are bigger than 0.8 because it is impossible to keep the state, $V_i = 1.0$ and $C_i = 1.0$ ($\forall i \in N$), due to high mutation rate 0.05.

The other important parameters and the payoff function of the dilemma game are shown in Table. 1. Under these conditions, we examine whether group dynamics accelerate cooperative behavior and what rules of group dynamics are effective for enhanceing the performance of systems.

4 Simulation

The number of times cooperation is established in 40 trials of four cases is shown in Table. 2. In regard to these results, we take up the average cooperativeness ($\bar{C}$) and vengefulness ($\bar{V}$) of all players after 5,000 generations and the average payoff of all players. Three typical transitions of the average cooperativeness and vengefulness of all players are shown in Figs. 1, 2, and 3. In these graphs, the horizontal axis represents the generation, and the vertical

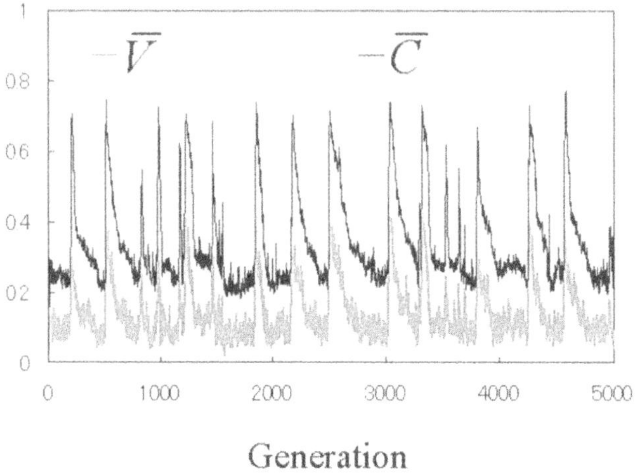

Fig. 2. Example of the failure of the establishment of cooperation in case 2 and 3: the transition of the average cooperativeness $\bar{C}$ and vengefulness $\bar{V}$ from 0 to 5,000 generations.

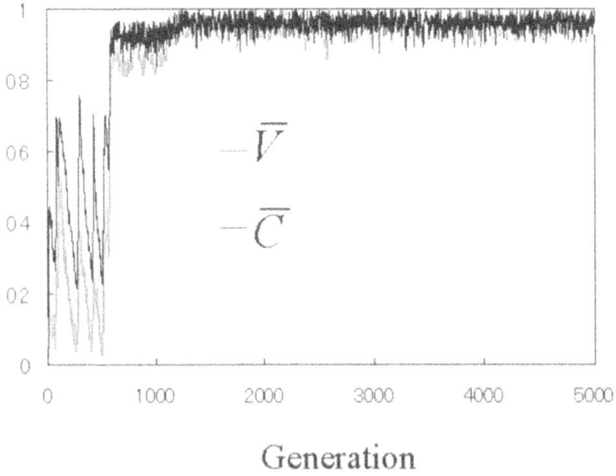

Fig. 3. Example of the establishment of cooperation in case 2, 3, 4: the transition of the average cooperativeness $\bar{C}$ and vengefulness $\bar{V}$ from 0 to 5,000 generations.

axis represents the average cooperativeness and vengefulness of all players. The transition of the average payoff of four cases is shown in Fig. 4. In these graphs, the x-axis is the generation, and the y-axis is the average payoff of all players.

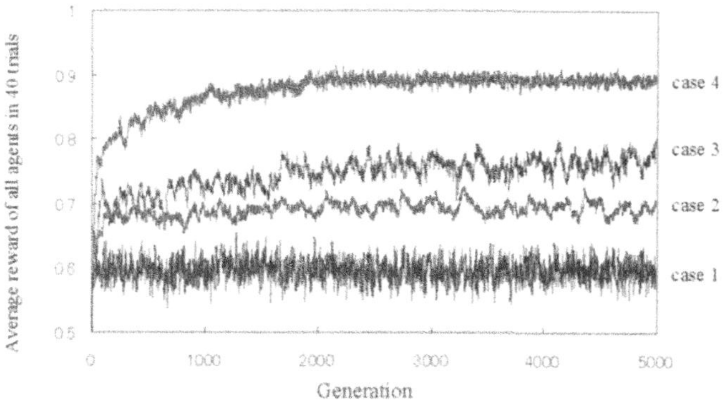

Fig. 4. Transition of the average payoff of all players in 40 trials of four cases of group dynamics.

4.1 Establishment of cooperation

In all trials of case 1, there were little cooperativeness and vengefulness, i.e., cooperation was not established at all within 5,000 generations. The typical behavior of $\bar{C}$ and $\bar{V}$ in case 1 for 5,000 generations is shown in Fig. 1. Throughout the generations, $\bar{C}$ and $\bar{V}$fluctuated in the range of 0.0 to 0.1. In 36 trials of case 2, cooperation was not established within 5,000 generations. In the remaining 4 trials, there were great deal of cooperativeness and vengefulness, i.e., cooperation was established. In 28 trials of case 3, cooperation was not established within 5,000 generations. In the remaining 12 trials, cooperation was established. In all trials of case 4, cooperation was established.

The typical behavior of $\bar{C}$ and $\bar{V}$ in case 2 and 3 when cooperation was not established within 5,000 generations is shown in Fig. 2. Usually, $\bar{C}$ remained in the range of 0.0 to 0.2 and $\bar{V}$ remained in the range of 0.2 to 0.4. However, occasionally $\bar{C}$ rose to 0.4 and $\bar{V}$ fell to 0.3, and then $\bar{C}$ and $\bar{V}$ returned to their initial states. This fluctuation was repeated throughout the generations.

The typical behavior of $\bar{C}$ and $\bar{V}$ in case 2, 3, 4 when cooperation was established within 5,000 generations is shown in Fig. 3. At first, $\bar{C}$ fluctuated in the range of 0.6 to 0.8 and $\bar{V}$ fluctuated in the range of 0.4 to 0.8, $\bar{C}$ and $\bar{V}$ became about 1.0 in the end. Once $\bar{C}$ and $\bar{V}$ reached 1.0, this state continued to remain there and did not transfer to another state.

4.2 Transition of average payoff

The average payoffs of all players in 40 trials of four cases are ranked in descending order as case 4, 3, 2, 1. In the graph of Fig. 4, throughout all generations, the average payoff of unilateral choice continued to fluctuate near 0.6. The average payoff of mutual choice also continued to be near 0.7. The average payoffs of mutual choice with the split rule continued to slightly rise from 0.7 to 0.8. The average payoffs of mutual choice with the split rule and re-offering rose to 0.9 until 2,000 generations. After 2,000 generations, it seldom changed.

5 Discussion

We discuss the establishment of cooperation based on the strategy (C_i and V_i) in four cases and the enhancement of systems' performance based on the average payoff of all players. In the following discussion, a player with a high level of cooperativeness is represented as C_{high}, and a player with a low level of cooperativeness as C_{low}. In the same way, a player with high and low levels of vengefulness are represented as V_{high} and V_{low}, respectively.

5.1 Establishment of cooperation

Case 1

In all trials of the group dynamics in case 1, why did the establishment of cooperation fail? A player with low cooperativeness by mutation, i.e., a player with C_{high}, cannot acquire a higher payoff than the players with C_{low}. The reason is that the players with C_{high} cannot refuse an offer from the players with C_{low} in group dynamics based on unilateral choice, and the players with C_{low} have a free-ride on the players with C_{high}. Accordingly, the players with C_{high} do not increase in the next generation. Therefore, cooperation is never established.

Case 2

In 36 trials of the group dynamics in case 2, why did the establishment of cooperation fail? We analyze the factors leading to the failure of cooperation based mutual choice.

First, we assumed that there was only one player with C_{high} and V_{high}. Mutation decreases cooperativeness or increases vengefulness because the initial condition is $V_i = 0$ and $C_i = 0$ ($\forall i \in N$). A player with cooperativeness decreased by mutation, i.e., a player with C_{high}, cannot acquire a higher payoff than the players with C_{low} because the players with C_{low} have a freeride on the players with C_{high}. Accordingly, the players with C_{high} do not increase in the next generation. A player with vengefulness increased by mutation, i.e., a player with V_{high}, cannot acquire a higher payoff than the players with C_{low} because players with V_{high} do not join a group consisting of players with C_{low}. Therefore, one player with C_{high} and V_{high} by mutation cannot acquire a higher payoff than the players with C_{low} and V_{low}. Consequently, the player with C_{high} and V_{high} is not selected in genetic operation, and it then perishes.

Next, we assumed that there were several players with C_{high} and V_{high}. If a group consists of only players with C_{high} and V_{high}, the group refuses the offers of players with C_{low}. If a group consists of both players with C_{high} and V_{high} and players with C_{high} and V_{low}, it is possible that a player with C_{low} would join this group and have a free-ride. The player with C_{low} can join the group because, while the players with C_{high} and V_{high} oppose the acceptance of his/her game offer, the players with C_{high} and V_{low} agree to it. If the players with C_{high} and V_{low} win the majority vote over the players with C_{high} and V_{high}, the player with C_{low} can join the group. In such a group, the players with C_{low} have a free-ride on the players with C_{high}. The players with C_{high} and V_{high} are not selected in the genetic operation and then perish because they cannot acquire higher payoffs than the free-rider. Although there are plural players with C_{high} and V_{high}, the players with C_{low} and the players with C_{high} and V_{low} prevent the establishment of cooperation. The players with C_{low} directly prevent the establishment of cooperation because they have a free-ride on the players with C_{high} and V_{high}. On the other hand, the players with C_{high} and V_{low} indirectly prevent the establishment of cooperation because they accept offers from the players with C_{low} who have a free-ride on the players with C_{high}. In group dynamics based on mutual choice, Therefore, the establishment of cooperation often fails.

On the other hand, in the remaining 4 trials, why did the establishment of cooperation succeed? Here, we analyze the factors leading to the establishment of cooperation in group dynamics based on mutual choice. The reason for the establishment of cooperation was that a player with C_{low} can join the group consisting of both players with C_{high} and V_{high} and players with C_{high} and V_{low}. If there are players with C_{high} and V_{high} but no player with C_{high} and V_{low}, the player with C_{low} cannot join the group, and then the players will defect from each other. As a result, the player with C_{low} acquires a lower payoff than the players with C_{high} and V_{high} who cooperate with each other. If the number of players with C_{high} and V_{high} increases, and the players predominate in the population for a few generations before the number of players with C_{high} and V_{low} increases by crossover or mutation, cooperation becomes established. Therefore, since the simulation results show that cooperation was established in 4 out of 40 trials, we can conclude that it is not impossible but difficult to realize the establishment of cooperation in group dynamics based on mutual choice.

Case 3

In 12 trials of group dynamics in case 3, why did the establishment of cooperation succeed? In case 3, the establishment of cooperation fails because the players with C_{high} and V_{low} accept the offer of the players with C_{low}. Here, we analyze the factors leading to the establishment of cooperation in group dynamics based on mutual choice with the split rule.

In group dynamics based on mutual choice with the split rule, if the players with C_{high} and V_{low} agree to accept the offer of a player with C_{low}, and the group as a whole also accepts it, the players with C_{high} and V_{high} leave the group based on the split rule; they refuse to play the dilemma game with those who play with defectors. The split rule prevents the player with C_{low} from having a free-ride on the players with C_{high} and V_{high}. This is because if the player with C_{low} joins the group, the players with C_{high} and V_{high} leave. As a result, if there are some players with C_{high} and V_{high}, they can form a group without the player with C_{low}. The players with C_{high} and V_{high} can acquire higher payoffs because they cooperate with each other. Throughout this process, the number of players with C_{high} and V_{high} increases and they predominate in the population. Therefore, cooperation becomes established.

Case 4

In all trials of group dynamics in case 4, why did the establishment of cooperation succeed? Based on group formation based on mutual choice and group split, a player with C_{high} and V_{high} sometimes leaves from the group and then joins a group consisting of only itself. In this case, the player with C_{high} and V_{high} acquires the payoff of the loner, which is lower than that in a group. If the player with C_{high} and V_{high} has a chance of re-offering, the player leaving from one group may be able to join another group. The player with C_{high} and V_{high} can avoid acquiring a lower payoff by mutual cooperation if another group consists of many players with C_{high}. The re-offering of a player leaving from a group increases the chance for players with C_{high} and V_{high} to acquire a higher payoff. Accordingly, the establishment of cooperation increases because the players with C_{high} and V_{high} do not decrease in the next generation.

5.2 Comparison of average payoffs

In this research, we compare the effect of the proposed group dynamics by the average payoff because the average payoff can be considered as a measure of the system performance. Based on the comparison of the average payoffs, the effect of four cases is ranked in descending order as case 4, 3, 2, 1. From the transition of the average payoffs, we can acquire the following results of group dynamics. In relatively early generations, the effect of the split rule doesn't provide good results for the establishment of cooperation because there is not a great difference between case 3 and 4.

6 Conclusions

In this paper, in order to enhance the performance of systems consisting of self-interest players, group dynamics was proposed. The partner choice mechanisms for the multiple 2-PD were extended to that for a multiple N-person dilemma game to realize group dynamics. Four kinds of group dynamics, case 1) only group formation based on unilateral choice, case 2) only group formation based on mutual choice, case 3) group formation based on mutual choice and group split, and case 4) group formation based on mutual choice, group split and re-offering were proposed based on the partner choice mechanisms. In order to measure the effect of the proposed group dynamics on the establishment of cooperation and the enhancement of system performance, an agent-based simulation was applied. Agent-based simulations with an evolutionary approach were conducted to confirm whether group dynamics with the split rule could promote cooperative behavior of players and enhance the performance of systems.

On the establishment of cooperation, the following results were confirmed: In group dynamics with only group formation based on unilateral choice, it is impossible to establish cooperation. In group dynamics with only group formation based on mutual choice, it is not impossible but difficult to establish cooperation. Similarly, in group dynamics with only group formation based on mutual choice and group formation, it is difficult to establish cooperation. In group dynamics with only group formation based on mutual choice and group formation and re-offering, it is possible to establish cooperation. Finally, it was confirmed that group dynamics has a large enough effect to increase the performance of systems if the group dynamics includes group split and re-offering.

References

1. R. Axelrod (1986) An Evolutionary Approach to Norms. *American Political Science Review.*, 80:1095–1111.
2. R. Axtell (2002) Non-cooperative Dynamics of Multi-agent Teams. In *Proceedings of The First International Joint Conference on Autonomous Agents and Multiagent Systems*, pages 1082–1089
3. L. Tesfatsion (1997) A Trade Network Game with Endogenous Partner Selection. *Kluwer Academic Publishers.*, pages 249–269
4. T. Yamashita and A. Ohuchi (2002) Analysis of Norms Game with Mutual Choice. In *Exploring New Frontiers on Artificial Intelligence*, pages 174–184. Springer-Verlag Tokyo

Evolution of Cooperative Behavior in C2C market: Effect of Reputation Management System

Hitoshi Yamamoto[1], Kazunari Ishida[2], and Toshizumi Ohta[1]

[1] The Graduate School of Information Systems, University of Electro-Communications, 1-5-1 Choufugaoka, Choufushi, Tokyo 182-8585, Japan
[2] Faculty of International Agriculture and Food Studies, Tokyo University of Agriculture, 1-1-1 Sakuragaoka, Setagayaku, Tokyo, 156-0054, Japan

Summary. We model an online consumer-to-consumer (C2C) market by employing the prisoner's dilemma. To discuss the characteristics of goods traded on a C2C market, we define temptation and contribution indexes based on the payoff matrix of the game. According to the results of the simulation with the model, we find that a positive reputation management system can promote cooperative behavior in online C2C markets. Moreover, we also find that such a system is especially effective for an online C2C market where expensive physical goods are traded, whereas a negative reputation management system is effective for an online C2C market where information goods are traded.

Key words. Reputation Management System, C2C market, Agent-Based Approach, Iterated Prisoner's Dilemma

1. Introduction

Thanks to the spread of the Internet throughout society, we can now buy and sell online goods and information that could not easily exchanged in the past due to small demand. The online consumer-to-consumer (C2C) market is a new kind of transaction place made possible through the popularization of the Internet. Although such a market provides an effective transaction facility, it is susceptible to fraud, because of its anonymity and ease of entry and exit. Thus, the attractive features of online trading have led to an increased risk of cheating, e.g., receiving goods without paying for them or receiving payments without sending goods. In short, there is a temptation to cheat others. On the other hand, communication through the Internet promotes voluntary contributions. The open source community for Linux and BBSs of various genres are good examples. However, the free-rider is a problem in these communities. Generally in on-line transactions, a participant can receive services without contributing somehow, which is not an incentive for cooperation.

In this paper, we show that the prisoner's dilemma is a suitable model to deal with this problem. Before we describe the model though, we should briefly review pertinent research on how to identify trustworthy participants and promote cooperative behavior. Participants tend to enter and exit online C2C markets frequently. Employing reputation to form trust among participants has been studied by many researchers. Rensnick et al. (2000) pointed out that using reputation information was one of the best ways to promote mutual trust between participants. Dellarocas (2000) discussed the robustness of reputation systems against unfair evaluations by malicious participants. Kollock (1999) provided a classification of positive and negative aspects concerning reputation information. Based on this classification, we will develop a model to analyze reputation management systems operationally. By employing an operational model, we can identify the conditions in which the reputation management system works efficiently.

2. Temptation and contribution in C2C markets

The Internet motivates users to contribute to online communities and tempts them to cheat of the transactions in those communities. It makes it easy for users to contribute to a community because of its low cost of communication, while it also tempts them to cheat on others because of its anonymity. In particular, ease of entry and exit may tempt users to receive goods without paying for them or to receive payments without sending goods. To promote efficient online transactions, we must give incentives to contribute and minimize the temptation to cheat. To explore viable systems for efficient online transactions, we formalize the situation according to game theory. In particular, we can define a stage in the online C2C transaction as the prisoner's dilemma.

2.1. Prisoner's Dilemma in a C2C market

A player who participates in a C2C online transaction always has an incentive to cheat on others (non-cooperation). In particular, a buyer may take goods from a seller without paying for them, and a seller may get a payment from a buyer without sending the goods to him or her.

The situation in C2C online transactions is representative of the prisoners' dilemma. If two player's cooperate, they can get the maximum total benefit. Yet one player cheating on the other is also a way to maximize self benefit. In its simplest incarnation, there are two players, and they cannot communicate with each other directly because they are in solitary confinement in a prison. Each player has two strategies, i.e., cooperation (C) and deception (D). We can consider a payoff matrix as shown in Table 1.

Table 1. Payoff matrix for prisoners' dilemma

		Action of player-2	
		C	D
Action of player-1	C	(S,S)	(W,B)
	D	(B,W)	(T,T)

The necessary conditions for the prisoners' dilemma are the following inequalities.

$$\begin{cases} B > S > T > W \\ 2S > B + W \end{cases} \tag{1}$$

In the prisoners' dilemma of a C2C online transaction, a seller can have two actions; i.e. he/she can cooperate with the buyer to give goods in exchange for payments or he/she can deceive him or her to get payments without sending goods. A buyer also can cooperate or deceive, i.e. pay for goods or get goods without paying for them. To explore viable policies to maximize cooperative behaviors and to eliminate non-cooperative ones, we must define indexes concerning contribution and temptation based on the payoff matrix of the prisoners' dilemma.

2.2. Temptation

Taylor (1976) defined the index γ as level of temptation to cheat others.

$$\gamma = \frac{B - S}{B - T} \tag{2}$$

When the denominator $B - T$ is small, the risk of cheating is small because there is only a small difference between the payoffs of the two situations, i.e., the case of (my action, the other's action) = (D,C) and (D,D). When $B - S$ is large, the incentive to cheat is large because there is a large difference between the payoffs of (D,C) and of (C,C). Hence, a large γ indicates a large temptation to cheat on others, whereas a small γ indicates a small temptation. The range of γ is (0,1), as defined in the inequalities (1).

2.3. Contribution

We define the index δ as the level of contribution as follows.

$$\delta = \frac{S - T}{S - W} \tag{3}$$

When the denominator $S - W$ is small, the risk of cooperating is small because there is only a small difference between the payoffs of (C,C) and of (C,D). When $S - T$ is large, the incentive to cooperate is large because there is a large difference between the payoffs of (C,C) and of (D,D). Hence, a large δ indicates a strong motivation for contribution, whereas a small δ indicates a weak motivation for contribution. The range of δ is (0,1), as defined in the inequalities (1).

2.4. Boundary Conditions

Based on the in-equalities (1) we can derive the boundary conditions in terms of δ and γ as follows.

$$\begin{cases} \gamma < 1/(1+\delta) \\ 0 < \gamma < 1 \\ 0 < \delta < 1 \end{cases} \tag{4}$$

Fig. 1 illustrates the area where the PD conditions of (4) are satisfied. Surprisingly, by employing the indexes, we can see that the boundary conditions of prisoners' dilemma can be plotted on the two-dimensional plane instead of plotting regions for the inequalities (1) in a four-dimensional parameter space fro representing the payoff matrix of the game. The mathematical simplicity of the two indexes is of obvious benefit to study the meaning of contribution and reputation.

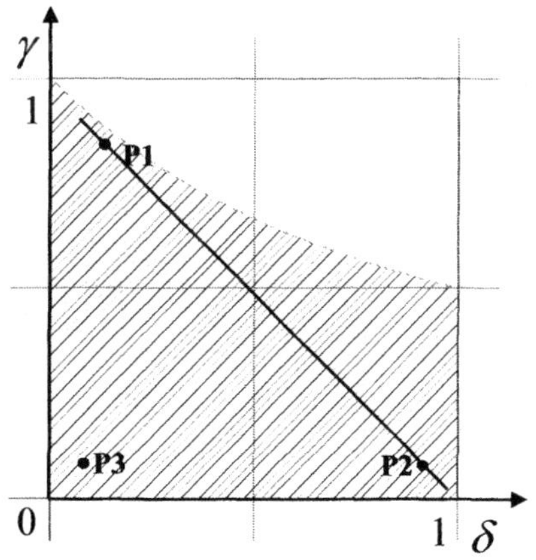

Fig. 1. The area that satisfies the boundary conditions on the contribution (δ) and temptation (γ) plane

2.5 Characteristics of goods in a market

In the area around point P1, γ is large but δ is small. The payoff matrix for this area indicates there is a large gain to cheating and large loss to being cheated. We can interpret the situation as transactions of high-price goods. In the area around point P2, γ is small but δ is large. The payoff matrix for this area indicates there is an incentive for cooperation because there is a small difference between the gain of cooperating S and that of cheating B. Moreover the incentive tends to be larger because there is a large difference between S and T. We can interpret the situation as being like that of the open source community where participants try to share information. In the area around point P3, γ and δ are small. In this situation, the risk to cooperate tends to be large because the difference between W and T is large, although the temptation to cheat tends to be small because the difference between B and S is small. Hence, it is difficult to cooperate, even though there is no temptation to cheat.

Thus by employing two axes, we can describe the characteristics of goods in a C2C market. In the next section, we will analyze the behavior of our model. The behavior on the line ($\gamma + \delta = 1$) in Fig. 1 will be useful to discuss the difference between physical goods and information. Based on this analysis, we will discuss the policy to develop the reputation management system.

3. Modeling Reputation Management System

To analyze and design a C2C online market, we developed our model based on an agent-based approach, because the analysis and design require detailed and dynamic explanations at the individual participants' level to exhibit social phenomena. Axelrod (1997) concluded that the agent-based approach would be effective for analyzing mechanisms that can promote global phenomena from local interactions between agents. By employing this approach, we describe C2C online transactions within the framework of the prisoners' dilemma in order to find the requisite conditions and market mechanism for promoting the emergence of cooperative behavior.

3.1. Procedure of Transactions

Our market model is for sellers and buyers dealing in goods through bids and awards. Transactions are performed by the following procedure.

1. The seller puts the "goods" which s/he has on the market.
2. The buyer chooses "goods" based on his or her preference (which is identical to "demand," here).
3. The buyer matches the "supply" with the "demand."
4. The buyer chooses a transaction partner by checking the seller's reputation.

5. The seller chooses a transaction partner by checking the buyer's reputation.
6. If a transaction partner is chosen, they will trade.
7. The profits of the seller and the buyer are found by consulting the prisoner's dilemma pay-off matrix.
8. A new participant enters the market every turn.
9. The new participant copies the strategy of the participant who has the highest current profit.

Under these circumstances, if there is no system to promote cooperation, a participant who does not always cooperate could exploit a participant who always cooperates with everyone. To promote cooperation, one can embed a reputation information management system into the C2C online transaction.

3.2. Formulation of Reputation Management System

To model the reputation management system, we define reputation in terms of positive and negative evaluations of a participant based on Kollock (1999). For simplicity, the reputation we deal with is the number of cooperative and non-cooperative actions in deals on a market.

An action of agent-i during a time period t (A_t^i) can be either cooperation (C) or defection (D).

$$A_t^i = \{C, D\} \tag{5}$$

A cooperative agent always chooses C, whereas a non-cooperative agent always chooses D. An agent with a tit for tat strategy selects his or her action based on the previous actions of the agent it is dealing with. A random agent cooperates or defects with others randomly. A transaction history (T_t^i) is recorded by the online transaction system.

$$T_t^i = \{A_k^i | k \in \{0,1,\cdots,t\}\} \tag{6}$$

To make a deal, agents who want to buy bid on goods offered by other agents; the agent who has received bids awards the goods to one of them. A bid or an award is decided by each agent based on the reputation it calculates by using the historical records of the actions of others. Based on the historical record, an agent can calculate the number of cooperative and non-cooperative actions in a certain time span, i.e., $T_{C,t}^i, T_{D,t}^i$ respectively.

$$T_{C,t}^i = \{k | A_k^i = C, k \in \{t - Scope + 1, t - Scope + 2, \cdots, t\}\} \tag{7}$$

$$T_{D,t}^i = \{k | A_k^i = D, k \in \{t - Scope + 1, t - Scope + 2, \cdots, t\}\} \tag{8}$$

The reputation of agent(i) is calculated based on focus of reputation (α) as described in equation (9).

$$R_t^i = \alpha |T_{C,t}^i| - (1 - \alpha) |T_{D,t}^i| \tag{9}$$

Positive or negative reputation systems can be described with α equaling 1 or 0, respectively. Based on the value calculated by (6), each agent makes his or her bid or award.

4. Simulation

Yamamoto et al. (2003) indicated the fundamental characteristics of reputation management systems in simulations with medium values of temptation and contribution, i.e., $(\gamma,\delta)=(0.4,0.6)$, and a variable the reputation cognitive parameter (α). According to their results, a positive reputation system can be more effective than a negative reputation system for an online transaction.

In this section, to discuss desirable reputation management system in terms of characteristics of goods on online C2C market, we will try to find what type of reputation management system can lead to the extinction of participants who cheat others. We will observe the behavior of the model on the $\gamma+\delta=1$ line in Fig. 1. A large γ means that a market deals with expensive physical goods. A small δ means that a market is a kind of a community to exchange information and knowledge. we will focus on cases with a high rate of entrance and exiting ($\alpha=30$), because we want to discuss the function of the reputation system.

The horizontal axes in Figs 2, 3, and 4 are δ. The vertical axes show average population after 200 simulation periods. The relation between γ and δ is $\gamma=1-\delta$. Fig. 2 shows the behavior with a positive reputation management system ($\alpha=1$).

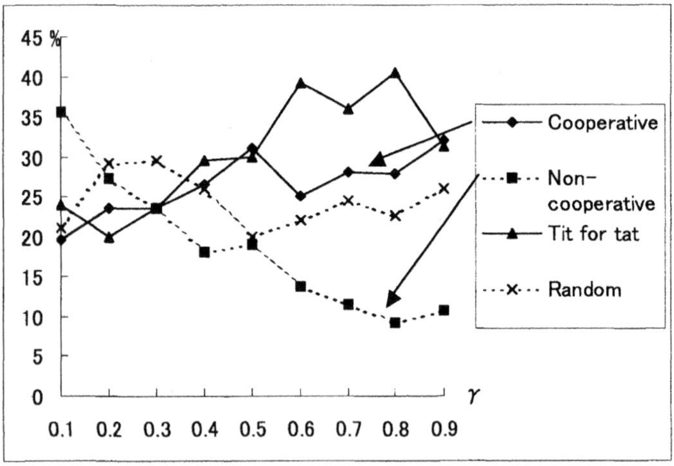

Fig. 2. Trajectories of populations on $\gamma+\delta=1$ when α is 1.0.

Fig. 3 shows the trajectories of populations for four types of strategy when the market employs positive and negative reputation management systems (α=0.5). Fig. 4 shows the trajectories of the populations when the market employs negative reputation management systems (α=0). All figures reflect the cooperative situation when δ is large. For example, a negative reputation management system can prevent non-cooperative behaviors when δ is 0.8, although the system can not prevent non-cooperative behavior when δ is 0.6.

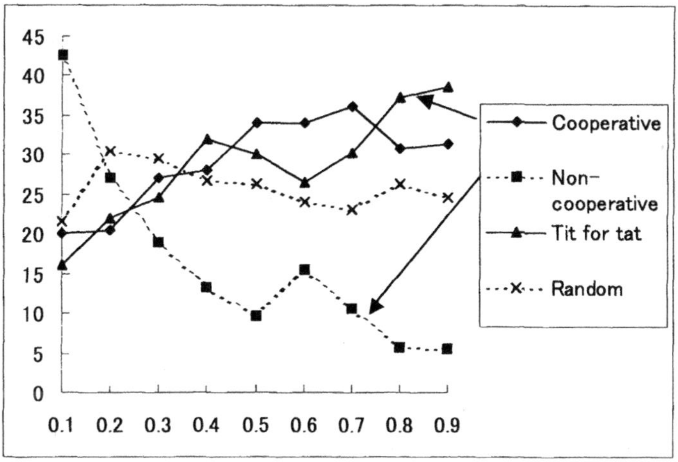

Fig. 3. Trajectories of populations on $\gamma+\delta=1$ when α is 0.5.

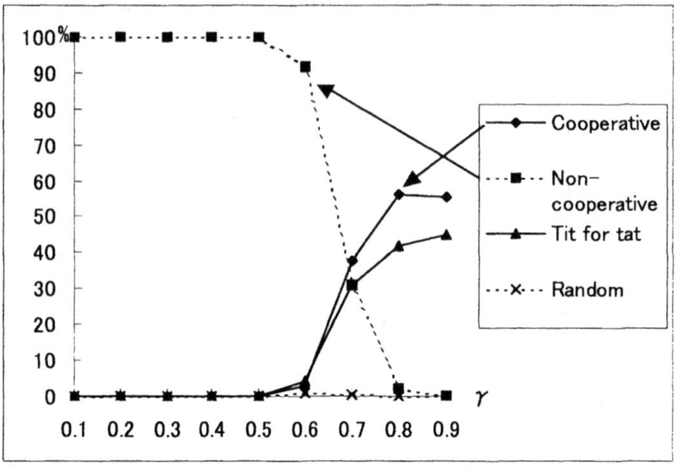

Fig. 4. Trajectories of populations on $\gamma+\delta=1$ when α is 0.0.

5. Discussion

According to Figs. 2 and 3, on the one hand, a positive reputation management system can prevent non-cooperative actions when there is a small to moderate temptation to cheat. On the other hand, Fig. 4 shows that the system can not prevent bad behavior when there is a large temptation. We thus find that a positive reputation management system is effective to promote good transactions in markets where expensive physical goods are exchanged.

On the other hand, the positive reputation management system prevents transactions by newcomers, whereas the negative system does not. Hence, the negative system is effective when it can promote cooperation, because of the characteristics concerning newcomers. In the area of $\delta>0.7$ of Fig. 3, there are many participants with the cooperative strategy. In this area, temptation is low and contribution is high, i.e., large benefit to cooperate and low risk to be cheated. Knowledge sharing markets such as K-square(www.ksquare.co.jp) and Chienowa.com(chienowa.com) where participants exchange their knowledge and money with invisible hands are relevant examples. If someone "free-rides" on the other's knowledge, the other might not suffer from it, because the other can still have his or her own information and knowledge despite the lack of compensation. Hence, in a online C2C knowledge market, a negative reputation management system would be better than positive one, because it can prevent non-cooperative actions, yet does not prevent transactions by newcomers to the market.

6. Conclusion

We showed the effectiveness of sharing information concerning reputation to ensure cooperative actions among participants in C2C online transactions by using an agent-based model in an experimental simulation. In a high turnover market that is typical of C2C online transactions of physical goods, a positive reputation system can be more effective than a negative reputation system. However, in a online C2C knowledge market, a negative reputation management system would be better than positive one because it does not prevent transactions by newcomers to the market.

We defined two indexes concerning temptation and contribution based on a payoff matrix, in order to deal with the characteristics of goods exchanged on C2C market. By employing the indexes, we can identify a viable policy to design an effective C2C market, because we can discuss what type of reputation management system is effective for trading certain goods, e.g. expensive physical goods or information goods.

References

Axelrod R (1997) The Complexity of Cooperation. Princeton University Press, pp 3 29

Dellarocas C (2000) Immunizing Online Reputation Reporting Systems Against Unfair Ratings and Discriminatory Behavior. Proceedings of the 2nd ACM Conference on Electronic Commerce

Kollock P (1999) The Production of Trust in Online Markets. Advances in Group Processes, 16: 99 123

Resnick P, Zeckhauser R, Friedman E and Kuwabara K (2000) Reputation Systems, Communications of the ACM, 43(12) 45 48

Tailor M (1976) The Prisoner's Dilemma Supergame. In: Anarchy and Cooperation, London: Wiley, pp 29 68

Yamamoto H, Ishida K and Ohta T (2003) Managing Online Trade by Reputation Circulation: An Agent-Based Approach to the C2C Market, Proc. of The 7th World Multi-Conference on Systemics, Cybernetics and Informatics, 1: 60 64

Constructing shared interpretations in a team of intelligent agents: the effects of communication intensity and structure

Davide Marchiori, Massimo Warglien

Department of Business Economics, Ca'Foscari University of Venezia, 873 Cannaregio 30121, Venezia, Italy

Summary. In this paper we explore a model of a team of intelligent agents constructing a shared interpretation of the state of their environment. Each agent is modeled as a constraint satisfaction network of the Hopfield (1982) type.

We show that in a noisy environment communication intensity often has a non-monotonic effect on team interpretive accuracy. We also investigate how team communication can correct erroneous individual interpretations stored in agents' memories – errors concerning what they know, not only what they perceive.

We also compare the effects of different communication structures, and show that communication structure matters only when agents are cognitively heterogeneous (each has a different repertoire of interpretations in his memory), while it has only a minor impact on team performance when agents are homogeneous.

Keywords. Team, Neural Nets, Hopfield Nets, Reliability, Groupthink

1. Introduction

Communication among agents is well known to improve the reliability of groups. In particular, it can correct individual misperceptions and help groups to achieve effective shared interpretations of their task environment (Weick and Roberts 1993). A the same time, it is also well known that groups are subject to "pressure to conform" pathologies that can lead individuals to converge on wrong judgments (Janis 1971). A good model of group interaction should account for both such virtues and pathologies.

In this paper we explore a model of a team of intelligent agents constructing a shared interpretation of the state of their environment. Each agent is modeled as a constraint satisfaction network of the Hopfield (1982) type. An individual interpretation is the stable state of a single agent in response to the perception of an environmental stimulus. A shared interpretation occurs when all agents converge to the same interpretation.

Agents have a repertoire of "typical" states of the environment stored in their associative memory. The communication among agents is modeled as connections from nodes of an agent to nodes of other agents, following an original proposal by Hutchins (1995). Communication intensity is the overall strength of such connections.

We study the behavior of such team in a noisy environment, which can cause individual misperception of the "true" state of the environment. We analyze the effects of communication intensity and structure, and of agents' cognitive heterogeneity, on the emergent collective interpretation of the state of the environment. In particular, we focus on the error-correcting or error-amplifying effects of communication in a team.

We show that in a noisy environment communication intensity often has a non-monotonic effect on the emergence of correct shared interpretations by the team. For low levels of communication intensity, increases in the intensity parameter are initially beneficial, fostering convergence between agents' interpretation and correcting noise. However, after a critical threshold is reached, increases in communication intensity generate overwhelming group pressure to conform, leading to convergence to arbitrary wrong interpretations. A simple "credulity theorem" shows that for a sufficiently large value of communication intensity every arbitrary shared interpretation is a fix-point of team behavior. This agrees with the intuition that peer pressure can lead to conformism.

We also investigate how team communication can correct erroneous individual interpretations stored in agents' memories – errors concerning what they know, not just what they perceive. We compare teams of homogeneously "wrong" agents (all agents have stored in their memory the same erroneous repertoire of states of the environment) with teams of heterogeneously "wrong" agents (different agents have stored different repertoires and are wrong on different features of the environment). Even in this case communication can actually rectify erroneous individual conceptions. Heterogeneous teams are slightly less reactive to increases in communication intensity, suggesting a moderating role of agents heterogeneity on collective credulity – a (minor) defect in the context of our simulations, but possibly a virtue in other contexts. We also compare the effects of different communication structures, and show that communication structure matters only when agents are heterogeneous, while it has only a minor impact on team performance when agents are homogeneous.

2. Structure of the model

Environment There is an environment which is characterized by N binary features. Each combination of such features is a possible state of the environment. In our simulations, there are always only three "true states" of the environment.

Environmental inputs The environment "sends" to each agent an input representing its state. The input is a string of N binary elements, each element corresponding to a feature of the environment.

Agents Agents are modeled as Hopfield (1982) neural networks of N nodes (a node for each feature of the environment). A Hopfield network is a set of nodes and connections representing interdependence between nodes. Nodes assume binary states (1, -1). Each node updates its state S_i autonomously, following a threshold decision rule using as input the states of connected nodes S_i weighted by the strength of corresponding connections w_{ij}.

$$S_i = \mathrm{sgn}\left(h_i\right) = \mathrm{sgn}\left(\sum_j w_{ij} S_j\right)$$

If connections are symmetric, the network always relaxes to a stable state (see Hertz et al. 1991 for a formal treatment). The stable states to which the network relaxes in response to environmental stimuli (its attractors) are the agents "interpretations" of the state of the environment. Each agent has stored in its memory 3 configurations of the environment.

Team A team is a set of n agents. Agents communicate with each other. Communication is feature-specific: each agent can communicate to others his current belief on the state of a specific feature of the environment, as represented by the current state of his node corresponding to such feature. Communication is modeled by introducing connections between each agent's nodes and the corresponding nodes of other agents (Hutchins 1995). Consequently, communication of the state of a node from one agent to another one is mediated by the existence of such connection and by its strength. The overall strength of communication connections in the team is defined as the communication intensity parameter. Intuitively, it reflects the "pressure" exerted by peer beliefs.

This allows us to model the team as a "network of networks" that still preserves the basic structure and formal properties of a Hopfield net. The net is constituted by a vector of nodes corresponding to the union of individual nodes, and a weight matrix containing both the individual memory weights and the communication connections. In the weight matrix, blocks along the main diagonal represent individual memories, while blocks outside the main diagonal represent communication structure. In this case, each i-th node of an agent k^* will update its state according to the following rule:

$$S_i^{k^*} = \mathrm{sgn}\left\{\sum_j w_{ij}^{k^*} S_j^{k^*} + \delta \sum_{k'=1}^{n} S_i^{k}\right\},$$

where δ is a parameter representing communication intensity and k′ is for all k different form k*.

3. Interpreting noisy environments

3.1 The simulation model

The first question we address is whether communication in a team can correct individual misperceptions of the environment. The problem is operationalized in our simulation model in the following way.

The environment has only 3 states. These three states are linearly independent and have the same Hamming distance between them. This allows minimizing perturbations due to *cross-talk* between agents (Hertz et al. 1991).

Agents have stored in their memory 3 configurations of the environments. The stored configurations are the same for all agents (the team is homogeneous). In this section, we assume that such configurations represent all possible "true" states of the environment. Thus, agents have an accurate knowledge of possible states of the environment.

However, the environment is noisy, i.e. inputs received by agents can be inaccurate: one or more features can be wrongly represented in the input. The Noise parameter in the simulation represents how many features are "wrong" in each input received by each agent. While all agents perceive the same level of noise, their misperceptions are independent (i.e. features to be misrepresented are independently drawn for each agent). The team is characterized by a "full communication" structure: all agents' nodes are connected to the corresponding nodes of other agents. Communication weights, representing communication intensity, are assumed to be the same for all communication connections. The value of such weights will be represented by a parameter δ. Thus, all communication blocks of the weight matrix will be multiples of the identity matrix: δI.

The performance of the team will be measured in two ways: as the percentage of shared correct interpretations over all runs of the simulation, and as the sum of individual errors (number of features misinterpreted) after the network has relaxed to a fix-point. A run consists in the presentation of an input and the subsequent process of relaxation of the team to a fix-point. Since true states of the world and memorized configurations are linearly independent and have the same Hamming distance among them, the problem is the same for all true states of the world, and we can present to the team only one (and no matter which one) true state of the environment with no loss of information. At each run, however, the noisy features will be randomly reassigned to each input perceived by each agent. For each simulation condition, 1000 runs were made.

3.2 Results and comments

In our simulations, we explore two parameters of the model: noise level (ν) is considered in the interval from 0 to 4, and communication intensity is considered in the interval from 0 to 14. Only integer values of both parameters are considered.

We have to distinguish three cases, according to the noise level ν.

For ν=0 (no noise), all agents converge always to the right interpretation. In the case of no communication (δ=0) this is an implication of the basic properties of Hopfield networks (each stored configuration is a fix-point). Even with positive communication intensity, since agents are in the right configuration since the beginning, nothing changes.

For ν=1 and no or low ($\delta\leq 2$) communication intensity, the behavior is the same. However, for $\delta\geq 3$, a limited deterioration in team performance is observed. This is due to the fact that there is a (low) probability that two agents are simultaneously wrong on the same feature. With δ large enough, this implies that the "wrong" agents will correct the "right" one, generating miscoordination and occasionally even collective convergence to a wrong interpretation.

Hence, for no noise or low noise level, the performance of non-communicating agents is always equivalent or better than the performance of a proper team.

For $\nu\geq 2$ communication the picture changes radically. Communication has a non-monotonic effect on team performance. For low levels of δ, communication corrects noise and improves the performance of the team as compared to disconnected individuals in terms of both shared interpretation and aggregate individual error. However, this beneficial effect is overwhelmed by pressures to conform as communication intensity increases. Figures 1 plot both the number of correct shared interpretations and those of all shared interpretations (no matter if wrong or right) for different noise levels. On the one hand, as an effect of the pressure exerted by communication, all shared interpretations increase monotonically with δ, reaching a maximum corresponding to shared interpretation in all runs for $\delta \geq 6$. In other words, for δ large enough, teams always converge to a shared interpretation. On the other hand, as pressure from other agents increases, there is an increasing probability that convergence of interpretations occur on arbitrary configurations, depending on the specific distribution of noise and the sequence of nodes drawn for update. Thus, the percent of correct shared interpretations declines. For $\delta\geq 6$ the performance stabilizes both in terms of aggregate error and correct shared interpretations.

In the subsequent section, we actually introduce a simple theorem stating that for δ large enough, all possible shared interpretation (in our case 2^{12}) are fix-points of the team network. As a result of such non-monotonic effect, for high communication intensity teams fall often prey of pressure to conform and behave as well if not worse than non-communicating agents.

3.3 The "credulous team" theorem

The theorem states some basic fix-point properties of team of agents modeled as networks of Hopfield networks. The theorem (for a proof, see appendix) has two parts.

The first part states that given a team, composed of n agents each modeled by an Hopfield network of N nodes, in which there is a full communication structure defined as above (see §2), it is always possible to determine a positive real value of δ, say δ_c, so that for all $\delta \geq \delta_c$ all shared interpretations are the fix-points of the team network.

The second part of the theorem shows that for all $\delta \geq \delta_c$ all shared interpretations are the only fix-points of such network. Thus, the team will always converge to a shared interpretation.

It can also be proved[1] that, for all $\delta \geq \delta_c$ all shared interpretations continue to be fix-points also in the case in which each agents' node is connected with those of others for a total of n-1 connections; in this case, however, it is not true in general that they are the unique fix-points.

However, shared interpretations are the unique fix-points in the particular case of teams composed of three agents, as in our simulations. This implies that, for large enough values of δ, all shared interpretations are fix-points in the case of the centralized and specialized structures of communication we consider in our model. With the random structure, instead, it is possible that not all nodes n-1 connections: in this case, the assumptions underlying the theorem are not respected.

4. Correcting wrong interpretations

In the former section we explored the noise-correcting effects of team communication. In this section we show that team communication can also correct erroneous individual interpretations stored in agents' memories – errors concerning what they know, not only what they perceive.

We consider two typologies of erroneous interpretations. In one case, all agents are wrong on the same features, i.e. the same two bits of each stored pattern are wrong (table 1). We label this case the "homogeneously wrong team".

[1] The proof is not reported here for reasons of space – but it is available at request.

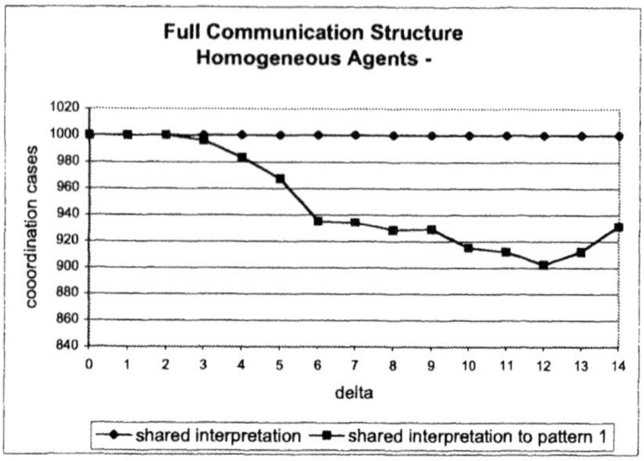

Fig.1.1

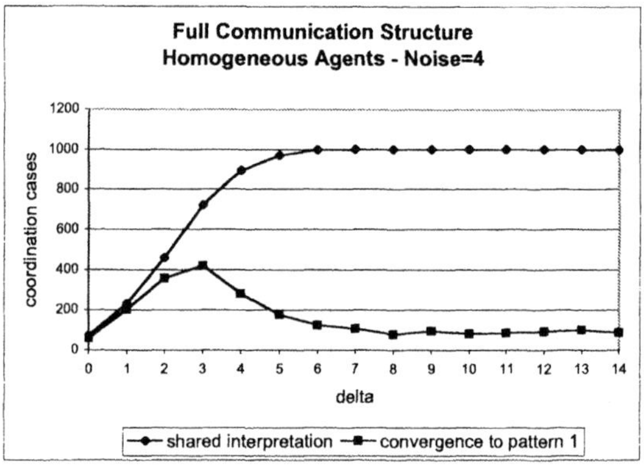

Fig. 1.2

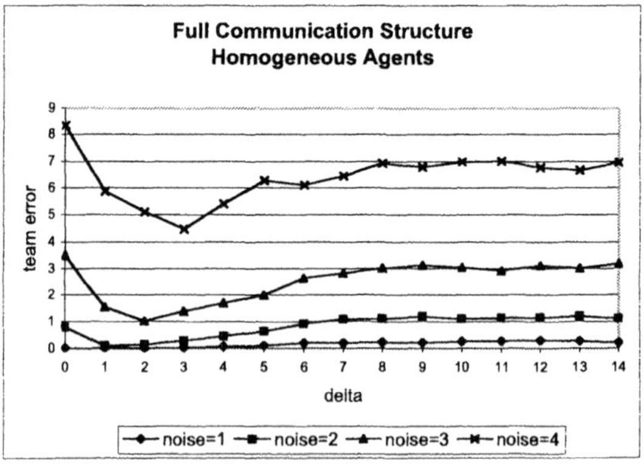

Fig. 1.3

In the other case, each agent is still always wrong on two features of the environment for each stored interpretation, but agents are wrong in different ways. We label this case the "heterogeneously wrong team".

We have divided the stored configurations in three segments of four features: each agent is wrong in two bits within a specific segment. The underlying intuition is that heterogeneity reflects specialization, i.e. each agent can correctly identify only part of the features of the environment. On the part he/she cannot correctly identify (four features), each agent has always the same interpretation, constituted by a series of 1 or –1 which is equidistant from the underlying set of "true" features (see table 1). Once more, this reflects the idea that on features outside his/her domain of specialization, an agent is unable to make meaningful distinctions.

The communication structure fully connects agents, exactly like in the previous simulations.

We explore again the same set of parameters of section 3: ν, noise level, and δ, communication intensity. Once more, it is useful to distinguish different cases.

Starting with the homogeneously wrong team, two different patterns emerge.

For δ=0 (no communication), agents individually converge to their stored patterns, which are by definition wrong. In the case of homogenously wrong agents, if noise is low enough, they converge on the same, shared wrong pattern. As noise increases, much coordination gets lost, and also aggregate error increases.

For δ>0, communication is always beneficial, although its benefits come to a plafond (once more, in rough correspondence with 100% convergence of the team to shared interpretations). In absence of noise, the performance improvement is discontinuous: the team jumps in one step from no coordination (δ≤3) to 100% coordination on the correct interpretation (δ≥4). In noisy environments, the improvement in performance is more gradual; of course, increased noise is reflected in lower asymptotic performance as communication intensity δ grows.

Table 1.1 Interpretations stored in each agent's memory

Homogeneously wrong teams	Heterogeneous teams
Agent 1:	Agent 1:
S_1=(-1,-1,-1,-1,1,-1,1,-1,-1,1,1,-1)	S_1=(1,1,-1,-1,1,-1,1,-1,1,1,1,1)
S_2=(1,-1,1,-1,1,1,-1,-1,1,-1,1,-1)	S_2=(-1,1,1,-1,1,1,-1,-1,1,1,1,1)
S_3=(-1,1,1,-1,-1,1,1,-1,1,1,-1,-1)	S_3=(1,-1,1,-1,-1,1,1,-1,1,1,1,1)
Agent 2:	Agent 2:
S_1=(-1,-1,-1,-1,1,-1,1,-1,-1,1,1,-1)	S_1=(1,1,-1,-1,1,1,1,1,-1,1,1,-1)
S_2=(1,-1,1,-1,1,1,-1,-1,1,-1,1,-1)	S_2=(-1,1,1,-1,1,1,1,1,1,-1,1,-1)
S_3=(-1,1,1,-1,-1,1,1,-1,1,1,-1,-1)	S_3=(1,-1,1,-1,1,1,1,1,1,1,-1,-1)
Agent 3:	Agent 3:
S_1=(-1,-1,-1,-1,1,-1,1,-1,-1,1,1,-1)	S_1=(1,1,1,1,1,-1,1,-1,-1,1,1,-1)
S_2=(1,-1,1,-1,1,1,-1,-1,1,-1,1,-1)	S_2=(1,1,1,1,1,1,-1,-1,1,-1,1,-1)
S_3=(-1,1,1,-1,-1,1,1,-1,1,1,-1,-1)	S_3=(1,1,1,1,-1,1,1,-1,1,1,-1,-1)

Table 1.2 The 3 Corrects Interpretations of the Environment:

S_1=(1,1,-1,-1,1,-1,1,-1,-1,1,1,-1)
S_2=(-1,1,1,-1,1,1,-1,-1,1,-1,1,-1)
S_3=(1,-1,1,-1,-1,1,1,-1,1,1,-1,-1)

The behavior of heterogeneously wrong teams is quite close to the one observed for homogenous teams. While aggregate error curves converge to approximately the same value as the homogenously wrong team ones, the main difference is in the speed of improvement. Heterogeneous teams respond more slowly to increases in δ, reflecting a moderating effect of heterogeneity on collective convergence (figures 2). In some way, heterogeneous teams are less credulous than homogeneous ones – in the context of our simulation tasks, however, this lack of credulity turns out to be a slight practical defect rather than a virtue.

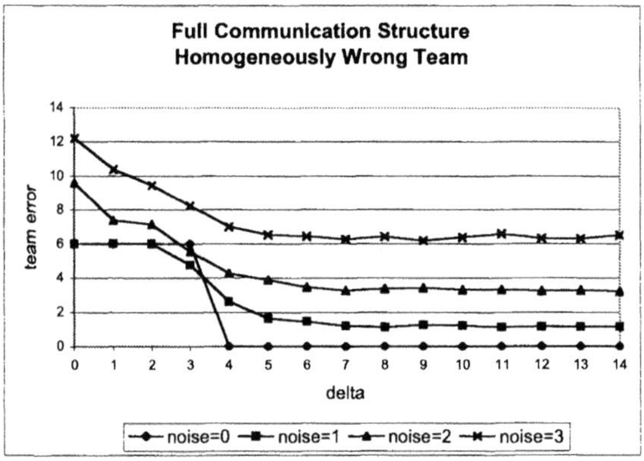

Fig 2.1

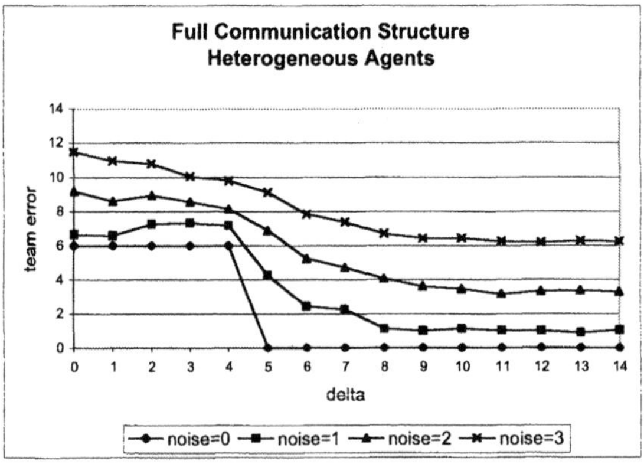

Fig. 2.2

5. Communication structure, cognitive heterogeneity and team performance

Up to now we have only considered the effects of communication intensity, given a full communicative connection among agents. We consider now the impact of different communication structures over team performance. In order to separate the effects of communication structure form those of communication intensity we consider three alternative structures with equal number of connections among agents and equal intensity of the δ parameter.

We consider three structures (see table 2): a centralized communication one, in which one agent communicates on all features with the other two, but the other two don't communicate between them; a specialized communication structure, in which all agents are allowed to communicate with each other but on specific subsets of features; and a random communication structure in which the structure of connections is randomly determined at the start of each simulation run. In all three structures the number of communicative connections is the same, i.e.2/3 of the fully connected structure.

We compare effects of communication structure on to different teams: teams with homogenously wrong interpretations, and teams with heterogeneously wrong interpretations. The underlying intuition is that the effects of structure on error correction might be very different according to the distribution of errors in individual interpretations.

Parameters considered are once more δ and v.

Simulation results show that heterogeneity greatly affects the impact of communication on team interpretations. While in the case of homogeneous agents structure matters indeed very little (there are almost negligible differences in performance between the centralized, the specialized and the random structure for all values of δ and v) great differences emerge in heterogeneous teams. In particular, differences are more relevant for intermediate values of δ and low-intermediate values of v (see figures 3 for an example), where we have already seen that also differences in convergence behavior differ mostly between homogeneous and heterogeneous teams. A plausible explanation is that in homogeneous teams there are no asymmetries among agents in stored interpretations, and thus the error correcting effect of communication is the same no matter how it is distributed. In heterogeneous teams, the existence of systematic differences in interpretation errors requires more structured error-correction processes. In particular, the specialized structure intensifies for each agent communications on the features on which he/she is wrong and unable to make meaningful distinctions. Not surprisingly, the order of effectiveness of structures is specialized>centralized>random, reflecting accurate structuring as a function of individual knowledge specialization.

Table 2 Communication Structures explored in the model

Full Communication Structure Scheme	Centralized Communication Structure Scheme	Specialized Communication Structure Scheme
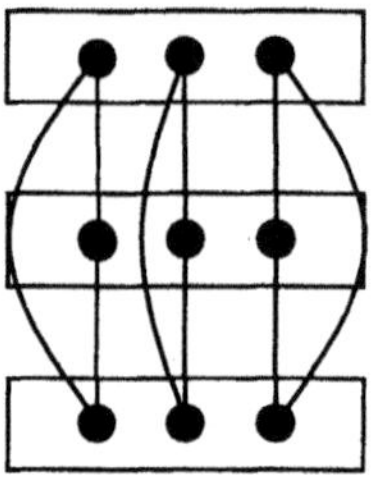	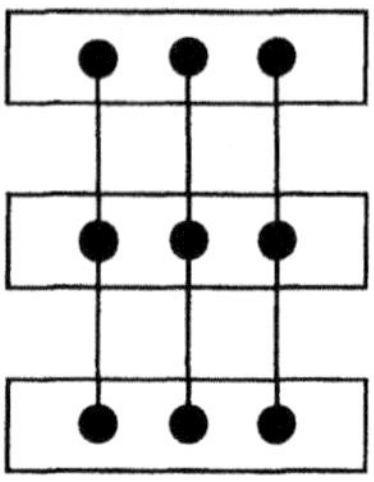	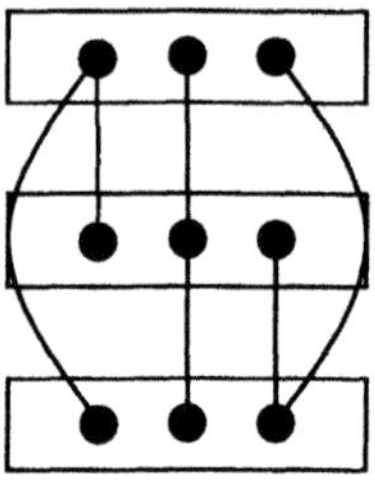

Each small circle on the refers to a subset of 4 features (nodes), each rectangle to an agent.

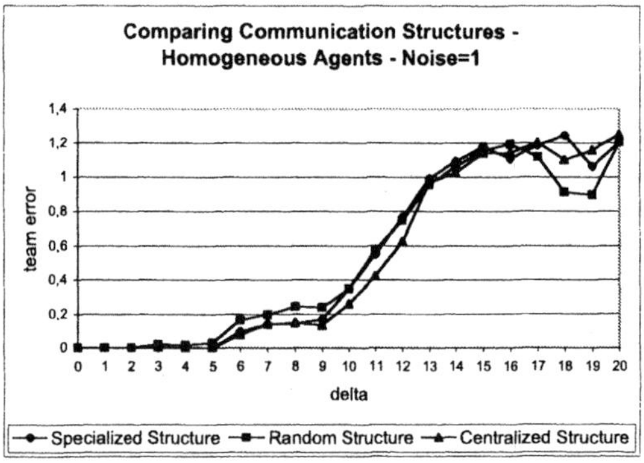

Fig. 3.1

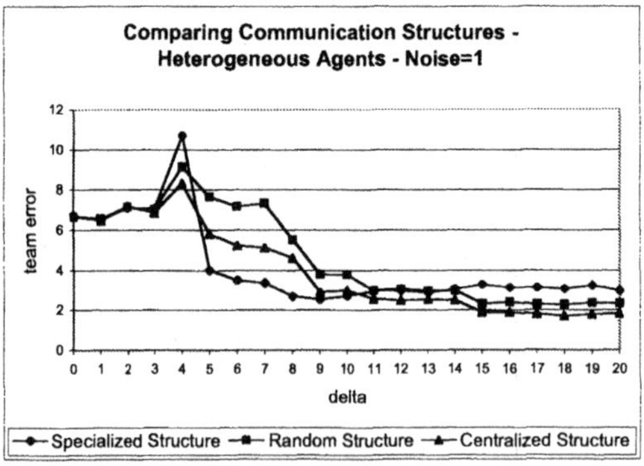

Fig. 3.2

6. Conclusions and further research

This paper is concerned with modeling the interpretive performance of teams in noisy environments. The recurrent theme of the paper is that communication may play an ambivalent role when teams have to correct individual misperceptions and misinterpretations of the state of the environment. In particular, while a moderate communication intensity can improve the error correction capabilities of a team, high levels of peer pressure will induce typical pathologies of group behavior.

The paper deals with the interactions of a few critical variables.

1. Interactions between noise in individual perception of the state of the environment and communication intensity. The main result is that beyond a critical noise level there is a non-monotonic effect of communication intensity on the performance of the team, with increasing collective credulity effects overriding the benefits of communicative interaction.

2. Interactions between types of misinterpretations stored in individual knowledge of the environment, noise levels and communication intensity. The most interesting result is the emergence of a moderating effect of cognitive heterogeneity of agents on their propensity to converge to arbitrary interpretations.

3. Interactions between cognitive heterogeneity and communication structures. While in cognitively homogeneous teams the structure of communication seems to play a minor role (only the density of communication ties matters), in cognitively heterogeneous teams matching the structure of communication with differences in individual cognitive repertoire improves the performance of the team.

We suggest a few future developments of our research. On the one hand, our model could be used to explain a variety of empirical results on the virtues and pathologies of team communication.

On the other one hand, the model might be extended constructing models of agents that do not just interpret but can also act on the environment on the ground of their interpretive process. This can be done by introducing action nodes to each agent network. Furthermore, communication structures with asymmetric connections should be considered – while this may introduce stability problems in the behavior of the team (Hertz et al. 1991), it would increase the realism of the model.

References

Hertz J, Krogh A, Palmer R (1991) Introduction to the theory of neural computation. Addison Wesley

Hopfield J J (1982) Neural networks and Physical Systems with Emergent Collective Computational Abilities. Proceedings of the National Academy of Sciences, 81, 3088-3092

Hutchins E, (1995) Cognition in the wild. MIT Press

Janis I (1971) Victims of Groupthink. Houghton Miffin

Weick K, Roberts K (1993) Collective Mind in Organizations: Heedful Interrelating on Flight Docks. Administrative Science Quarterly, 38, 357-81

Appendix: The "credulous team" theorem – a proof.

Part I: we show that if S is any shared interpretation then there exists a positive real value of δ, δ_c, such that for every $\delta \geq \delta_c$ S is a fix-point. S will be a vector of the type:

$$S = \left(S_1^1, S_2^1, \ldots, S_N^1, \ldots, S_1^k, S_2^k, \ldots, S_N^k, \ldots, S_1^n, S_2^n, \ldots, S_N^n\right)$$

with $S_i^1 = S_i^2 = \ldots = S_i^n$, $\forall \; i=1,\ldots,N$ and where n is the number of agents and N the number of nodes for each individual agent. For the i-th unit of the k-th agent network the Hopfield dynamic rule gives:

$$S_i^k = \operatorname{sgn}\left\{\Sigma_j w_{ij}^k S_j^k + \delta(n-1)S_i^k\right\}.$$

This allows us to state that $\exists \; \delta_C' \in \Re \;\mid\; \forall \delta \geq \delta_c'$:

$$\Sigma_j w_{ij}^k S_j^k \leq \delta(n-1)S_i^k, \quad \forall k$$

and for the same values of δ:

$$S_i^k = \operatorname{sgn}\left\{\Sigma_j w_{ij}^k S_j^k + \delta(n-1)S_i^k\right\} = \operatorname{sgn}\left\{\delta(n-1)S_i^k\right\} = \operatorname{sgn}\left\{S_i^k\right\} = S_i^k.$$

thus S_i^k is stable. Repeating the procedure for all $i=1,\ldots,N$ we can conclude that S is a fix-point for the team network and the first part is demonstrated.

Part II: we show that if S is a fix-point then there exists a positive real value of δ, δ_c, so that for every $\delta \geq \delta_c$ S is a shared interpretation. We can write S as in the Part I, and for the i-th unit of the k-th network the dynamic rule gives:

$$S_i^k = \operatorname{sgn}\left\{\Sigma_j w_{ij}^k S_j^k + \delta \sum_{p'=1}^{n} S_i^p\right\}. \quad (*)$$

where p' is for all p different from k. Suppose that S is a fix-point but not a shared interpretation. We distinguish two cases.

a) n is odd. Suppose that S_i^k has the opposite sign of that of the majority part of its correspondent nodes. In this case the second sum in (*) is different from zero and has the opposite sign of S_i^k. We can write:

$$S_i^k = \mathrm{sgn}\left\{\sum_j w_{ij}^k S_j^k - a\delta S_i^k\right\},$$

where a is the (positive) number of nodes over the half that has opposite sign respect to S_i^k. Thus $\exists\ \delta_c'' \in \Re \mid \forall \delta \geq \delta_c''$:

$$S_i^k = \mathrm{sgn}\left\{\sum_j w_{ij}^k S_j^k - a\delta S_i^k\right\} = \mathrm{sgn}\left\{-a\delta S_i^k\right\} = \mathrm{sgn}\left\{-S_i^k\right\} = -S_i^k, \quad \forall k$$

which means that S is not a fixed point, which is absurd. Thus a non-shared interpretation cannot be a fix-point for the team network.

b) n is even. If S_i^k has the opposite sign of that of the majority of nodes, we can reconduct this case to the case a). Then let us consider the case in which S_i^k has the same sign of one half of the nodes, and for example let it be (without loss of generality):

$$S_i^k = \mathrm{sgn}\left\{\sum_j w_{ij}^k S_j^k + \underbrace{\delta S_i^k + \ldots + \delta S_i^k}_{\frac{n}{2}-1\ times} \underbrace{-\delta S_i^k - \ldots - \delta S_i^k}_{\frac{n}{2}\ times}\right\} = \mathrm{sgn}\left\{\sum_j w_{ij}^k S_j^k - \delta S_i^k\right\}$$

We could therefore say that $\exists\ \delta_c'' \in \Re \mid \forall \delta \geq \delta_c''$:

$$S_i^k = \mathrm{sgn}\left\{\sum_j w_{ij}^k S_j^k - \delta S_j^k\right\} = \mathrm{sgn}\left\{-\delta S_i^k\right\} = \mathrm{sgn}\left\{-S_i^k\right\} = -S_i^k, \quad \forall k$$

and once more we face an absurd: S is not a fix-point and thus a non-shared interpretation can not be a fix-point for the team network.

The theorem is verified for all threshold values of δ:

$$\delta_C = \max\left\{\delta_C', \delta_C''\right\}.$$

Gaming simulation of the international CO2 emission trading under the Kyoto Protocol

Hideyuki Mizuta[1] and Yoshiki Yamagata[2]

[1] IBM Tokyo Research Laboratory, 1623-14 Shimotsuruma, Yamato-shi, Kanagawa-ken 242-8502, Japan e28193@jp.ibm.com

[2] Climate Change Research Project, National Institute for Environmental Studies, 16-2 Onogawa, Tsukuba, Ibaraki 305-0053, Japan yamagata@nies.go.jp

Summary. In response to the Kyoto Protocol, an international greenhouse gas (CO2) emission trading market is likely to be created. Computational and gaming simulations are expected to be able to reproduce complex phenomena in economics and society, and helps us to experiment with various controlling methods, to evaluate systematic designs, and to extract the fundamental elements which produce the interesting phenomena in depth analysis. In a series of works, we developed a simple agent-based simulation framework and its applications for economic and environmental studies including the international CO2 emission trading, and constructed a Web application for the gaming simulation of the emission trading with human players to investigate and improve the behavior model for agents. In this paper, we show results of our gaming simulation experiments performed in 2002 and 2003 as a part of a lecture course for environmental studies in university.

Key words: Kyoto Protocol, Agent-based Approach, Gaming Simulation, Emission Trading

1 Introduction

In response to the Kyoto Protocol, an international CO2 emission trading market is likely to be created. However, after the US withdrawal from the Kyoto Protocol and the revisions of national emission reduction targets in the Bonn and Marrakesh agreements, a low price of CO2 emission permits are expected to be the outcome of implementation. There are demands for analyzing several different scenarios, mainly in relation to the Russian participation and Hot air trading. Certain economical analyses are conducted on the basis of assumptions that the strategic options open to the supply side of the permit market and Russia would potentially a dominating seller of emission permits under the Kyoto Protocol.

International emission trading simulations have been conducted worldwide as a tool for understanding and explaining the concepts of tradable permits to industrialists, policy-makers and students. These simulations allow us to understand how the market will evolve. In order to simulate complicated realistic trading behavior, an agent-based model of the CO2 trading market has been developed and applied. As an experimental tool, especially our simulation analysis benefits from using a realistic economical data on marginal abatement cost and initial allocation of tradable permits among countries based on the agreement of the Kyoto Protocol. Due to this arrangement, it enables us to grasp the implication of Hot Air and strategic trading behaviors of selling countries.

In fact, international communities are now facing the risk of Kyoto's not entering into force (collapse of the protocol) due to the non-ratification by Russia. Our trading simulation suggested that, in some cases, such a strategic behavior of countries in the market is likely to occur, however it is interesting that such behavior was actually observed even before the international emission trading regime is created. The simulation could also provide substantial insights into the evolution of the CO2 emission trading market, particularly related to the evolution of trade volume, permit prices and country strategies.

As the USA will not ratify the Kyoto Protocol at least for the first commitment period, potentially largest buyer in the emission trading market is out of the market. The participation of Australia, another large buyer, also is unlikely. On the other hand, EU has determined the rules for EU wide emissions trading, and Russia, Ukraine, and other countries in Eastern Europe have huge Hot Air. If the large amount of Hot Air is traded in the first commitment period, permit price will go downwards.

However, if Russia and other countries restrict hot air trading, in order to bring about higher permit prices, simulations indicate that such strategic behaviors would have a major impact on the outcome of the first commitment period [1, 2, 3, 4, 11].

In this paper, we introduce a system for the agent-based simulation and web-based gaming simulation for complex social interaction such as the international CO2 emission trading under the Kyoto Protocol and show results of the gaming simulation experiments performed in 2002 and 2003.

2 Agent-based simulation of the international CO2 emission trading

In a series of works [10, 6, 7, 8, 9], we considered agent-based simulations including the international CO2 emission trading.

We are utilizing our simple Java framework for effective implementation of the agent-based simulation constructed with the layered structure as follows. The Agent Layer contains a basic agent class and the fundamental environment for the agents. The environment provides the fundamental facilities for agents and users to create agents, to dispose of agents, and to send messages through a MessageManager class. The Social Layer describes the basic role of agents in the society and gives the example of message exchanges for trade. We implemented Central, Participant, and Watcher agents and a simple market process using RFB and BID messages. The Central agent creates, registers and initiates Participant agents and Watcher agents.

With this framework, we have been investigating the CO2 emission trading under the Kyoto Protocol. COP agent is a subclass of the Central agent and manages the international trading. Nation agent is also a subclass of the Participant agent and correspond to countries or regional groups. In this model, we created 12 Nations; 6 are Annex I countries who are assigned reduction targets in the level of emission in 1990, and 6 are Non Annex I countries who are not assigned targets for reduction as in the CERT model [5]. Fig. 1 shows the main trading procedure. We consider dynamic market development through the first commitment period 2008-2012. In each trading year, the COP agent sends Request for Bid (RFB) messages to all Nations which have an asking price.

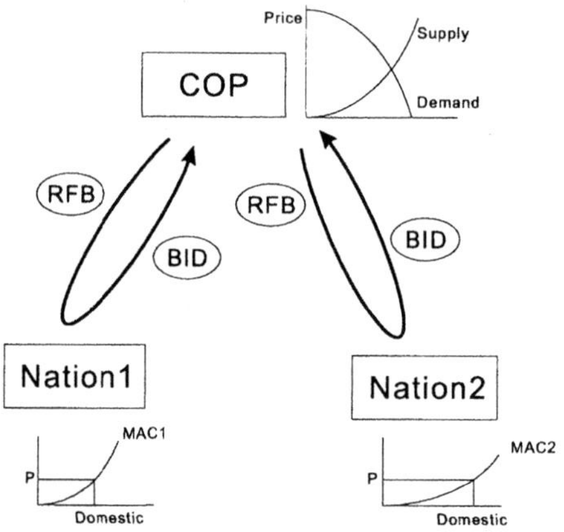

Fig. 1. Trading procedure.

Upon receiving the RFB message, a Nation agent examines the asking price and his Marginal Abatement Cost (MAC) to decide the amount of the domestic reduction. Then he sends back a Bid message to the COP agent which says how much he wants to buy or to sell at the asked price. After repeating this RFB-BID process, the COP model will find the equilibrium price where the demand and the supply balance, and send the Trade message to approve the trades for the year. Thus, the equilibrium price for each year is determined when the MAC functions and the assigned reductions of all of the participants are given.

For the multiple trading periods, we considered a partition of the assigned reduction as a strategy of agents. The dynamics of MAC is given by the technology function $t_{in}(p)$ which gives the amount of reduction using the available technology at a given cost p for the Nation i at the year n.

As a simple dynamic process for the reduction technology $t_{in}(p)$, we adopt reusability $0 \leq \alpha \leq 1$ and deflation $0 \leq \gamma \equiv 1/\beta \leq 1$. Once the technology whose cost is lower than the price P^* is used, the reusability of the technology will be restricted with the coefficient α. On the other hand, the technical innovations and deflation decreases the cost of the technology. With $\bar{P}_{in} \equiv \max\{\gamma_i^n P_0^*, \gamma_i^{n-1} P_1^*, \ldots, \gamma_i P_{n-1}^*\}$, we can obtain the technology function as

$$t_{in}(p) \equiv \begin{cases} \alpha_i \beta_i^n t_{i0}(\beta_i^n p) & p < \bar{P}_{in} \\ \beta_i^n t_{i0}(\beta_i^n p) & \text{otherwise.} \end{cases}$$

We assume the initial technology function $t_{i0}(p)$ with two coefficients a_i and b_i to reproduce the quadratic MAC function in the CERT model,

$$t_{i0}(p) \equiv \frac{1}{\sqrt{b_i^2 + 4a_i p}}.$$

Fig. 2 shows an example of the simulation views. We can see brief reports on 12 agents and price changes from 2008 to 2012.

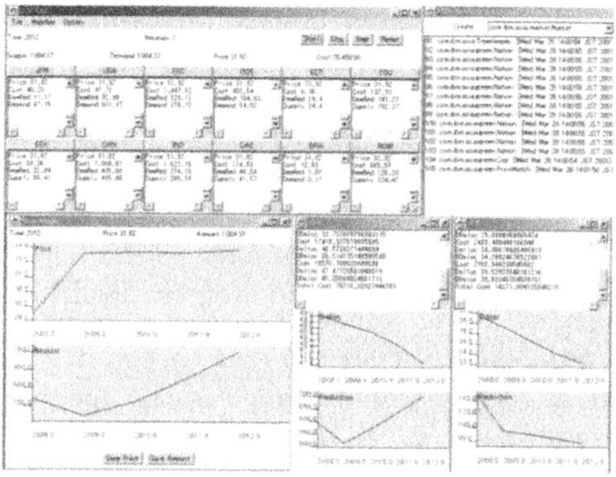

Fig. 2. Dynamic CO2 emission trading over the commitment period, 2008–2012.

3 Web-based gaming system

Gaming simulations with human players in an environment similar to the agents' environment are expected to help us in constructing plausible behavior models and extracting the essential dynamics. We implemented a remote accessing interface in the agent framework which enables human players to collaborate with software agents, and constructed a Web application for a gaming simulation modeling international emission trading. In this section,

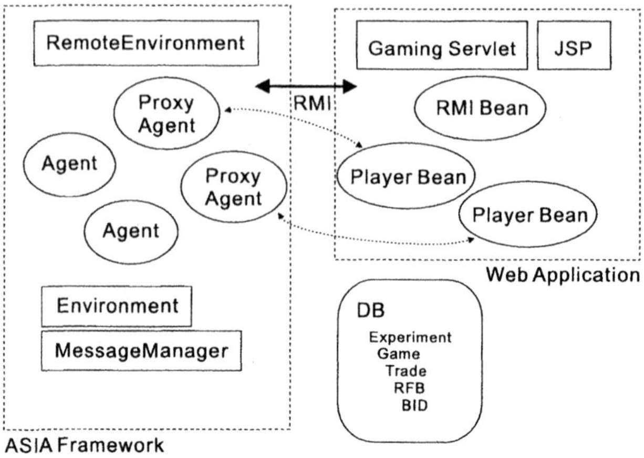

Fig. 3. Web application and the agent system

we briefly introduce this gaming system (see Fig. 3) used for the gaming simulations in the following sections.

For remote access, we use RMI services and proxy agents at the Agent Layer. Through the RMI server, remote clients can create and dispose of agents. The RMI server also provides the naming service for agents and proxy messaging. A remote client who wants to talk with these agents needs to create a proxy agent with a message queue. The proxy agent acts in the same way as a normal agent in the framework, sends messages on behalf of the remote client, and passes the received messages back to the remote client. We also provide proxy versions of Participant and Watcher agents in the Social Layer.

We have developed a Web application using servlets for gaming so that most client PCs with Web browsers can easily access it.

In this system, as with typical Web applications, the servlets work as controllers and JSPs provide views. To retain information about the players, this application also requires Java beans corresponding to proxy agents. Messages like RFBs received by the agents are passed to the beans for the players in XML format, are interpreted, and displayed by servlets and JSPs. On the other side, player's inputs such as BIDs are packed into messages and sent through the proxy agent. In this simulation, players determine the amounts of the domestic reduction of CO2 and the amounts of the excess demand for international emission trading according to the presented price in the RFB at each iteration. Information such as the cost graph, the MAC, the total reduction target and the trading history are also given (see Fig. 3).

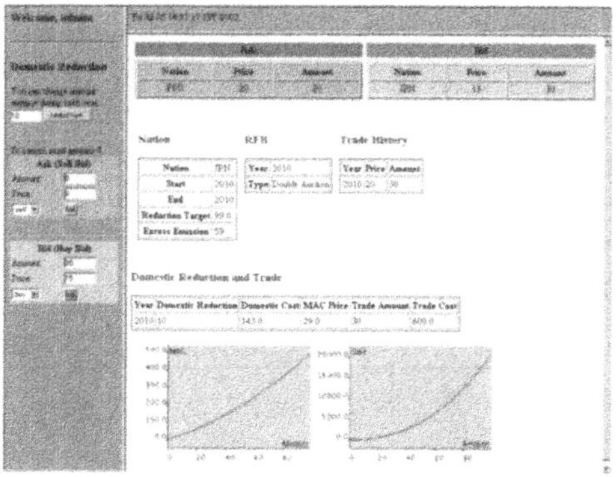

Fig. 4. Gaming client for double auction

4 Gaming simulation

We presented preliminary results of the gaming simulation at AESCS'02 [12] and CS'02 [13].

In the simulation, we tried two type of trading model; Walras equilibrium price and Double Auction (DA). For trading among computational agents, we used Walras trading for one or five trading years to find the equilibrium price and cost effective strategies. On the other hand, we introduced DA trading for human players since the iterative process of Walras trading is too troublesome for human and will not converge with dishonest and irrational bids. In reality, we tried the Walras trading for only one trading year with students in the preliminary gaming experiment in 2002, which could not reach the equilibrium. With DA trading, gaming players enjoyed free trading, and sell/buy permits to achieve the target positively.

The most characteristic behavior emerged in the game was price control by sellers. Sellers (EET[3]and FSU[4]) were unwilling to sell until the market price became very high, and buyers (JPN, EEC[5], OOE[6]) were forced to pay more than the equilibrium. Even after we changed assigned countries of players, this tendency of high price controlled by sellers was sustained and sellers obtained greater revenue than the equilibrium trading of computational agents.

We summarized the results in Table. 1

After the preliminary experiments, we performed the gaming simulation of the international CO2 emission trading again with different students on June 2003. We assigned 6 groups of countries including USA to 6 groups of 11 students. One group contains one student and other five groups contain

[3] EET: Economies in Transition of Eastern Europe

[4] FSU: Former Soviet Union

[5] EEC: 15 EU members

[6] OOE: Rest OECD

Table 1. Gaming simulation 2002 summary

Reference (1 Year, Equilibrium Price = $66.44)					
Nation	JPN	EEC	OOE	EET	FSU
Cost	5883	16932	2166	-3664	-11503
Gaming 02-1 (DA 1 Year)					
Nation	JPN	EEC	OOE	EET	FSU
Cost	6991	20542	2231	-2020	-15237
Performance	-18.83%	-21.32%	-3.00%	-44.87%	32.46%
Price	$81.34	$84.29	-$84.00	-$92.45	-$82.65
Gaming 02-2 (DA 1 Year)					
Nation	JPN	EEC	OOE	EET	FSU
Cost	6320	18387	2209	-4323	-12769
Performance	-7.43%	-8.59%	-1.99%	17.99%	11.01%
Price	$72.47	$73.58	$73.67	-$73.67	-$73.13
Reference (5 Years)					
Nation	JPN	EEC	OOE	EET	FSU
Cost	11489	34648	5667	-6443	-21067
Gaming 02-3 (DA 5 Years)					
Nation	JPN	EEC	OOE	EET	FSU
Cost	22191	69780	7088	-16549	-25852
Performance	-93.15%	-101.40%	-25.07%	156.85%	22.71%

two students. In this experiment, we introduced uncertainty of future circumstances by changing the technology innovation factor. We set relatively high value $\beta_i = 2$ for the factor with first and second games which caused significant deflation of domestic reduction cost (and MAC) after years. Then we set relatively small value $\beta_i = 1.2$ for the factor with third and fourth games.

We used the same gaming system with the first experiment in 2002. Players and the game controller accessed to the gaming system with web browser. The game controller predefined the game nation's parameter, and controlled the procession of games. One game consists of 5 trading years and one trading year takes about 10 minutes in the real world. This web-based gaming system collaborated with the agent-based simulation framework. Hence, we can investigate the behavior of trading using the computational agents with the same factors given to game players. We consider the performance of students relatively by comparing their total cost to achieve the Kyoto targets with the results of the agent-based simulation with Walras equilibrium price.

The gaming simulation was held for two days. Each day, we gave a lecture of the Kyoto Protocol and performed two gaming simulation. Results of the gaming are shown in Table. 2, Table. 3 and Fig. 4. We let students calculate their own performance in the end of each day and surveyed their strategy and comment together with students openly.

Through the gaming and comments, we noticed most significant difference in 2003 was unpopularity of naked price control by sellers observed in 2002. Instead, players were mostly concerned about technology innovation and made their trading plan under their expectation though many of them had to correct errors at last two trading years with higher cost. It seems that an emerged trend becomes dominant in the class rapidly in both cases.

On the other hand, it is common in the series of course that students felt MAC difficult to understand at first and learned it through the gaming simulation as improvement in performances expressed. Thus, such a gaming simulation also seems efficient for the teaching of complicated social interaction.

Table 2. Gaming simulation 2003 summary 1st day

Reference (innovation factor: 2.0)

Nation	JPN	USA	EEC	OOE	EET	FSU
Cost (M$)	21426	108737	64248	7774	-19324	-55689

Gaming 03-1

Nation	JPN	USA	EEC	OOE	EET	FSU
Cost (M$)	60092	165663	146465	10962	-18002	-97294
Performance	-180%	-52%	-128%	-41%	-7%	75%

Gaming 03-2

Nation	JPN	USA	EEC	OOE	EET	FSU
Cost (M$)	52803	153881	105308	-1475	-27239	-33480
Performance	-146%	-42%	-64%	119%	41%	-40%

Table 3. Gaming simulation 2003 summary 2nd day

Reference (innovation factor: 1.2)

Nation	JPN	USA	EEC	OOE	EET	FSU
Cost (M$)	84275	413347	247139	27408	-80651	-223364

Gaming 03-3

Nation	JPN	USA	EEC	OOE	EET	FSU
Cost (M$)	51432	739291	243159	24153	-33570	-93102
Performance	-39%	-79%	-2%	12%	-58%	-58%

Gaming 03-2

Nation	JPN	USA	EEC	OOE	EET	FSU
Cost (M$)	56876	340911	261912	25987	-45891	-103696
Performance	33%	18%	-6%	5%	-43%	-54%

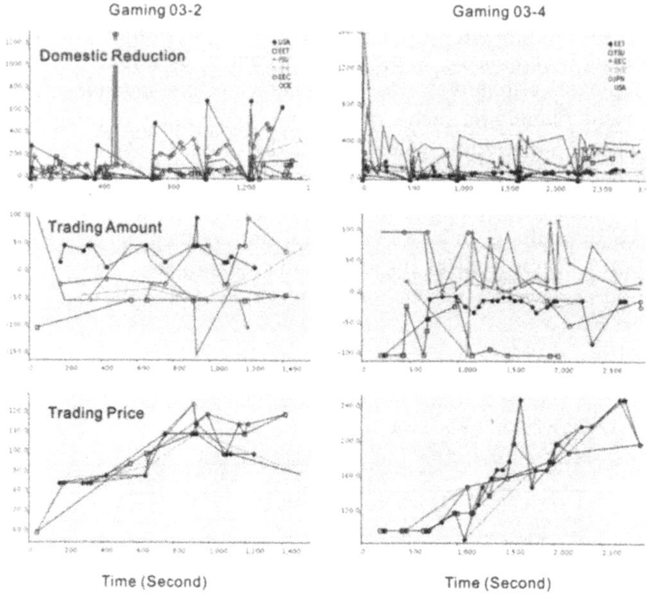

Fig. 5. Domestic reduction and international trading

5 Concluding remarks

In response to the Kyoto Protocol, an international CO2 emission trading market is likely to be created. International emission trading simulations have been conducted worldwide as a tool for understanding and explaining the concepts of tradable permits to industrialists, policy-makers and students. These simulations allow us to understand how the market will evolve. In order to simulate complicated realistic trading behavior, an agent-based model of the CO2 trading market has been developed and applied.

We considered a dynamical simulation for the international CO2 emission trading with our agent-based simulation framework, and developed a Web application for the gaming simulation of the emission trading which works along with the agent system through network to study realistic human behavior. We executed the first prototyping gaming simulation in June, 2002 and then in June, 2003 with strong support of Prof. Rokugawa and undergraduate students in University of Tokyo. The series of the gaming simulation showed emergence of dominant trend and learning by students.

We are also developing an integrated system for collaboration between computational agents and human players by implementing automated bidding capabilities in the proxy agent to examine more intelligent and complicated trading. We are expecting that such a gaming simulation with this system helps us to construct improved heterogeneous behavior models and to propose more stable and low-cost trading process for the Kyoto Protocol.

References

1. Babiker HB, Jacoby DH, Reilly JM, Reiner DM (2002) The evolution of a climate regime: Kyoto to Marrakech and beyond. Environmetal Science & Policy 5:195–206
2. Buchner B, Carraro C, Cersosimo I (2002) Economic consequences of the US withdrawal from the Kyoto/Bonn Protocol. Climate Policy 2:273–292
3. den Elzen MGJ, de Moor APG (2003) Analyzing the Kyoto Protocol under the Marrakesh accords: economic efficiency and environmental effectiveness. Ecological Economics 43:141–158
4. Grütter J, Kappel R, Staub P (2002) The GHG Market on the Eve of Kyoto Ratification. Report. Eidgennössische Technische Hochshule, Zürich, Switzerland
5. Grütter JM (2000) World Market for GHG Emission Reductions. Prepared for the World Bank's National AIJ/JI/CDM Strategy Studies Program
6. Mizuta H, Steiglitz K (2000) Agent-based Simulation of Dynamic Online Auctions. In: Joines JA, Barton RR, Kang K, Fishwick PA (Eds) Proceedings of the 2000 Winter Simulation Conference, pp 1772–1777
7. Mizuta H, Yamagata Y (2001) Agent-based Simulation and Greenhouse Gas Emissions Trading. In: Peters BA, Smith JS, Medeiros DJ, Rohrer MW (Eds) Proceedings of the 2001 Winter Simulation Conference, pp 535–540
8. Mizuta H, Yamagata Y (2002) Transaction Cycle of Agents and Web-Based Gaming Simulation for International Emissions Trading. In: Yucesan E, Chen CH, Snowdon JL, Charnes JM (Eds) Proceedings of the 2002 Winter Simulation Conference, pp 801–806
9. Mizuta H, Yamagata Y (2002) Agent-based Simulation and Gaming System for International Emissions Trading. In: Namatame A, Terano T, Kurumatani K (Eds) Agent-based Approaches in Economic and Social Complex Systems, IOS Press, pp 69–78
10. Mizuta H, Steiglitz K, Lirov E (1999) Effects of Price Signal Choices on Market Stability. The 4th Workshop on Economics with Heterogeneous Interacting Agents (WEHIA'99), Genoa, Italy, June 4–June 5
11. Springer U, Varilek M (2003) Estimating the price of tradable permits for greenhouse gas emission in 2008–12. Energy Policy
12. Yamagata Y, Mizuta H (2002) An International Regime Design Regarding the Kyoto Protocol: The Role of Multi-Agent Simulation. The Second International Workshop on Agent-based Approaches in Economic and Social Complex Systems (AESCS'02), Tokyo, Japan, August 16
13. Yamagata Y, Mizuta H (2002) Agent-based simulation of hte International CO2 Emission Trading : Emergent behavior of countries. The 6th International Conference on Complex Systems(CS02), Tokyo, Japan, September 9-11

A Report of U-Mart Experiments as an Educational Courseware

Kazuhisa Taniguchi[1], Yoshihiro Nakajima[2], and Fumihiko Hashimoto[2]

[1]Faculty of Economics, Kinki University, 3-4-1 Kowakae, Higashiosaka, Osaka 577-8502 Japan
[2]Graduate School of Economics, Osaka City University, 3-3-138 Sugimoto, Sumiyoshi-ku, Osaka, 558-8585 Japan

Summary. This article reports results of a series of U-Mart experiments as an educational courseware. The participants in the experiments were 22 third year university students and 20 computer programmed software machine agents. This series of the experiments is the first test which was performed systematically by more than 20 human trader agents.

First, conditions of the experiments are explained; second, results of the series of the experiments are reported. Contents of the acquired results are as follows; settled profits, order volume, rate of contracted volume, volume of order, and position control. Though the obtained consequences may be definitive, they would enlighten tendencies and peculiarities of human conducts in financial market such as U-Mart system.

Key words. U-Mart, Human trader, Simulation, Educational Courseware

Introduction

The purpose of this article is to report an educational consequence as a courseware of U-mart system which is a manifold simulation system. The system can be used as both an educational courseware and a research program. Regarding the educational use, economic majors, who learn stock market or financial system, can trade the futures by the U-Mart virtual trading game and obtain practical information. A programming skill can be improved by developing a machine agent for engineering majors. In this report, a series of U-Mart experiments were conducted by human trader agents, who were third year university students, to learn a future market. Computer programmed software machine which were of a random trading type.

The course and conditions of the U-Mart Experiments

Participants were 22 third year university students, economic majors, who belonged to the author's seminar class and 20 computer programmed software machine agents which were supplied by U-Mart developing members (Sato et al.2001). The students attended the seminars which were held by the author. They learned about futures markets and stock exchanges in addition to the history of futures markets, the stock exchange in Japan, the Tokyo, New York and other world stock exchanges systems before the U-Mart experiments. They also acquired technical terms regarding futures markets and trading strategies according to technical analysis and fundamental analysis. These students were taught how to use the GUI-Client monitor, which is a graphical user interface of U-Mart system for people. It needed 4 seminars classes of 90 minutes each to comprehend the whole of the contents. After this preliminary course, these 22 students participated in the series of experiments with 20 computer programmed software machine agents which were a random trading type. This series of experiments were conducted 9 times from the beginning of June to the middle of July 2002. Each experiment runs about 50 minutes.

The futures market of this U-Mart system opens in a fixed time session trading which is called "Itayose". All orders are dealt at the same time. The length of the trading day in the futures market of these U-Mart experiments is a virtual 24 days. It needs about 50 minutes for one futures market session to be completed in real time. Itayose is held 8 times a virtual day and the interval time of Itayose is 10 seconds in real time. Though this interval time may be too short to trade for beginner human agents, it was enough time for the proficient students. Itayose, under which all orders are dealt as simultaneous orders, refers to the method of determining the prices. Theses experimental conditions were determined by several preliminary experiments. Fig.1 shows the example of a series of spot price and future price in the second experiment. In the second experiment, as a series of spot price data, J30 which was supplied by the Mainichi Press was adapted. There are 20 random trading type machine agents and these agents make limit orders, with a maximum of 20 yen, randomly around spot prices. They order 5 volumes for each order and order 5 times during every one Itayose.

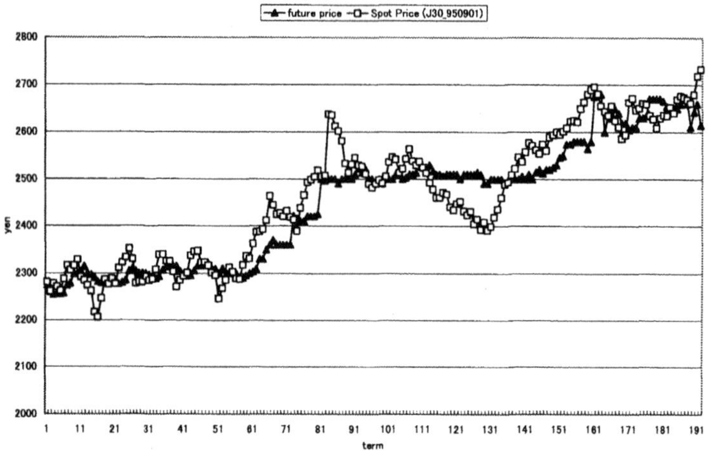

Fig. 1. A series of future price and spot price of the second experiment

Results and observations on the Experiments

Settled profits

On average, the random trading machine agents were superior to human agents and gained the profits. According to the results of a questionnaire after the completion of all nine experiments, there were a lot of different strategies for human agents, and the strategy which human agents adopted was greatly contingent on his or her character and attitude to the market. Before the trade, each agent was given virtual one billion yen. Some of the human agents were superior to machine agents and most of them were inferior to machine agents. The Average settled profits of each experiment by human were illustrated in Fig.2.

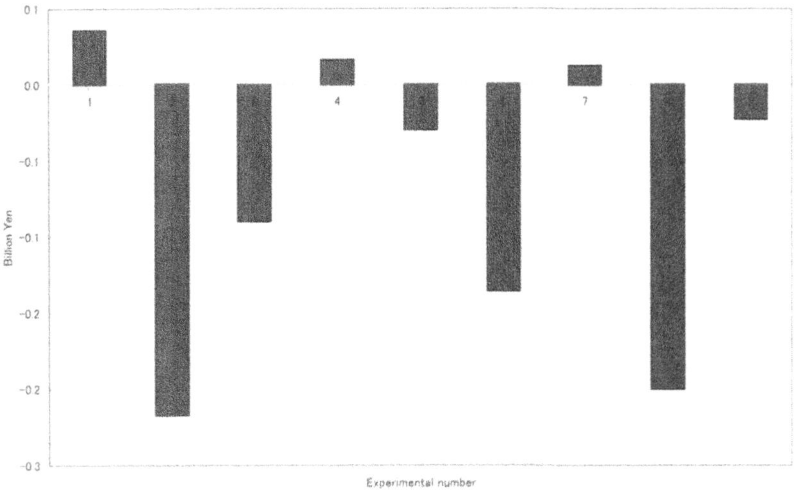

Fig. 2. The Average settled profits of each experiment by human agents

The order volume

Order volume consists of sell-order volume and buy-order volume. The order volume trended upward through the series of experiments. The order volume of the last experiment session was about three and a half times compared with the order volume of the first experiment session. The frequencies of orders were nearly constant compared to the order volume except the first experiment. Human agents seemed to have learned how to determine the order volume through the series of experiments. See Fig.3.

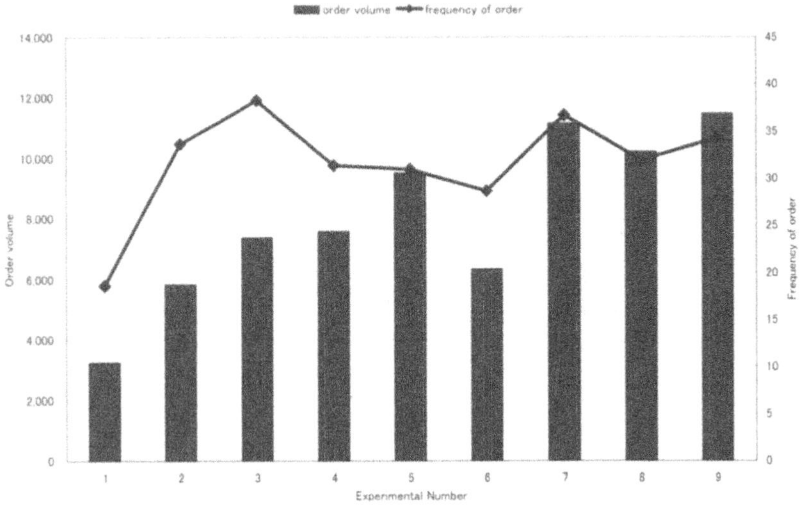

Fig. 3. Order Volume and the frequency of order by human agents

The rate of contracted volume per volume of order

The contracted volume increased as the order volume increased, but the rate of contracted volume per volume of order remained almost constant. Market orders were not prohibited in the first experiment session, therefore, in this one only, the rate of contracted volume is high. See Fig.4.

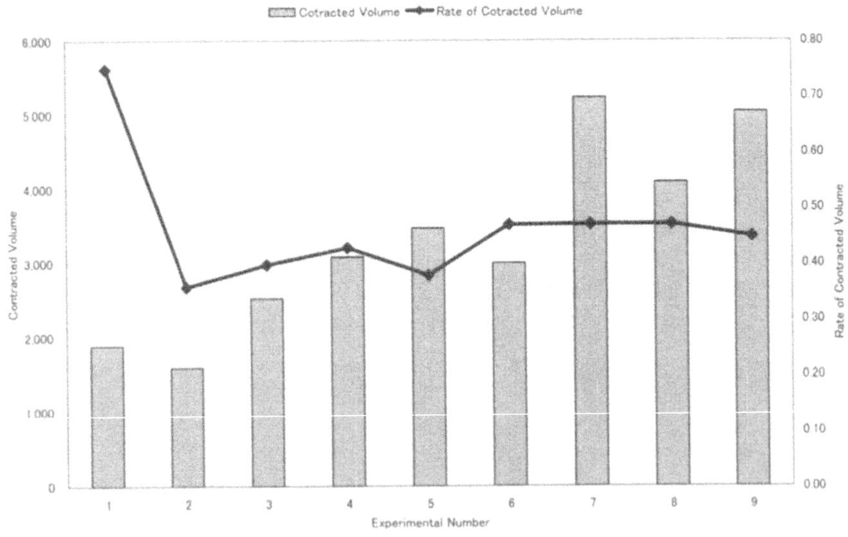

Fig.4. Contracted Volume and Rate of Contracted Volume per Volume of order

Position Control

All futures contracts must be settled by offsetting in future market. Agents are required to buy or sell to cover their transactions by the final clearing day. A short position must be bought and the long position must be sold, which is referred to as the position control. Human agents learned the importance of position control in our seminar, but it is not easy to control it practically in the trading market. In general, human agents became to control the position after a few experimental trainings, but it depended on the personal character of each individual human. Even after the completion of the experiments, some human agents could not perfectly control the position. See fig.5.

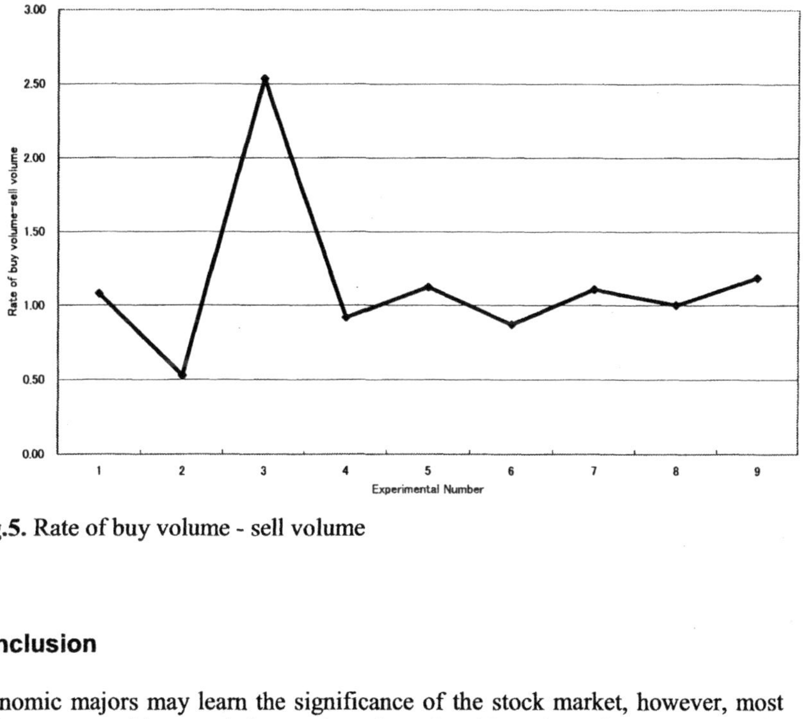

Fig.5. Rate of buy volume - sell volume

Conclusion

Economic majors may learn the significance of the stock market, however, most of them are not able to trade in a real stock market. Nowadays, there are many virtual investment web sites, which have been administrated by a private stock company, and these web sites may be useful to learn the stock market. But it takes a long term to finish a trade, such as a few months. It is difficult to deal them as a courseware, particularly in a several times of lectures or seminars.

One of the excellent features of the U-Mart system is to trade the futures index practically as a virtual trading game, and the trading results can be obtained instantly. The obtained experimental data are useful to analyze human economic behaviors. For example, in this series of these experiments, the frequencies of order and the rate of contacted volume per order volume were nearly constant. But, both order volume and contracted volume trended upward. Therefore, theses obtained results suggest that there are two kinds of economic variables in this virtual market. The one depends on human learning processes through these experiments, and the other does not contingent upon the human learning behaviors but other experimental conditions which are not revealed so far. This is the first U-Mart experiments which were performed systematically by more than 20 human trader agents. The number of experimental data is not so large-scale, so the obtained results are definitive. The furthermore experimental-data are required to enrich our understanding about the financial market.

Reference

[1]H.Sato, H.Matsui, I.Ono, H.Kita, T.Terano, H.Deguchi, and Y.Shiozawa(2001): "U-Mart project: learning economic principles from the bottom by both human and software agents", New frontiers in artificial intelligence . pp 121-131, Springer.

Evaluation Criteria for Learning Mechanisms applied to Agents in a Cross-Cultural Simulation

Yutaka I. Leon Suematsu[1,2], Keiki Takadama[1,3], Katsunori Shimohara[1,2], Osamu Katai[2] and Kiyoshi Arai[4]

[1] ATR International - Network Informatics Labs. 2-2-2 Hikari-dai, Seika-cho, Soraku-gun, Kyoto 619-0288, JAPAN. {yutaka, keiki, katsu}@atr.jp
[2] Graduate School of Informatics, Kyoto University, Yoshida-honmachi, Sakyo-ku, Kyoto 606-8501, JAPAN. Email: katai@i.kyoto-u.ac.jp
[3] Interdisciplinary Graduate School of Science and Engineering, Department of Computational Intelligence and Systems Science, Tokyo Institute of Technology, 4259 Nagatsuta-cho, Midori-ku, Yokohama, Kanagawa 226-8502, JAPAN
[4] School of Project Management, Chiba Institute of Technology, 2-17-1 Tsuda-numa Narashino-shi, 275, JAPAN. Email: k-arai@pf.it-chiba.ac.jp

Summary. In problems with non-specific equilibrium, common in social sciences, the processes involved in learning mechanisms can produce quite different outcomes. However, it is quite difficult to define which of the learning mechanisms is the best. When considering the case of a cross-cultural environment, it is necessary to evaluate how adaptation to different cultures occurs while keeping, at some level, the cultural diversity among the groups. This paper focuses on identifying an evaluation criterion using a comparison of various learning mechanisms that can manage the *trade-off* between adaptation to a new culture and the preservation of cultural diversity. Results show that: (a) For small and gradual accuracy from a less accurate learning mechanism, there is a tiny reduction in the diversity while the convergence time drops rapidly. For an accuracy level close to the most accurate learning mechanism, a reduction of the convergence time can be minor, while the diversity drops rapidly; (b) The evaluation of learning mechanism that performs better for fast converging while simultaneously keeping a good diversity before the convergence was performed graphically.

Key words: Agent-based model, learning mechanism, cross-cultural environments, gaming simulation, BARNGA

1 Introduction

Social sciences commonly deal with situations that do not have an explicit equilibrium. In order to analyze such systems, Agent-Based Modelling (ABM)

has become a powerful tool, enhancing the study of various fields of the social sciences [1, 2, 6]. In agent design, not only do agents behave according to pre-defined rules, but also possess learning mechanisms that allow them to adapt to dynamic environments. When facing systems without a specific equilibrium, a trade-off exists between convergence and diversity. In a cross-cultural environment, the trade-off is between adaptation to a new culture and the preservation of culture diversity. Investigations into the learning mechanisms that affect this trade-off and their level of influence are significant. In our previous work [5], three learning mechanisms where implemented in order to evaluate their influence on a trade-off. These mechanisms where developed by increasing the conditions in performing the learning necessary to improve accuracy. It was found that the more accurate the learning is, the faster the convergence to a common culture. However, diversity can be retained in the opposite order. From these results, it is quite difficult to define which one of the mechanisms is best to deal with the trade-off. This paper focuses on defining an evaluation criterion for a better comparison between various learning mechanisms. This paper explores the possibility of finding a learning mechanism that converges faster as an accurate learning process while retaining higher diversity. The paper is organized as follows: Section 2 introduces BARNGA, a card game used as the test-bed. In Section 3, the ABM model architecture is outlined, followed by the simulation results in Section 4. Discussions are presented in Section 5 and finally, the conclusions and future work are provided in Section 6.

2 BARNGA

BARNGA[8] is a card game developed in the field of *gaming simulation*[3] and it was created for participants to experience difficulties due to cultural differences. The players are grouped in tables in which the initial rules for each table are slightly different to represent cross-cultural diversity. It should be noted that the players are not allowed to speak to one another, restricting communication to a minimum. When the players change tables they have to learn and overcome the difficulties raised by the cultural differences reflected in the changing rules of the game in order to effectively work in cross-cultural groups.

When players are initially assigned to tables, they receive the instructions and rules of the game and practice for a while in order to understand and get used them. After practice, the instructions provided are removed and the simulation game starts.

Players play for a certain number of games. A migration process then takes place. The player who wins or loses the most games for each table are moved clockwise and counter-clockwise, respectively, to the neighboring tables. This process is repeated for a certain number of migrations. When the game is restarted, players experience difficulties since the players from different tables play according to different rules. However, after a certain number of games or migrations, some players are able to distinguish the differences and will try to adapt to the rules played by the others or to negotiate to define some common rules for the table. Significantly, the players are not allowed to speak, limiting communication and simulating natural language barriers so that they must adapt using intuition, reasoning and insight. Negotiations are carried out using only body language or facial expressions.

The game is played as follows: For each *game* [1], a *dealer*, who is the player that has won the most *tricks* in the previous game or who has been chosen by *paper-rock-scissors* when there is no winner, is designated. The dealer shuffles the cards and deals them out one at a time. Each player receives around 5-7 cards, depending on the number of players. The first player of a trick plays any card. The other players then follow in the same way by playing a card of the same suit. In the case where there are no cards from the original suit, a card from any suit can be played. The winner of the trick is the player who places the highest or lowest card from the original suit. This parameter is called the *order*. However, deviation rules such as *trumps* are allowed. If a player does not have a card from the original suit, they can play a trump card, *i.e.*, a card from the strongest suit so that the winner of the trick is the player who places the highest or lowest trump card in the trick. The combinations of order and trumps allow the representation of different cultures. In other words, the differences between the tables are: (1) The order of the card that wins the trick, *i.e.*, whether it is the highest or lowest and; (2) The trumps that win the trick from four possible suits. For instance, one table plays with the clubs as trumps and the highest card is the order that wins the trick, while for others, the clubs are the trumps and the lowest card is the order, and other tables have hearts as trumps while others have spades. What the players do not know is that there are slight differences in the rules between the tables. Therefore, conflicts arise when players play with different rules since everyone thinks that their opponents have a good understanding of the same rules although they are actually different. Since the players do not know the existence of the differences in the rules, several reactions such as confusion or anger can be observed. Some people may think "What is wrong with these people?", "Don't they know the rules?" After several games or exchanges, some players may realize the existence of these differences and try to learn the new rules for that table, *i.e.*, a new culture. However, the players who do not realize the existence of such differences will continue playing according to their original rules, getting angry or frustrated when they cannot win.

This game illustrates how prejudice can arise over customs and cultural differences between people, showing how people can misunderstand each other

---

[1] In this study, *trick* represents a turn where all players of the table have played a card, while a *game* is when all the tricks or cards are played. For simplicity the number tricks played between migrations are used instead of the number of games between migrations.

and think they should behave by common rules. For instance, players can understand the feelings of cultural shock when entering a new culture, and learn that they should be patient while attempting to understand and identify their new surroundings. For a more detailed description of the game, refer to [5].

3 Agent-based model

The implementation of the game previously explained considers two main elements, the *table* where the game is held, and *players* - called agents in this model - that represent human players. Due to its importance, only the agent model is described. The designed agent contains the following components as shown in Figure 1:

< **Knowledge** >

- **Game rules** represent the knowledge of all possible rules that may govern a game. Each rule contains the *order* and the *trump*, which define how to evaluate the winner in every trick, and the weight that represents the degree of belief the agent has that the rules are valid for the table he is playing in.
- **Strategic rules** are a collection of *if-then* rules that define the strategies the agent has on how to play the game in order to win [2].

< **Mechanism** >

- **Card selection** performs the selection of the card the agent will play according to the information received from the table. This information includes the cards played in the current trick by other players, number of players and the player number in the current trick. After receiving such information, the agent selects the game rule he believes the table is governed by, with a probabilistic selection according to the weight of the rules. Based on this information and the strategic rules, the card to be played is selected.
- **Projections on the winner** evaluates who should be the winner of the trick based on the selected game rule the agent believes the table is governed by.
- **Table adaptation** modifies the weight of the selected game rule, which the agent believes the table is governed by in the current trick, according to its correctness. Weight modification is carried out by Equation 1, where W represents the weight of the rule r at time t, flexibility indicates the degree of adaptation to the selected game rule[3], while the reward is valued in the range $[0:1]$ that represents the punishment or the prize the agent receives

[2] In the current stage of this research, strategic rules are predetermined by a human designer, but further studies on the learning mechanism for strategic rules are planned.

[3] In the field of Machine Learning, this parameter is known as the learning rate.

based on the incorrectness or correctness of the rules, respectively[4]. The correctness of a rule is calculated based on whether the projections of who should be the winner of the trick is correct. The learning mechanism used is reinforcement learning [7] since it can tune or redefine rules as a consequence of the interactions in the game.

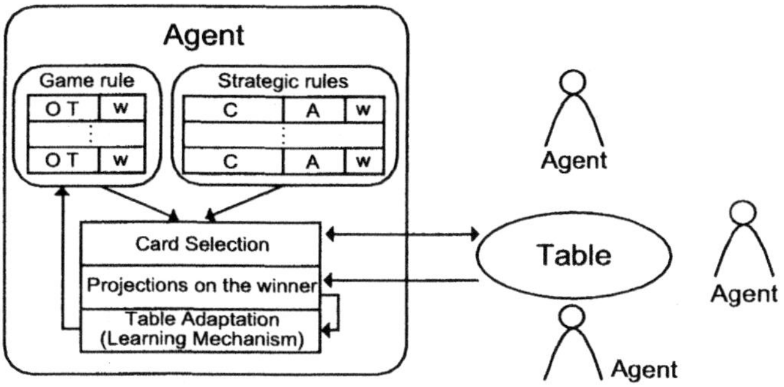

Fig. 1. Agent architecture

$$W_t^r = (1 - \mathit{flexibility}) * W_{t-1}^r + \mathit{flexibility} * \mathit{reward} \qquad (1)$$

4 Simulation results

4.1 Simulation Setting

Several experiments using different learning mechanisms were performed to identify the most suitable learning mechanism that can manage the relationship between cultural preservation and adaptation to new cultures. Five types of algorithms were constructed, which were based on how correct the projection of the winning player of the trick is. These algorithms were designed incrementing the complexity of evaluations to perform learning. The weights of the game rules are updated when:

- Agent projection is incorrect or correct (**A**)
- Agent projection is incorrect or, if correct, two or more cards of the trump must be present in the trick (**B**)
- Agent projection is incorrect or, if correct, two or more cards of the trump are presented and the first suit is different from the trump(**C**)
- First, learning A is used during the first 10 tricks after each migration, continued by learning B and for the rest of the tricks (**AB**)

[4] Incorrectness reduces the weight of the agent-selected game rule, while correctness increases it.

- First, learning B is used during the first 10 tricks after each migration, continued by learning C and for the rest of the tricks (**BC**)

The definition of the rule at each table is determined probabilistically among the rules with the 1st, 2nd, 3rd, 5th or 8th highest weights of all players participating in the table. The parameters of the model were defined as shown in Table 1. Each table starts with one of the 8 possible game rules (combinations of two possible orders and the four possible trumps) defined at random. The experiments were executed 10 times. It should be noted that the number of tricks per migration is used instead of the number of games per migration.

Table 1. Parameter setting

parameters for barnga game		
TABLES	number of tables	8
PLAYER/TABLE	number of player per table	4
MIGRATIONS	number of migrations	1000
GAMES/MIGRATION	number of games played before each migration	4
TRICKS/GAME	number of tricks per game	5
FLEXIBILITY	learning flexibility	0.1, 0.2, 0.3, 0.5

4.2 Experimental Results

The experimental results are shown in Figures 2 and 3. Figure 2 shows the dynamics of the diversity of rules among tables. Each line represents the change of diversity influenced by each learning mechanism, the x-axis represents the number of migrations in a logarithmic scale and the y-axis represents the number of different rules among the tables.

Finally, Figure 3 shows the comparison between the learning mechanisms and their influence on the convergence and diversity among groups. The x-axis represents the learning mechanisms used (A, AB, B, BC and C). The straight lines and dotted-lines represent the normalized values of the convergence and diversity average among 10 executions, respectively. The normalization was performed by using Equation 2. Where i and j represent the learning algorithm used. C_N_i and D_N_i represent the normalized convergence and diversity of learning i, respectively, while C_i and D_i represent the convergence and diversity measure of learning i, respectively. C_i was measured by the time needed to converge all the tables for algorithm i, while D_i shows the number of different rules that are used among all tables within a certain time for learning i. It should be noted that the influence of the different flexibilities used in the normalized convergence and diversity tendencies were very small. Therefore, all results are presented in average among flexibilities 0.01, 0.1, 0.2, 0.3 and 0.5.

$$C\_N_i = \frac{C_i - \min_j(C_j)}{\max_j(C_j) - \min_j(C_j)} \qquad D\_N_i = \frac{D_i - \min_j(D_j)}{\max_j(D_j) - \min_j(D_j)} \tag{2}$$

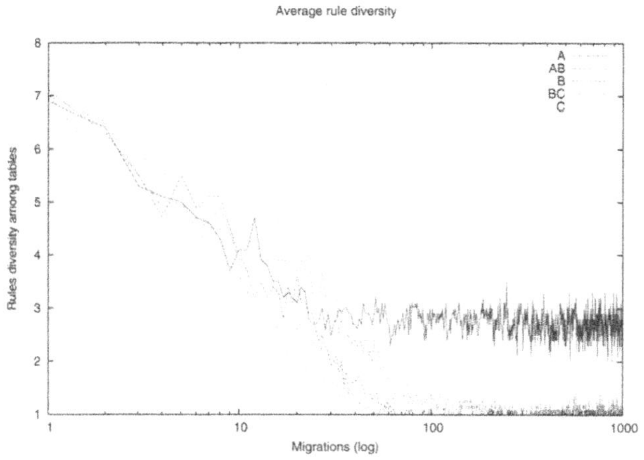

Fig. 2. Table dynamics

5 Discussions

Culture diversity

Figure 2 shows the dynamics of the culture diversity over time. These results show that learning A does not converge and the diversity is kept around 2-3 rules. This is due to some incorrect learning performed by A. However, for the other cases, all tables play with the same rules before 100 migrations, even though B sometimes performed some incorrect learning. Additionally, it shows little difference for the preservation of cultural diversity by learning B, BC and C. When applying the logarithmic scale, some slight differences between those learning mechanisms can be observed. Learning C converges faster than BC which is faster than B. B also is faster than AB. These results clearly showed that, regardless of the learning mechanism used, all of the tables converge to one rule after a certain number of migrations.

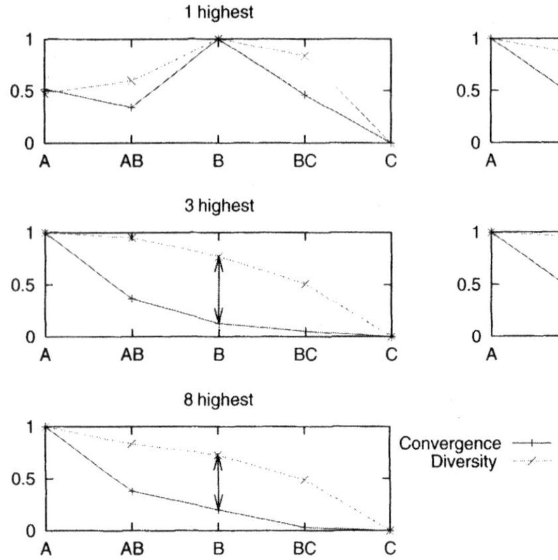

Fig. 3. Learning comparisons

Trade-off management

It is quite difficult to say which is the best learning mechanism, due to their different results. In this model, the difficulty is how to evaluate which learning mechanism performs better at adapting faster to the table and at the same time can keep at some level the cultural diversity. Results in Figure 3 show that the more elaborate the evaluation for learning is, the faster the convergence and consequently the reduction of diversity is. The exception is when using the rule with the highest weight of every agent to define the game rule of the table. In order to understand the reason for this exception, further analysis is required. One interesting observation is that the increase of complexity in the learning mechanisms influences the convergence speed and the diversity of groups in different ways. For small gradual accuracy from the less accurate learning mechanism A, there is a tiny reduction in the diversity even though the convergence time drops rapidly. For accuracy close to the most accurate learning mechanism C, the reduction of the convergence time is minor, while the diversity drops rapidly. Learning with middle accuracy B shows the highest difference between diversity preservation and the convergence time. Analysis in identifying the best mechanism that allows adaptation to a new culture and, at the same time, the retaining of cultural diversity among the tables, can be carried out graphically by simultaneous observations of the influence of the learning mechanisms on the convergence and diversity tendencies, this can be observed by the arrows in Figure 3.

6 Conclusions

Through analysis of an ABM model of the card game BARNGA, it was shown how different learning mechanisms influence the relationship between the preservation of cultural diversity and the processes involved in adaptation to new cultures. Through our analysis, the following implications have been found: (1) For small gradual accuracy from the less accurate learning mechanism A, there is a tiny reduction in the diversity even though the convergence time drops rapidly. For accuracy close to the most accurate learning mechanism C, the reduction of the convergence time is minor, while the diversity drops rapidly. (2) Learning with middle accuracy B shows the highest difference between diversity preservation and the convergence time. (3) Analysis in identifying the best mechanism that allows adaptation to a new culture and, at the same time, the retaining of cultural diversity among the tables, can be carried out graphically by simultaneous observations of the influence of the learning mechanisms on the convergence and diversity tendencies. Future research will consider: (1) Investigations of the influences of migration topology; (2) Further explorations of the BARNGA model for the study of cross-cultural differences and; (3) Evaluations of the influence of different types of learning in the various problems seen in the social sciences.

Acknowledge

This research was conducted as part of the 'Research on Human Communication' with funding from the National Institute of Information and Communications Technology (NICT), Japan. This research also was supported in part by the 'Foundation for the Fusion of Science and Technology' (FOST). We would like to express our thanks for all of the above support.

References

1. Axelrod, R. M. (1997) The complexity of cooperation: Agent-based models of competition and collaboration. Princeton University Press
2. Axelrod, R. M. and Cohen M. D. (2000) Harnessing complexity: Organizational implications of a scientific frontier. The Free Press
3. Greenblat, C. S. (1987) Designing games and simulations: An illustrated handbook. New-bury Park: Saga Publications
4. Leon, Y., Takadama, K., Nawa, N., Shimohara, K. and Katai, O. (2003) Analyzing the agent-based model simulation and its implications. Advances in Complex Systems, Vol.6, No. 3: 331–348

5. Leon, Y., Takadama, K., Shimohara, K., Katai, O. and Arai, K. (2003) Analyzing BARNGA Gaming Simulation Using an Agent-Based Model. In: Proceeding of The 34th Annual Conference of the International Simulation and Gaming Association (ISAGA), pp. 817–876
6. Moss, S. and Davidsson, P. (2001) Multi-Agent-Based Simulation. Lecture Notes in Artificial Intelligence. Springer-Verlag, Vol. 1979
7. Sutton, R. S., Barto A.G. (1998) Reinforcement Learning: An Introduction, MIT Press
8. Thiagarajan, S. and Steinwachs B. (1990) Barnga: A Simulation Game on Cultural Clashes, Intercultural Press,

Agent-based simulation of adaptive organizational structures to environmental change

Shingo Takahashi and Yusuke Goto

Department of Industrial and Management Systems Engineering, Waseda University, 3-4-1 Okubo, Shinjuku, Tokyo 169-8555, Japan

Summary. This paper proposes an agent-based simulation model for analyzing adaptive processes of organizational structures to environmental changes. The model is based on a framework of computational organization theory (COT) and performed using the method of inverse simulation with genetic algorithm. The model specifies an activity process in organization that is composed of tasks, agents and environments. The roles of agents: normal and leader, are defined based on some basic tasks of agents: recognizing tasks from environment, sharing knowledge required for processing tasks, and coordinating tasks among agents. Organizational structures are distinguished according to the configuration of the roles of agents resolving the tasks recognized. Adaptation process is represented as learning process of agents' internal models of environments. Environments are expressed as task generators and fall into 5 types. This paper shows some fundamental relationships between organizational structures and dynamically changing environments.

Key words. organizational structure, agent-based simulation, inverse simulation

1 Introduction

The purposes of this paper are to present an agent-based model for analyzing adaptive processes of organizational structures to environmental changes, and to show some simulation results on organizational adaptation. The model developed in this paper is intended to investigate the dynamical change of organizational structures adapted along with dynamically changing environments.

Organizational adaptation has been researched mainly in organization theory. Contingency theory developed by Lawrence and Lorsch (1967) are concerned with static aspects of the relationships between organizational structures and environments, based on empirical studies.

In computational organization theory (Carley and Gasser 1999), though there has been many researches based on agent-based approaches (Deguchi 2000) to analyze learning and adaptation processes in organization (March 1991; Takadama et al. 1999), few research has dealt with similar problems of adaptive organizational structures as in this paper.

Carley and Svoboda (1996) developed a model of adaptive process of organization to environment by applying simulated annealing method. Their model does not consider the processes of formation and convergence of organizational structures adapting specific environments, and does not deal with different types of environments that dynamically change in time.

In our model each organization adapts its structure to environments by selecting autonomously and dynamically its form. We model an organization as a task-based system, which is mainly applied in computational organization theory. Then we use inverse simulation method to classify organizational structures that adapt virtually provided environments and observe adaptive processes of learning in organization.

Each agent in the model is planned to learn his role in an organization for resolving tasks that are supposed to require knowledge. This paper considers an organizational structure to be determined by the formation of the roles of agents in the organization. In our simulation model genetic algorithm and inverse simulation method are used when agents in an organization learn their roles and decision rules in an evolutionary manner.

2 Model of organization

2.1 Activity process in organization

The agents in an organization manage, in a cooperative manner, tasks generated in the environment of the organization. How much tasks are successfully managed in the organization depends on the knowledge and skills the agents have.

The main activity process in an organization for the management of tasks is given in the following flow. Tasks are generated in the environment of the organization.

1. Some agents as leaders in the organization recognize the properties of the tasks that should be processed in the organization.
2. The results of the agents' recognition of the tasks are exchanged with the other agents, and each agent revises his recognition of the tasks if necessary. The exchanged recognition of the tasks is defined as the organizational recognition of the tasks.
3. The leader agents coordinate the assignments of tasks to agents.
4. According to the assignments, the agents exchange the required knowledge necessary to resolve the tasks.
5. Each agent resolves tasks by using his knowledge resource, and gets a positive evaluation if the tasks are successfully done.
6. After a series of tasks, the organization makes some action to the environment and gets some evaluation representing how good the result of the activity is for the current environment.

2.2 Task

We define a task as a set of components of knowledge that are required for resolving the task. In the simulation in this paper, each task is characterized by specifying 8 elements of knowledge. For example, a task characterized as having the 1st and 3rd elements of knowledge represents that the task requires the 1st and 3rd elements of knowledge to resolve it.

A task is expressed by l bits strings, each of which is either 1 or 0. If a bit in a task is 1, then the knowledge of that bit is required to resolve the task. For example, a task expressed by (1,0,0,1,1,0,0,0) requires the 1st, 4th and 5th elements of knowledge to resolve it.

2.3 Agent

In an organization we suppose there are an enough number of agents to manage tasks. Each organization is composed of one leader agent and the other normal agents. A normal agent recognizes and specifies what knowledge is required for tasks, and then exchanges the recognized tasks with other agents in an organization. A leader agent coordinates tasks as well as the role of a normal agent, and has a set of decision rules as his internal model for organizational decision making. The rules are (1) how many agents participate in recognizing tasks, (2) tasks of concern are coordinated or not, and (3) how many agents participate in exchanging knowledge to resolve the recognized tasks.

2.4 Organizational structure

Basically there are two types of organizational structures: hierarchical structure and network structure. Every organization lies between hierarchical and network structure. In this paper we represent an organizational structure as a specification of the decision rules of leader agents.

We put two basic provisions for organizational hierarchy. In an upper stratum of an organizational hierarchy tasks are recognized to be resolved. In a lower stratum of an organizational hierarchy tasks are actually resolved, after the required knowledge is exchanged among the agents whom the leader agent assigns to resolve the tasks.

In a typical hierarchical structure one leader agent recognizes tasks and in a typical network structure many agents participate in recognizing tasks.

We classify organizational structures by specifying the values of the decision rules mentioned above. If the number of agents who recognize tasks and exchange the knowledge with other agents is small, then the organizational structure becomes hierarchical.

2.5 Environments

An organization is surrounded by environment that is dynamically changing. We here model environment as a task generator and a response function. An environment as a task generator provides an organization with tasks. An environment as a response function evaluates the output of the activities of an organization. The environment evaluates the output of an organization based on three indicators: quality, cost, delivery. Quality indicator expresses how much complex tasks succeeded. Cost indicator expresses how small number of agents engage in resolving tasks. Delivery indicator expresses how many tasks succeeded.

We consider 5 types of environments according to the marketing concepts in the standard theory of marketing (Cotler and Armstrong 1999): production-oriented environment, sales-oriented environment, consumer-oriented environment, society-oriented environment, environment-oriented environment.

The weighting characteristics of the 5 types of environments are shown (Table 1).

Table 1. Characteristics of environments

Environment	Quality	Cost	Delivery
Production-oriented	very low weighting	high weighting	high weighting
Sales-oriented	low weighting	high weighting	high weighting
Consumer-oriented	medium weighting	medium weighting	medium weighting
Society-oriented	high weighting	low weighting	low weighting
Environment-oriented	very high weighting	very low weighting	very low weighting

Five types of environments are defined by evaluation functions that evaluate the results of organizational activities. The evaluation functions are expressed with a combination of weights for quality of tasks, cost of resolving tasks and delivery evaluation.

2.6 Adaptation process

This paper basically uses the inverse simulation method, which was proposed by Kurahashi, Minami and Terano (1999), to investigate the adaptation process of organization that simulates autonomous organizational learning, structural change of organization by revising decision making rules in organizational activities. Our model of adaptation of organization is composed of the following 5 steps.

1. Organizations as population in simulation are produced from the given gene pool of organizations.
2. Each organization has the given number of agents each of whom has his own initial characteristic values.
3. Each agent makes a series of activities in a given period in accordance with the rules of activity in the organization to which the agent belongs.
4. An environment of which we are interested in investigating the property is represented by an evaluation function to evaluate the results of organizational activities.
5. After the evaluation of the organizational activities, organizations as population revise their genes by applying the genetic operators in genetic algorithm.

Here we should notice an interpretation of the adaptation process on actual organizations. Each organization is described as a chromosome in a gene pool. The adaptation process is applied to the given gene pool. This seems that the adaptation process modeled might be effective for not a single organization but some amount of population of oraganizations. Our model, however, does not necessarily intend such adaptation process for a set of „real" organizations.

The gene pool could give executives as decision makers some set of alternatives to be selected in making a decision of an organizational structure adaptive to a currently recognized environment. Then the gene pool represents a „virtual" set of organizations as alternatives. The whole process of adaptation shows that of executives' adaptive decision making.

3 Simulation model

3.1 Chromosome of organization

The chromosome of an organization C_{org} is composed of genetic attributes P_{gen} and activity attributes $P_{act} : C_{org} = (P_{gen}, P_{act})$. The genetic attributes are specified at the initial stage of the simulation and revised according with the adaptation process. The activity attributes represent the results of the activities of agents in every period of the simulation steps. The initial values of the activity attributes are set as 0, and rewritten in the processes of organization.

The genetic attributes are defined as gene sequences:

$$P_{gen} = (n_p, n_k, cord, AK, AP),$$

where n_p is the number of agents participating in recognizing tasks, n_k the number of agents participating in sharing knowledge, $cord$ expresses the leader's decision on coordination: 1 for coordinating, and 0 for non-coordinating,

$AK = \{ak^1,...,ak^{n_a} \mid ak^m =< ak_1^m,...,ak_l^m >, ak_i^m \in \{0,1\}\}$ the knowledge structure of agents (l=8 in this paper) for resolving tasks, $AP = \{ap^1,...,ap^{n_a} \mid ap^i \in \{0.90, 0.93, 0.96, 0.99\}\}$ the accuracy indicator of each agent, which provides the possibility to recognize tasks. In the knowledge structure of agents, $ak_i^m = 1$ means that agent m has the i th knowledge. The leader agent has all the elements of P_{gen}, but other normal agents i has only ak^i and ap^i. The accuracy indicator ap^i is coded as $00, 01, 10, 11$ corresponding to $0.90, 0.93, 0.96, 0.99$ respectively.

3.2 Simulation process

In the simulation each organization first performs tasks during the period that is predetermined as a parameter of the experiment, and the gene pool of the chromosomes of organizations are revised during the generations also predetermined as an experimental parameter.

The simulation is basically composed of 10 steps with two phases.

Table 2. Parameters in environments

Environment	Types of tasks		Weights for evaluation		
	Complexity	Variety of generation dynamics	w_q	w_c	w_d
Production-oriented	simple	constantly	0.1	0.7	0.2
Sales-oriented	simple	gradually	0.2	0.5	0.3
Consumer-oriented	complex	phased	0.3	0.4	0.3
Society-oriented	complex	random	0.5	0.2	0.3
Environment-oriented	complex	random	0.6	0.1	0.3

Types of tasks are defined by the complexity of tasks and the variety of task generation dynamics. The weights for evaluation depict the values w_q, w_c, and w_d used in the evaluation function in each environment.

Task resolution phase.

1. Generation of tasks. Tasks are characterized by complexity and variety of change. What kinds of tasks are generated depends on the environment that generates the tasks (Table 2).
2. Recognition of tasks. Each agent of selected n_p agents recognizes each task by scanning every bit of the task. The possibility that an agent i correctly recog-

nizes a bit of a task is defined by $ap^i \cdot ap_c$, where ap_c is 0.99 or 0.9 that depends on the difficulty of the task. Then $T_a = \{ta_i \mid i = 1,...,n_p\}$ is obtained.

3. Constructing organizational recognition of tasks. The results of the recognition of a task are exchanged to be common in the agents. Comparing each bit of the recognized tasks by the agents, the organizational recognition T_{org} of the task is defined by using the majority rule for the bits of the agents' recognition.
4. Coordination. Each agent can perform only one bit in a task. If a task is complex and $cord = 1$, then the leader agent coordinates who should perform the task.
5. Sharing knowledge. The agents who actually resolve the organizationally recognized task T_{org} are randomly selected. The number of agents is n_k. The bit of T_{org} that has the value 1 is needed to be resolved by some agent. Such a bit with 1 of. T_{org} is assigned to the agent whose corresponding bit is 1, which means that he can actually resolve that bit of T_{org}. If no agent has a bit of 1, there is no assignment of that bit.
6. Resolving tasks. Based on the sharing knowledge and assignment of a task to the n_k agents, the task is actually resolved. This resolution succeeds if all the bits of T_{org} are assigned to some agent, otherwise the resolution fails. If the resolution of the task succeeds, then 1 adds to $succ$ or $h-succ$ according to the complexity of the task. If the period of task resolution phase does not terminate, repeat from the step 1, otherwise go to the next phase.

Adaptation phase.

7. Evaluation of results. The results of the task activities in an organization are evaluated with a fitness function representing how much the organization adapts the environment of concern. The fitness function is defined by $f = w_q q + w_c c + w_d d$. The values of the weight parameters depend on the environmental types (Table 2). The detail definition of the fitness function is given by

$$f = w_q \cdot \frac{hsucc}{t_c} + w_c \cdot \left(1 - \frac{\sqrt{n_p}\sqrt{n_k \cdot cord}}{n_a}\right) + w_d \cdot \frac{succ}{t}$$

   If the termination condition does not satisfy, go to the next step, otherwise the simulation ends.
8. Selection of organizations. By using the roulette rule of genetic algorithm, organization genes for the next generation are selected. The simulation in this paper a linear scaling is applied to the fitness functions. The activity attributes are initialized for the next generation process of task resolution.
9. Crossover of genetic attributes. A two-point crossover is applied on the genetic attributes of organization genes. The crossover probability is set to 0.6.

10. Mutation of genetic attributes. Mutation with the probability 0.01 is applied on the genetic attributes of organization genes. The steps are iterated for the next generation.

4 Experimental results

We show three types of experimental results concerning the relationships between adaptive organizational structures and environments. The parameters of the experiments are; the number of generations: 500, the number of activity processes of resolving tasks in each generation: 500, the population of organizations: 100, the population of agents: 30.

Table 3. Organizational structures adaptive to environments

Environment	Participants for recognizing tasks	Coordination	Participants for sharing knowledge	Fitness value
Production-oriented	1	1	7	0.94
Sales-oriented	1	1	11	0.94
Consumer-oriented	3	1	28	0.83
Society-oriented	7	1	29	0.90
Environment-oriented	11	1	30	0.94

Participants for recognizing tasks and sharing knowledge mean the number of agents who participate in these activities. The Coordination with value 1 means that the leader agent coordinates who should perform the task.

4.1 Adaptive organizational structure for environment

First we show the result of the experiment in which we search the organizational structures most adaptive to each of the 5 types of environments. The result is shown in Table 3.

From the result on the number of participants for recognizing tasks, we see that in production-oriented and sales-oriented environments hierarchal structures are most adaptive, and in environment-oriented environment network-structures are most adaptive.

4.2 Adaptation process for changing environment

The second experiment is to see the adaptation processes of organizational structures when the type of an environment changes to another type, while in the first experiment the environment is fixed through the adaptation process. We here show the results on two types of the environmental changes: change from production-oriented to sales-oriented, and change from sales-oriented to society-oriented (Fig. 1, 2).

In the experiment, the environments change at 300th generation. The results shown in Fig. 1 and 2 imply that the differences on characteristics between changing environments are critical for the adaptation process of the organization. Though the production-oriented environment and the sales-oriented environment are not so effective to the adaptation process, the characteristics of society-oriented environment are effectively different from those of sales-oriented environment.

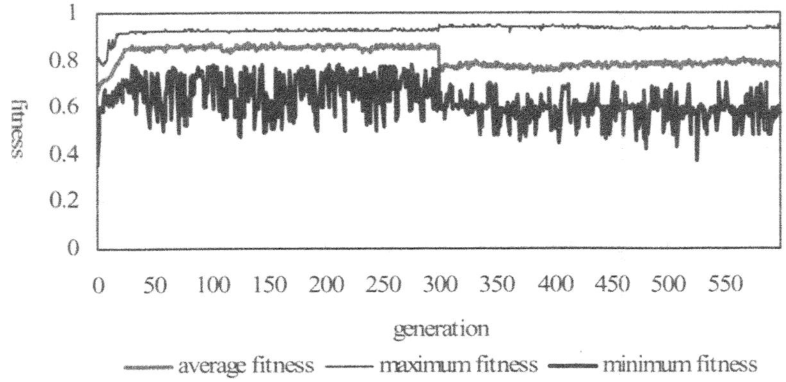

Fig. 1. Adaptation process in changing environment from production-oriented to sales-oriented
The environment changes from production-oriented to sales-oriented at 300th generation.

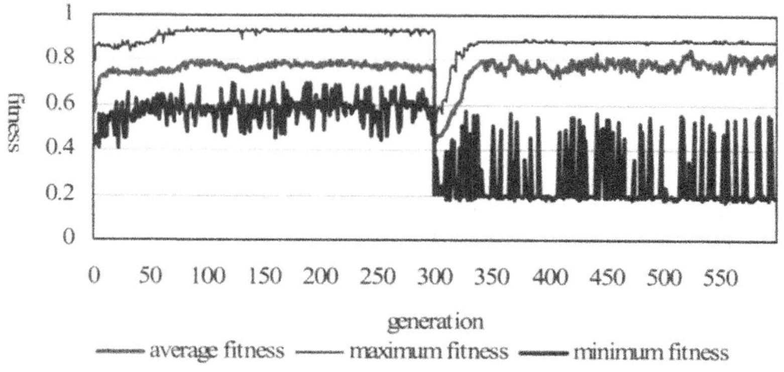

Fig. 2. Adaptation process in changing environment form sales-oriented to society-oriented The environment changes from sales-oriented to society-oriented at 300th generation

4.3 Sensitive analysis of adaptive organizational structure

In this experiment, we compare the characteristics of organizational structures and adaptive organizational structures to environment. We are here concerned with the scale of an organization and industrial properties: labor-concentrated industry or knowledge-concentrated industry. The results are shown in Table 4 and 5.

Table 4. Adaptive structure in participants

Environment	Group (n_a=10, l=4)			Section (n_a=30, l=7)			Branch (n_a=60, l=10)		
	n_p	c	n_s	n_p	c	n_s	n_p	c	n_s
Production-oriented	1	0	X	1	1	6	1	1	9
Sales-oriented	1	1	6	1	1	8	1	1	12
Consumer-oriented	3	1	8	3	1	27	5	1	60
Society-oriented	5	1	8	7	1	28	11	1	60
Environment-oriented	7	1	9	9	1	30	11	1	60

Notation: n_a shows a degree to how many agents participate in the activities of recognition of tasks and sharing knowledge; l knowledge length; n_p and n_s the numbers of participants for recognizing tasks and sharing knowledge respectively; and c coordination value taking 1 if the leader agent coordinates who should perform the task, 0 otherwise.

The adaptive organizational structure in a group, which has small number of agents for activities, shows the largest variety concerning the environmental differences.

The number of agents, n_a, can be considered as a degree to how much agents participate in the activities of recognition of tasks and sharing knowledge. The smaller the number of agents is in an organizational structure, to the greater degree agents participate in the activities.

A remarkable result in adaptive organizational structure concerning types of industries can be seen in the relationship of the labor-concentrated industry and the environment-oriented environment, in which a group structure can be found in recognizing tasks and sharing knowledge.

We can also see a general relationship between industry types and knowledge length l. The larger l is, the more agents participate in sharing knowledge.

Table 5. Adaptive structure in industries

Environment	Labor-con. (n_a=40, l=3)			Average (n_a=40, l=6)			Knowledge-con. (n_a=40, l=9)		
	n_p	c	n_s	n_p	c	n_s	n_p	c	n_s
Production-oriented	1	1	6	1	1	7	1	1	7
Sales-oriented	1	1	8	1	1	10	1	1	10
Consumer-oriented	7	1	8	5	1	20	5	1	40
Society-oriented	9	1	10	11	1	29	9	1	40
Environment-oriented	11	1	10	15	1	31	12	1	40

The meaning of notations are similar as in table 4. Three types of industries: labor-concentrated, knowledge-concentrated and average, are specified according to the complexity of knowledge lengths.

5 Conclusion

In this paper we developed an agent-based model for investigating adaptive organizational structures, which seek the structure with the maximum fitness value to environment. We defined 5 types of environments by specifying 3 aspects of quality, cost and delivery. The simulation results partly showed the most adaptive organizational structure for each type of environments. We obtained other simulation results concerning the fundamental relationships between the changing environments and the characteristics of organizational structures. These results are basically consistent with well-known things in the theory of organization. The main contribution of this paper is to provide rigid agent-based framework to build a model to get adaptation processes of organization in dynamically changing, i.e. non-stationary environment.

The model developed in this paper could become more sophisticated for further research on organizational adaptation in several folds. In theoretical treatments of organization, our model could provide a basic way to consider organizational learning, especially double-loop learning. From a positivism point of view, by adding to the current model more detailed properties of specific organizations that we are actually concerned with, we could get more deep insights on actual problem situations in organizations.

References

Carley KM, Gasser L (1999) Computational Organization Theory. in Multiagent Systems - A Modern Approach to Distributed Artificial Intelligence - (G. Weiss ed.). MIT Press.

Carley KM, Svoboda DM (1996) Modeling Organizational Adaptation as a Simulated Annealing Process. Sociological Methods & Research, Vol.25, No.1, pp.138-168.

Cotler P, Armstrong G (1999) Marketing: An Introduction(4th ed.). Prentice-Hall.

Deguchi H (ed.) (2000) Special Issue: Agent-based Approach. J. of Organizational Science, Vol.34, No.2 (in Japanese).

Kurahashi S, Minami U, Terano T (1999) Inverse Simulation for Analyzing Emergent Behaviors in Artificial Societies. J. of The Society of Instrument and Control Engineers, Vol.35, No.11, pp.1454-1461 (in Japanese).

Lawrence PR, Lorsch JW (1967) Organization and Environment: Managing Differentiation and Integration. Harvard University Press.

March JG (1991) Exploration and Exploitation in Organizational Learning. Organization Science, Vol.2, No.1, pp.71-87.

Takadama K, Terano T, Shimohara K, Hori K, and Nakasuka S (1999) Making Organizational Learning Operational: Implications from Learning Classifier Systems. Computational & Mathematical Organization Theory, Vol.5, No.3, pp.229-252.

A Study on alliance analysis in civil aviation industry based on fuzzy landscape theory

Shigemasa Suganuma[1], Jian Chen[2], and Yoshiteru Nakamori[1]

[1]School of Knowledge Science, Japan Advanced Institute of Science and Technology, 1-1 Asahidai, Tatsunokuchi, Ishikawa 923-1292, Japan
[2]School of Economics and Management, Tsinghua University, Beijing, 100084, China

Summary. The concept of landscape theory provides a way of thinking about the many possible ways in which elements of a system can fit together, predicting which configurations are most likely to occur, how much dissatisfaction with the outcomes is inevitable, and how the system will respond to changes in the relationship between the elements. Recently we extended landscape theory using the notion of fuzzy partitions.

In this paper we study the formation of competing alliances by companies who wish to increase their own business efficiency in the civil aviation industry. The purpose of this paper is to evaluate the fuzzy landscape theory by using an airline industry case.

Key words. Landscape theory, Global alliance, civil aviation, Membership value

Introduction

Global alliances have major influences on spurring competitiveness and rationalizing the management of member companies.

Commercial airlines form global alliances in several ways. A regulatory body with enforcement powers or a single dominant state sometimes can impose a rule on a market. As a result, it is increasingly common for carriers to join together into one or more global alliances in order to improve business efficiency. Global alliances formed before 2000 to increase the business efficiency of the members are examples of this phenomenon. Little attention has been given to research on how a carrier decides which airline alliance to join. Increasing our understanding of the process by which carriers choose a global alliance would provide insights into both the formation of global alliances and the structures that emerge from such alliances.

The concept of landscape theory provides a way of thinking about the many possible ways in which elements of a system can fit together, predicting which configurations are most likely to occur, how much dissatisfaction with the outcomes is inevitable, and how the system will respond to changes in the relationship between the elements (Axelrod 1997). Recently we extended landscape theory using the notion of fuzzy partitions (Suganuma et al. 2005).

In this paper we study the formation of competing alliances by companies who wish to increase their own business efficiency in the civil aviation industry. The purpose of this paper is to evaluate the fuzzy landscape theory by using an airline industry case.

Preliminaries of landscape theory

This section briefly recalls key concepts from landscape theory. More detailed discussions of the theory as well as its applications are referred from landscape theory, as described by Axelrod (Axelrod 1997).

Landscape theory begins with a finite set of actors, denoted by $\mathrm{A} = \{A_1,\ldots,A_n\}$. Each actor A_i has its own *size*, $s_i > 0$, that reflects the importance of that actor to others. In addition, each pair of actors A_i and A_j has a *propensity* p_{ij} that is a measure of how willing the two actors are to be in the same coalition. For example, in the language of international alignments, the propensity number is positive and large if the two nations get along well together and negative if they have many sources of potential conflict. Further, if one country has a source of conflict with another, then the second country typically has the same source of conflict with the first. Thus the theory assumes that propensity is symmetric, that is $p_{ij} = p_{ji}$.

By a *configuration* we mean a partition of the set of actors. That is, each actor is placed into one and only one group. Given a configuration X, we then define the distance between any two actors A_i and A_j within X, denoted by $d_{ij}(X)$. For example, assume that $X = \{X_1,\ldots,X_m\}$ is a configuration, then the simplest measure of distance can be defined as follows:

$$d_{ij}(X) = \begin{cases} 0, \text{if } A_i, A_j \in X_k \text{ for some } X_k \\ 1, \text{otherwise} \end{cases} \quad (1)$$

Using distance and propensity, the so-called *frustration* of an actor A_i is defined as the measure of how poorly or well a given configuration satisfies the propensities of a given actor to be near or far from each other actor. Formally, the frustration of an actor A_i in a configuration X is defined by

$$F_i(X) = \sum_{i \neq j} s_j p_{ij} d_{ij}(X) \qquad (2)$$

where s_j is the size of A_j, p_{ij} is the propensity of A_i to be close to A_j, and $d_{ij}(X)$ is the distance between A_i and A_j in X.

Finally, the so-called *energy*, E of an entire configuration X is now defined as the weighted sum of the frustrations of each actor in a configuration, where the weights are the sizes of the actors. More precisely, the energy of a configuration X is as follows :

$$E(X) = \sum_{i} s_i F_i(X) \qquad (3)$$

Equivalently, the following equation defines the energy of a configuration in terms of the size of the actors, their propensities to work together, and their distances in the configuration:

$$E(X) = \sum_{i,j} s_i s_j p_{ij} d_{ij}(X) \qquad (4)$$

where the summation is over all ordered pairs of distinct actors. Now the predicted configurations are based on the attempts of actors to minimize their frustrations based on their pairwise propensities to align with some actors and oppose others. These attempts lead to a local minimum in the energy landscape of the entire system.

Fuzzification of landscape theory

In this section, we propose an extension of landscape theory based on the notion of fuzzy partitions. It should be also noted that in landscape theory, the measure of distance in a configuration can be defined differently according to various applied situations. In Kijima (Kijima 2001a, 2001b), the author has extended landscape theory by introducing another measure of distance. In our research, as mentioned in the introduction, we extend the theory by relaxing the notion of membership grades in the definition of a configuration. We can now mathematically restate landscape theory in terms of an optimized problem with constraints. Given

- $\mathrm{A} = \{A_1, \ldots, A_n\}$
  - A set of n actors and each A_i has its size s_i, $i = 1, \ldots, n$,
- $\lfloor p_{ij} \rfloor_{n \times n}$
  - The symmetric matrix of propensities,

- $X = \{X_1, \ldots, X_m\}$
  - A configuration, where $1 < m < n$.

For any $A_i \in A, X_k \in X$, let us denote

$$u_{ik} := \mu_{X_k}(A_i) = \begin{cases} 1, \text{if } A_i \in X_k \\ 0, \text{otherwise} \end{cases} \quad (5)$$

where μ_{X_k} denotes the characteristic function of X_k.

It is easily seen that the measure of distance defined by (1) can be stated in terms of membership grades as follows:

$$d_{ij}(X) = \frac{1}{2}\sum_{k=1}^{m}(u_{ik} - u_{jk})^2 \quad (6)$$

Substituting (6) into (4) yields the following expression of the energy of a configuration:

$$E(X) = \frac{1}{2}\sum_{i=1}^{n}\sum_{i \neq j=1}^{n} s_i s_j p_{ij} \sum_{k=1}^{m}(u_{ik} - u_{jk})^2 \quad (7)$$

As mentioned in the preceding section, the problem is to find predicted configurations which are local minima in the entire system's energy landscape. Mathematically, the theory now aims at minimizing the objective function (7) under the constraints (8), (9) and (10) below

$$1 < m < n; u_{ik} \in \{0,1\}, \text{ for all } i \in \{1,\ldots,n\}, k \in \{1,\ldots,m\} \quad (8)$$

and

$$\sum_{i=1}^{n} u_{ik} > 0 \quad \text{for all } k \in \{1,\ldots,m\} \quad (9)$$

and

$$\sum_{k=1}^{m} u_{ik} = 1 \quad \text{for all } i \in \{1,\ldots,n\} \quad (10)$$

It is interesting to see that the principles of landscape theory are similar to those of clustering based on objective functions with the well-known *c*-means algorithms 1(Kaufman L. & Rousseeu 1990).

Under such a formulation, we can extend the theory by relaxing the notion of a configuration to a fuzzy one. Now we aim at finding fuzzy configurations that minimize function (7) subject to constraints

$$\begin{cases} u_{ik} \in [0,1], & \text{for all } i \in \{1,\dots,n\}, k \in \{1,\dots,m\} \\ \sum_{i=1}^{n} u_{ik} > 0, & \text{for all } k \in \{1,\dots,m\} \\ \sum_{k=1}^{m} u_{ik} = 1, & \text{for all } i \in \{1,\dots,n\} \end{cases} \tag{11}$$

Let us denote

$$u = \{U = [u_{ik}]_{n\times m} \mid u_{ik} \in [0,1] \wedge \sum_{k=1}^{m} u_{ik} = 1 \wedge \sum_{i=1}^{n} u_{ik} > 0, \forall i,k\}$$

In the next section we develop a GA-based algorithm to find near-optimized solutions corresponding to predicted fuzzy configurations. Previously, we made two simulations with the proposed algorithm, one for the problem of international alignments in the Second World War in Europe, and the other for the problem of coalition formation in standard-setting alliances in the UNIX operating system case (Suganuma 2005).

An algorithm and simulation results

The algorithm proposed to solve the optimized problem discussed above is described as follows.

Input:

The set of sizes of actors $\{s_1 \dots, s_n\}$, the propensity matrix $\lfloor p_{ij} \rfloor_{n\times n}$

Output:

$U \in \mu$ that minimizes the energy function E.

1: Set $t=0$, initiate the first configuration U_0 randomly, set a value for T.

2: Calculate the energy value for $U_0 = \left[u\binom{(0)}{ik}\right]_{n\times m}$

by $E(U_0) = \frac{1}{2}\sum_{i=1}\sum_{i\neq j=1} s_i s_j p_{ij} \sum_{k=1}^{m}\left(u_{ik}^{(0)} - u_{jk}^{(0)}\right)^2$

3: $t= t+1$.

4: Use GA to generate the next configuration U_t from the preceding configuration.

5: Calculate the energy value $E(U_t)$.

6: While $|E(U_t) - E(U_{t-1})| \geq \varepsilon$ and $t \geq T$ do

IF $E(U_t) < E(U_{t-1})$ Then go to step 3.

Else set t: =t-1 go to step 3.

To illustrate the applicability of our approach and to test the proposed algorithm, we have used a case study from the civil aviation industry.

Application to the civil aviation industry

In the civil aviation industry, business alliances are usually studied in terms of global alliances. The dominant approach to explaining airline alliances is that carriers form alliances primarily in opposition to the partnerships formed by other powerful carriers. This balancing process tends to increase business efficiency, spur competitiveness, and increase the rationalization of management. As a result, it will be increasingly common for carriers to join together in one or more global alliances in order to promote business efficiency.

Little research has been done on how a commercial airline decides which alliance group to join. Increasing our understanding of the process by which commercial airlines choose an alliance would provide insights into the character of these carrier groups. In our research we study the formation of competing alliances to increase business efficiency. Because global alliances must induce individual carriers to join them in order to succeed, we concentrate on the consortia formation process, in which carriers join such global alliances. Our basic assumptions are that a carrier prefers to join a large alliance group in order to increase the probability of successfully sharing systems, resources, and routes, and to avoid groups with direct rivals, especially rivals of the same size, in order to maximize its own benefits.

By applying the principles of landscape theory, we can describe the composition of airline alliances. We analyze the effectiveness of our assumption by using 1997 and 2001 alliance data for measuring competitiveness. The experiment verifies that Fuzzy Landscape Theory also can apply to the asymmetric propensity, and to the existence of any number of alliances. The research proceeds as follows.

First, we briefly describe the global alliances and introduce the rationale for alliance formation in the civil aviation industry. The illustration shows that our model does quite well at explaining the membership decisions of the carriers involved.

Global alliances are powerful strategies for increasing competitiveness and promoting the synergistic rationalization of management. The first global alliance was formed in 1989 after the Airline Deregulation Act of 1978 (see Table 1.).

Table 1. Five major alliance*

STAR Alliance (since 1997)	
Air Canada	Canada
Air New Zealand	New Zealand
All Nippon Airways	Japan
Ansett Australia	Australia
Austrian Airlines	Austria
bmi british midland	UK
Lauda air	Austria
Lufthansa	Germany
Mexicana	Mexico
SAS	Scandinavia
Singapore Airlines	Singapore
Thai Airways	Thailand
Tyrolean	Austria
United Airlines	USA
Varig	Brazil

OneWorld Alliance (since 1998)	
Aer Lingus	Ireland
American Airlines	USA
British Airways	UK
Cathay Pacific	Hong Kong
Finnair	Finland
Iberia	Spain
Lanchile	Chile
Quantas	Australia

Sky Team (since 1999)	
Air France	France
Aero Mexico	Mexico
Alitalia	Italy
Czech Airlines	Czech Republic
Delta	USA
Korean Airlines	South Korea

Qualiflyer (since 1998)	
Air Portugal	Portugal
Air Littoral	France
Air Europe	Italy
Air Liberte	France
Cross Air	Switzerland
LOT	Poland
PGA	Portugal
Sabena	Belgium
Swissair	Switzerland
Volare Airlines	Italy

North West Airlines/KLM (since 1989)	
North West Airlines	USA
KLM	The Netherlands

*These alliances reflect the situation until Oct. 2001. Several changes have occurred since that time.

A key aspect of global alliance design is the free competition policy established by the Airline Deregulation Act of 1978 and Open Sky, which intensified consortia formation in the US. In this process many mergers and acquisitions and capital tie-ups were ruled out because of the enforcement of anti-monopoly laws. As a result, the U.S. international airlines are in an oligopoly state dominated by four carriers, namely American Airlines, Delta, Northwest Airlines, and United Airlines.

In Europe, also, EU integration and airline service and capital tie-ups have come to be performed regionally, in each country. In order to secure a place in a market, each carrier searches for a better partner and the tie-up partnerships do not remain within Europe, but expand even to airlines in the U.S., which share the huge transatlantic market. As a result of this trend, Europe and the United States formed five main alliances by 1999. The objective of our test is to predict the airline industry alignment that actually occurred after the Airline Deregulation Act of 1978. The first task for our analysis was to identify the relevant carriers.

We identified the carriers with the potential to play an important role in grouping Global Alliances, the year on Sky Team formed. We selected ten carriers: five major American/British carriers and five other carriers that compete in the civil aviation industry. The five main carriers were United Airlines, American Airlines, Delta, Northwest Airlines, and British Airways; the other carriers were Lufthansa, Thai Airways, Cathay Pacific, KLM, and SAS. All of the companies are among the top 25 carriers (Sugiura 1990) in the world. Next, we required a measure for individual carrier size. However, there is no one unequivocal measure of carrier size in the civil aviation industry. Air Transport World (1990) specifies several measures of carrier size, using various rankings. For this research, we used two generally used indexes, Revenue Passenger Miles (RPMs) and Annual Number of Passengers.

To determine the size of the ten carriers, we used each carrier's 1997 Annual Number of Passengers and 2001 Revenue Passenger Kilometers (RPKs) and Annual Passenger. Revenue Passenger Miles (RPMs) is the numerical value obtained by multiplying the annual number of passengers and annual flight distances. Table 2 displays the target carriers, including the number of passengers and Revenue Passenger Kilometers in 2001. 1997 data is referred to as Kijima's data, and 2001 data was compiled by the Japan Aircraft Development Corporation (2003).

Table 2. Target carriers and size data

No	Flight Carrier	1999's RPNs (1,000peoples)	2001's RPNs (1,000,000Km)	2001's RPKs (1,000,000Km)
1	American Airlines	110,147	78,178	170,883
2	British Airways	73,334	40,004	106,270
3	Cathay Pacific	25,747	11,269	44,792
4	United Airlines	125,372	75,457	187,666
5	Lufthansa	53,535	39,694	86,695
6	SAS (Scandinavian Airline Systems)	13,200	23,244	23,295
7	Thai Airways International	23,827	18,271	44,039
8	Northwest Airlines	74,168	54,056	117,658
9	KLM Royal Dutch Airlines	36,110	15,995	57,848
10	Delta Air Lines	104,699	104,943	163,663

Kijima has proposed a model which extends the asymmetric propensity and existence of alliances of any number, using the civil aviation industry as an application case. The number of passengers in 1997 is important in order to perform a comparison with Kijima's results, which is one index for measuring the validity of our result. From this comparison, we examines whether a fuzzy landscape is valid for asymmetric propensity, and the existence of any number of alliances. Moreover, because a suitable scale is specified from Kijima's simulation results, our simulation is performed using RPM and Annual Passenger Number data. As noted previously, we believe that increasing their own networks is an important factor that carriers consider when making alignment choices. Kijima (2001a, 2001b) takes a similar view. Therefore, we considered that the airline networks' propensity is as described by Kijima. That is, it aims at the 1997 flight table excluding code sharing flights between the carriers. 1997 data and measures of propensity are quoted from Kijima's article.

Result analysis

Table 3 displays the simulation results, which include the equilibrium configuration that is close to the actual alliance configuration in the end of 1999. The top 10 configurations are arranged by order of energy. The alignment of the configuration numbers specifies the configurations, to quote Kijima, "For example, 1112222334 implies that in this equilibrium configuration there are four alliances, each of which consists of carriers 1, 2 and 3; 4, 5, 6, and 7; 8 and 9; and 10, where each number represents the flight carrier listed in Table 2". Additionally, the table also reports the error number. The actual configuration is as described in Table-1; in Table 3, the nearest configuration suggested by the simulation is No.2, in which the only difference is that Cathay Pacific and SAS are interchanged. Since the four main companies in the United States are standard, this result suggests not constructing a mutually beneficial tie-up. If the configuration is considered on the basis of the amount of energy, this result was approximate value as Kijima's.

Table 3. Simulation results* (Based on size of 1999yrs Annual Number of Passengers)

No.	Configuration										ERR no.	Energy
	American	British	Cathay	United	Lufthansa	SAS	Thai	Northwest	KLM	Delta		
1	1	2	1	3	4	3	1	2	2	4	3ERR	-112,597,473,880.42
2	1	2	1	3	3	1	3	2	2	4	2ERR	-110,397,367,547.80
3	1	1	2	3	3	2	1	2	1	4	4ERR	-110,271,212,626.28
4	1	2	1	3	1	2	1	2	1	4	4ERR	-108,995,556,695.66
5	1	2	2	3	2	1	2	2	1	4	4ERR	-108,352,501,728.29
6	1	2	2	3	3	3	2	2	1	4	3ERR	-107,258,064,058.70
7	1	1	2	2	2	2	3	4	2	3	3ERR	-105,461,762,672.37
8	1	2	2	2	1	3	4	3	4	4	5ERR	-104,897,539,611.36
9	1	2	1	2	3	1	3	3	4	4	5ERR	-104,878,359,952.81
10	1	1	2	3	2	3	2	4	1	2	4ERR	-104,862,102,391.40

Note: In Configuration,((0,0,0)(0,0,0,0)(0,0)(0)) is correct.
It is grouped by using the same number. (e.g. 1112222334)

Table 4 furnishes us with information regarding the fuzzification of results. In the table, each column shows the membership values of the corresponding airline company, and each row shows the membership grades of the companies belonging to the alliance.

In alliance 1, American Airlines and Cathay Pacific have been estimated correctly. Thai Airways International (Thai) is incorrectly assigned, and this group lacks British Airways. In alliance 2, Northwest Airlines and KLM Royal Dutch

Airlines are selected correctly; only British Airways is incorrect. In alliance 3, United Airlines and SAS are correctly selected, but Lufthansa and Thai have been omitted. In alliance 4, Delta is correct, but Lufthansa is incorrect.

Table 4. Membership values on No.1 of table 3

Alliance Groups	American	British	Cathay	United	Lufthansa	SAS	Thai	Northwest	KLM	Delta
1	0.008232	0.157707	0.21373	0.883458	0.234324	0.363533	0.261959	0.033067	0.140856	0.002457
2	0.944114	0.348291	0.387164	0.036657	0.271435	0.223237	0.318173	0.006167	0.055609	0.016531
3	0.003513	0.07669	0.337723	0.005481	0.384586	0.234078	0.270087	0.001235	0.206609	0.966747
4	0.04414	0.417312	0.061383	0.074404	0.109655	0.179152	0.149782	0.959531	0.596926	0.014265

From the membership values, we find that US companies are the main partners in their alliances. We also carried out the same analysis using 2001 RPKs and Annual Number of Passengers, finding that the RPKs lead to actual alliance configurations more accurately than Annual Number of Passengers (see Tables 5. and 6.). Table 5 reports the configurations based on Annual Number of Passengers; the configuration in alliance 4 is very near an actual alliance, the exceptions being Thai and KLM which were incorrect. That is, we find that four carriers of United States independently form their own alliance groups. Table 6 shows the result using RPKs, finding that the No.2 is close to the actual alliance configuration exceptions being Cathay, which was incorrect.

Comparing Table 5 with Table 6 shows that the RPK data are better suited to represent size. This superiority leads to two interpretations. First, RPKs produce better results compared to number of passengers. Second, RPKs clearly produce lower energies.

Table 5. Simulation result (Based on size of 2001yrs annual number of passengers)

No	Configuration	ERR no.	Energy
1	1232342314	5ERR	-97,407,424,686.04
2	1233322442	4ERR	-96,388,517,127.17
3	1232231433	6ERR	-96,022,365,291.57
4	1112221324	2ERR	-95,917,499,866.12
5	1234441332	3ERR	-95,024,716,496.37
6	1213424412	5ERR	-94,237,740,235.37
7	1123334412	3ERR	-94,154,902,572.81
8	1234111322	4ERR	-94,017,392,042.74
9	1234424223	3ERR	-93,905,845,979.58
10	1222231443	4ERR	-93,848,644,920.40

Table 6. Simulation result (Based on size of 2001yrs RPKs)

No	Configuration	ERR no.	Energy
1	1223442412	4ERR	-418,606,993,746.02
2	1123333224	1ERR	-405,055,379,986.43
3	1222232344	4ERR	-404,099,702,485.82
4	1122222334	1ERR	-401,462,595,056.39
5	1112231443	2ERR	-400,275,934,133.81
6	1232121443	4ERR	-395,765,614,790.18
7	1234414243	4ERR	-393,136,141,845.16
8	1222223433	4ERR	-391,424,709,183.18
9	1123442432	4ERR	-387,342,197,433.36
10	1232134443	5ERR	-380,789,954,749.94

Conclusion

In this research, we have verified and illustrated the effectiveness of our assumption, using 1997 and 2001 airline data. Given a plausible set of assumptions concerning carrier size and propensity, we have achieved configurations near the actual alliances. That is, our model allows asymmetric propensities and thereby the methodology can be extended to instances in which one carrier wants to join another but the second does not want to join the first. It also can apply to any number of alliances. The success indicates that this approach provides a practical method for suggesting which carriers in a civil aviation industry will ally. As well as being a useful illustration of the approach, the empirical analysis provided useful insights into the size of agents in the civil aviation industry.

Using only maker's size and propensity, we estimated the probable alliance configurations. Further development of the model presented in this paper should enhance the factors that determine alliance formation in other settings, as is the case with an original theory.

This work is supported by a 21st century COE program called "Scientific Knowledge Creation Based on Knowledge Science" at the Japan Advanced Institute of Science and Technology.

References

Air Transport World (2004) (http://www.atwonline.com/)

Axelrod R (1997) The Complexity of Cooperation. Princeton University Press, Princeton, New Jersey, USA

Japan Aircraft Development Corporation (2003) Associated information's of civil aviation on 2002yrs, (in Japanese), 4-3 (http://www.jadc.or.jp/)

Kijima K (2001) Generalized landscape theory: Agent- based approach to alliance formations, Civil Aviation Industry, Journal of Systems Science and Complexity 14 (2) pp. 113-123

Kijima K (2001) Invitation to Drama Theory Ohmsha, (in Japanese), pp. 58-63, pp.140-156

Kaufman L, Rousseeuw P J (1990) Finding Groups in Data - An Introduction to Cluster Analysis New York: Wiley

Sugiura K (1999) Big Airlines of the World (in Japanese), Chuuou Shoin

Suganuma S, V N Huynh, Wang S, Y. Nakamori (2005) A Fuzzy Set Based Approach to Generalized Landscape Theory of Aggregation Journal of New Generation Computing: Computing Paradigms and Computational Intelligence, Vol. 23 No. 1, Ohmsha, pp.57-66

The Defense of Disruptive Technologies

David Meyer[1], Christian Buchta[2], Andreas Mild[3], and Alfred Taudes[3]

[1] Department of Information Systems
Vienna University of Economics and Business Administration
david.meyer@wu-wien.ac.at
[2] Department of Tourism and Leisure Studies
Vienna University of Economics and Business Administration
christian.buchta@wu-wien.ac.at
[3] Department of Production Management
Vienna University of Economics and Business Administration
andreas.mild@wu-wien.ac.at, alfred.taudes@wu-wien.ac.at

Summary. We present an extension to an existing work that investigates conditions for "disruptive technologies" to cause the failure of a former monopolist (incumbent) to the advent of new firm (entrant). This paper shows that 1. the forecast of the positions of the entrant technology allows the incumbent to detect threatening entrant technologies, and 2. cloning the entrant firm allows the incumbent to participate in the new market and assures the survival of the incumbent firm group.

Key words: strategic management, organizational decision making, disruptive technologies, agent-based simulations

1 Introduction

Based on extensive long-term studies of the disk drive and other industries, Christensen (1997) introduced the concept of "disruptive technology". According to Christensen, initially such a technology is employed in a novel market segment and, when judged according to the features most relevant to the incumbents' current customers, is inferior to the technology used by the incumbents in the established market segment. Nevertheless, over time the firms using the disruptive technology are able to successfully invade the established market segment from the lower end of the market and industry leadership changes.

Buchta et al. (2004) introduced a formal model studying the influence of technological efficiency and organizational inertia on the emergence of competition when firms decide myopically. Using an agent-based computer simulation model, they observe the competitive reaction of a former monopolist to the advent of a new competitor. While the entrant uses a new technology, the monopolist is free either to stick to his former technology or to switch to the new one. They find that—irrespective of details regarding the demand side—a change of industry leadership occurs only if the new ("disruptive") technology is not too efficient and organizations are inert. The present article investigates defensive strategies allowing the incumbent to survive. To this end, the model is extended in two ways. First, we use a simple forecasting mechanism to predict the positions of the entrant technology, allowing the incumbent to better detect threatening entrant technologies. Second, the incumbent can "clone" the entrant rather than having to completely switch to the disruptive technology to defend disruption.

2 The Basic Model

The model introduced in Buchta et al. (2004) consists of 3 components: technology, market and a firm's decision. The technology part connects product performance (features) to a firm's investment, i.e. the movement of the product position in the feature space as a function of the investment of the firm. The market describes the consumers' choice, their preferences and market dynamics. In the firm's decision part, the firm's objective function and decision-making process is described. In the following, let i, j, k, l denote indices of consumers, firms, technologies, and features, respectively.

2.1 Technology

A firm's product combines two basic model elements: a (linear) trajectory of possible product positions, and a (non-linear) function that maps cumulated investments to the actual position in the product life cycle. A technological path α_k is a vector that specifies a linear trajectory of possible product positions in a two-dimensional feature space that are reachable through investments in product development over time:

$$\alpha_k = \lambda_k(\sin\delta_k, \cos\delta_k), \tag{1}$$

where $\delta_k \in (0, \pi/2)$ describes the direction (feature mix) and $\lambda_k > 0$ the efficiency of the technology, i.e., the larger λ_k, the higher the feature levels of a product for a given investment sum.

There are two technologies available: at first, only α_1 used by the incumbent is available. α_2 is the (potentially) disruptive technology and the only choice available to the entrant. By the time of entry τ, the incumbent firm is free to choose either of the two technologies. Let technology choice be denoted by index variables $c_{j,t} \in \{0, 1, 2\}$, where $c_{1,t} = 1, t < \tau$ for the incumbent and $c_{2,t} = 2, t \geq \tau$ for the entrant. A zero choice indicates absence of a firm from the market, such as in the initial period of a simulation $t = 0$.

The total investment in the current technology of a firm, $E_{j,t}$, is the sum of investments $e_{j,t}$ over time. It is assumed that the incumbent has to give up his former technology and forfeit his prior investments, if he decides to switch to the disruptive technology:

$$E_{j,t} = \begin{cases} E_{j,t-1} + e_{j,t} & \text{if} \quad c_{j,t} = c_{j,t-1} \\ e_{j,t} & \text{otherwise} \end{cases}, \tag{2}$$

where in the initial period of a simulation $E_{j,0} = 0$.

A firm's product position, a vector with components $x_{j1,t}$ and $x_{j2,t}$, is defined as the firm's effective investment multiplied by the technological path chosen:

$$\mathbf{x}_{j,t} = \ln(1 + E_{j,t})\alpha_{c_{j,t}}. \tag{3}$$

The effectiveness of investments is implemented as a logarithmic transformation of the total investments. That is, the authors assume that the simulations start when both technologies have reached the state of maturity, and that successive investments in a technology show decreasing returns to scale. Thus, only the second, decreasing part of a simplified S-curve is modeled.

A firm's total cost consists of two components: fixed cost and investment cost. Regarding the fixed cost, we assume a factor $\gamma > 0$ on total investments. Through the investment cost, we model organizational inertia by introducing a factor $\kappa \geq 1$ that scales the investments of a firm without inertia:

$$C_{j,t} = \gamma E_{j,t} + \kappa^{e_{j,t}} e_{j,t}. \tag{4}$$

Thus, while a level of $\kappa = 1$ describes a situation where a firm is faced with linear increases in cost for linear improvements of its technological position in a single period, $\kappa > 1$ punishes fast technological progress by exponentially increasing investment cost. This means, it is cheaper for a firm to reach a specific level of investment within more periods, i.e., the organization is inert. However, as a consequence of the simplified S-curve model, a linear increase in a firm's position leads to an exponential increase in total cost, even if the firm is not inert. Therefore, cost acts as a bound on investments.

2.2 Market

Following Adner (2003), the behavior of a consumer is assumed to be guided by a Cobb-Douglas utility function with two arguments: product performance $y_{ij,t}$ and price $p_{j,t} > 0$ with the parameter $\beta > 0$ balancing the importance of product performance versus price:

$$u_{ij,t} = y_{ij,t}^{(1-\beta)}(1/p_{j,t})^{\beta} \tag{5}$$

Product performance depends on the feature levels $x_{jl,t}$, performance thresholds $d_{il,t} > 0$, and the relative preferences for the features $\eta \geq 0$, again in the form of a Cobb-Douglas function:

$$y_{ij,t} = \begin{cases} 1 + (x_{j1,t} - d_{i1,t})^{\eta}(x_{j2,t} - d_{i2,t})^{1-\eta} & \text{if} \quad x_{jl,t} > d_{il,t}, \\ & \qquad l \in \{1,2\} \\ 0 & \text{otherwise} \end{cases} . \tag{6}$$

A consumer considers a product for choice only if its utility exceeds an overall utility threshold $u > 0$, i.e. $u_{ij,t} > u$, and chooses one unit of the product with maximum utility (denoted by $s_{i,t} \in \{1,2\}$), where ties are broken with equal probability.

The Parameters η, β and u describe general market conditions and are thus assumed equal for all consumers. Consumer heterogeneity is introduced by a distribution of $(d_{i1,t}, d_{i2,t})$.

Both time-constant and adaptive consumer thresholds are studied. Using time-invariant preferences, consumers are not influenced in their preferences by technological progress, i.e., $d_{i,t} = d_{i,0}$. In the case of adaptive consumer behavior, which we indicate by the switch variable $\zeta \in \{0,1\}$, the minimal performance thresholds are adapted according to the direction and rate of improvement of the product purchased, that is such that, with $\rho_t(x_I) = \frac{x_{I,t}}{x_{I,t-1}}$ for arbitrary index set I,

$$\rho_{t+1}(d_{il}) = \begin{cases} \rho_t(x_{c_{i,t}l}) & \text{if} \quad \zeta,\, x_{c_{i,t}l,t-1} > 0 \\ 1 & \text{otherwise} \end{cases} \tag{7}$$

holds. This means that if the features of a product increase by, say 10%, the buyers of this product also increase their minimal performance requirements by the same percentage. In case the product was just launched, consumers do not change their requirements as there was no improvement.

2.3 Firm's Decision

Besides technology choice, in each period of time a firm has to decide on a proper level of investment and price. Firms are assumed to be well-informed—i.e., they know the consumers' utility functions and their competitors' past actions—to be rational—that is, they make optimal best response decisions—and myopic—that means that they have a one-period forecast horizon.

The equations from the preceding paragraphs can be reformulated so as to express a consumer's reservation price for a product as a function of a firm's investment and price, given the consumer's current preference and the utility of the competitor's product. For ease of presentation, let $\hat{D}_{c_{j,t},t}$ denote the demand forecast of firm j using technology $c_{j,t}$ in period t, based on the information about the market up to period $t-1$. Then the profit maximization problem of a firm can be summarized as follows:

$$\hat{\pi}_{j,t} = p_{j,t}\hat{D}_{c_{j,t},t} - C_{j,t} \rightarrow \max_{c_{j,t},e_{j,t},p_{j,t}} \tag{8}$$
$$\text{s.t. } c_{1,t} = 1 \text{ if } t < \tau,$$
$$c_{2,t} = 0 \text{ if } t < \tau,$$
$$c_{2,t} = 2 \text{ if } t \geq \tau,$$
$$e_{j,t} \leq F_{j,t}.$$

$F_{j,t}$ denotes a firm's current funds, that is cumulated profits plus initial funds. A firm leaves the market if it does not expect a positive profit or if its funds have become negative.

2.4 Summary of Main Results

Using a multi-agent computer simulation implementing the model described above, the authors have shown that the entrant is never able to outperform the incumbent, if organizational inertia does not exist. Furthermore, they have found that outperformance of the incumbent firm depends on a specific range of the entrant's (relative) technological efficiency. If the new (disruptive) technology's efficiency is too low, the entrant is not able to reach a satisfactory product performance and, thus, is unable to capture a significant share of the market. On the other hand, if the efficiency is very high, it is more attractive to the incumbent to switch to the new technology than to continue with his initial one. The result is a duopolistic market where price competition between similar products prevails. Finally, differentials in organizational inertia seem to expose the incumbent to an increased risk of disruption. Both results regarding technological efficiency and organizational inertia hold independently of the demand structure (cf. Adner (2003)).

3 Defending Disruption

The key to disruption in the basic setting seems to be the short planning horizon in conjunction with inertia, which leads the incumbent to an uneres-timation of the danger of disruption. In addition, even when the incumbent becomes aware of the peculiar situation, its 'defending' strategy—switching to the entrant technology—is not practical: a real incumbent firm is unlikely to sink all its former investments, resulting in giving up its leading position in the high-end of the market, with the additional risk of failure due to in-appropriate organization and cost structures. In this paper, we investigate Christensen's main suggestions for incumbent managers, facing this kind of situation:

1. Try to predict the technological path of the entrant product in order to assess its competitive threat potential.

2. When a potential competitor is detected, do not try to change your firm, but create a new, efficient entrant instead and accept possible cannibalization effects.

We now explain how these suggestions are operationalized in the artificial environment, and present the results of new experiments.

3.1 Model Extensions

Better forecast of the entrant's product position:

First, we allow the incumbent to make a better forecast of the entrant position. In the base model, the incumbent's estimate of the future entrant position was just its current position. We now replace this crude guess by a model-based approach, assuming that each dimension of the entrant technology follows an exponential model, that is, given the entrant's product $\boldsymbol{x}_{E,t} = (f_{1,t}, f_{2,t})$, we assume:

$$f_{i,t} = a_i t^{b_i}, \; i = 1, 2 \tag{9}$$

which is a simple linear regression model (it is linear in the parameters: after using a logarithmic transformation, a_i and b_i can be estimated using, e.g., the well-known Ordinary Least Squares estimator). This model accounts for decreasing steps on the technology path, that is, assumes a simplified S-curve model. We need at least two observations to estimate the two parameters a_i and b_i. Using this model, the incumbent is able to make a prediction of the entrant's future position. To keep things simple, we use the average of the entrant product's last two prices as an estimate for the future price. For its own product, the incumbent assumes an investment rate increase of 10%, which is what approximately happened in the base simulations (in real life situations, the incumbent will simply use the figures from its investment plan. The aim here is a conservative, worst-case estimation of the future situation). Now, as the demand function is supposed to be known, the incumbent can forecast the optimal price for its product, and also the future profits and market shares. This allows the incumbent to assess the entrant product for any future period.

Cloning of the Entrant Firm

In our simulation, the incumbent considers the entrant technology as dangerous in period t if its market share in period $t + 3$ drops to under 50%. But instead of switching to the new technology, we assume the incumbent has the ability to create a new firm similar to the entrant—called 'clone' in the following—that is, with the same technology, but with 80% of the incumbent's budget (We choose 80% because we want to explore an experimental setting in which the clone's investments in the first period are maximized. When the clone has normal, optimizing, behavior, the budget size effectively does not matter, because only a small part of it is used). The role of this 'cloned' firm is to catch up with the entrant's position and thus to participate in the better product performance and the new market segment. On the other hand, the incumbent can no longer choose to switch to the new technology.

As an example for the firm dynamics, consider the four plots in Figure 1 illustrating a simulation with parameters $\kappa = 1.3$, $\lambda = 1.2$, and budget = 10. Each plot illustrates the market: the consumers' performance thresholds are drawn as crosses. The lines mark the technological trajectories for the incumbent (close to the vertical axis) and the entrant/clone technology (45°), respectively. Points on these lines depict product positions corresponding to linearly increasing levels of total investment $(0, 1, 2, \ldots)$ given equal technological efficiency. The letters 'I', 'E', and 'P' represent consumers buying a product from the incumbent, entrant, and (persecuting) clone firm, respectively.

In the top left plot, we see the situation in period $t = 3$: the incumbent has already conquered part of the targeted market segment. In period $t = 4$, the entrant firm appears; the top right plot illustrates its position in period $t = 6$. Clearly, the incumbent is outperformed by the new technology which covers a larger market segment. But now, the incumbent reacts by creating a new firm: in the bottom left plot, we see the advent of the pursuing clone: only one period after its creation, its product is chosen by many of the consumers of the lower left part of the market quadrant. Note that the incumbent loses some of its customers to the new firm, too. Finally, in period $t = 30$, we see that entrant and clone share approximately 50% of their market segment, as expected.

3.2 Virtual Experiment and Results

In order to see whether the new defense mechanism is effective, we run the simulation within the parameter ranges of κ, entrant λ, and incumbent budget associated with disruptive outcomes in the basic model. Alternatively, we test the assumption of a more 'aggressive' clone, investing its whole endowment in the first period to make up the initial technological disadvantage. We stop the simulations after 30 periods. The experimental setup thus follows the full-factorial design defined by the factors in Table 1.

Table 1. Experimental Design Factors

factor	levels
incumbent budget	100 1000 10000
entrant λ	0.6 0.8 1.0 1.2
κ	1.1 1.2 1.3
aggressive?	YES NO

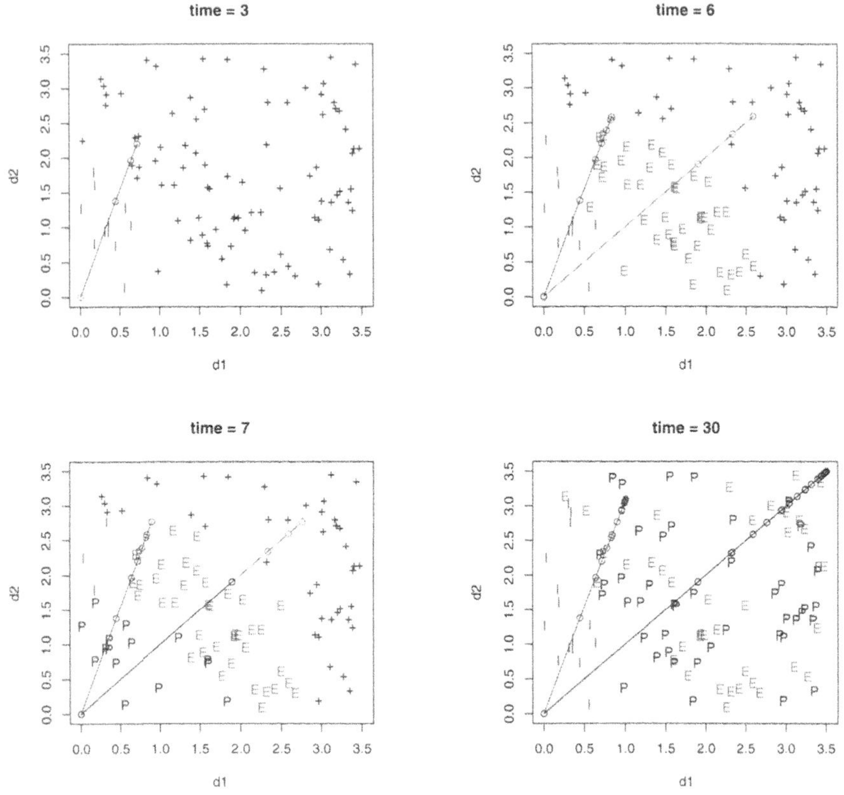

Fig. 1. A typical simulation with incumbent, entrant, and clone firm

In all cases where the entrant has the potential to defeat the incumbent (which is not the case for most settings with $\lambda = 0.6$), the firm dynamics are similar to the one illustrated in Figure 1: the pursuing firm catches up with the entrant and finally gets half of the market. Hence, the incumbent firm group survives in all settings. However, as can be seen from Figure 2 which summarizes the cumulated profits for all firms at the end of the simulations, the overall profits are lower if the pursuing firm is created than if it is not. This is due to the more pronounced price competition, initiated by the clone which tries to reach the entrant firm, and aggravated by the incumbent firm lowering its price in response to the advent of the entrant firm. The price level is also higher in the basic model when the incumbent switches to the entrant technology, resulting in a duopolistic competition which is well known to have a higher equilibrium price than settings with full competition (Cournot game). Figure 3 illustrates these two differing price dynamics. This also explains why the combined profits of incumbent and clone are lower than the cumulated profits of the entrant at the end of the simulation. From Figure 2, we finally see that neither λ nor the incumbent starting budget are of great influence, except the trivial effects that the overall cumulated profits increase with λ (i.e., the product's efficiency), and that the cumulated profits are higher in the quasi-monopolistic cases when the incumbent has a huge starting budget.

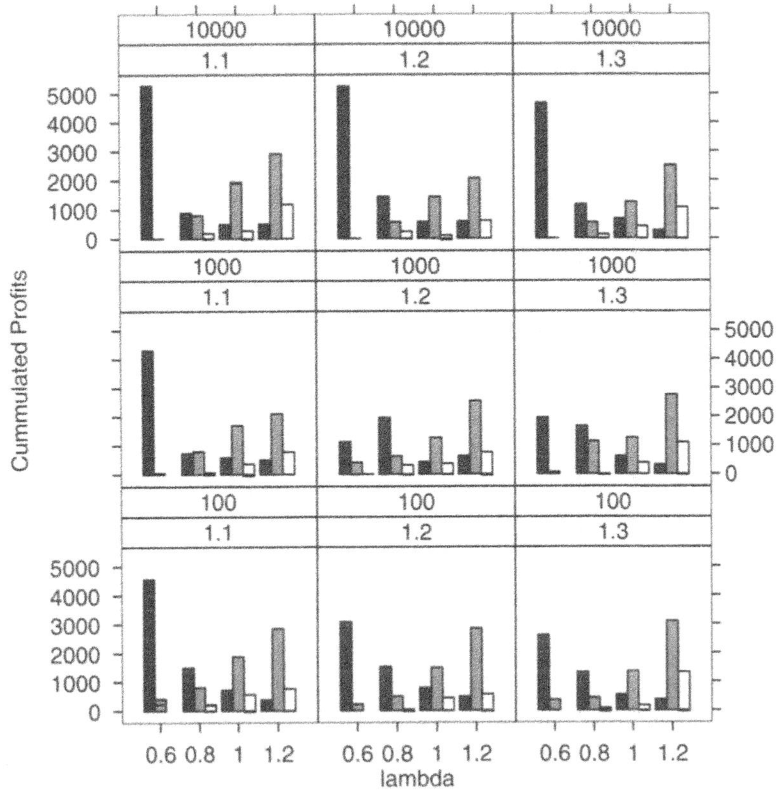

Fig. 2. Cumulated profits for all scenarios. The incumbent firm is colored black, the entrant gray, and the clone white.

As to the final market shares, the picture has more nuances: as can be seen from Figure 4 summarizing the mean profits of the last four periods, the value of λ is most influential, whereas κ and incumbent starting budget are not. For λ=0.6, the entrant—most of the times—is not menacing: no clone is created, and the incumbent keeps the whole market. For $\lambda \geq 0.8$, however, the incumbent's assessment of the future situation leads to the creation of a clone. For $\lambda = 0.8$, the incumbent still stays in the leading position, but for $\lambda \geq 1$, it has vanished from the market at the end of the simulation (!) and the market

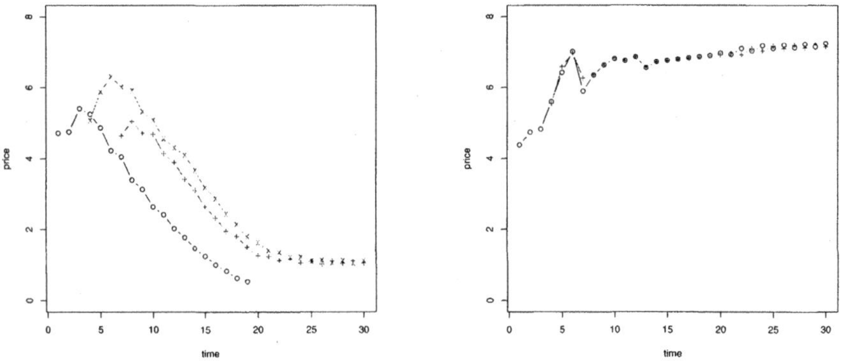

Fig. 3. Price dynamics both for the base (switching) model and the extended model for the same parameter settings ($\lambda = 1.2$, $\kappa = 1.3$, incumbent budget = 100). Legend: incumbent (o), entrant (+), clone (x).

becomes a duopol with entrant and clone firm. Interestingly, the results for settings with aggressive investing behavior do not show an advantage for the clone: despite the faster catch-up, it is not able to defeat the entrant whose budget is already important enough to survive periods without or with low profits. On the contrary, due to the exponentially increasing costs, the clone makes a huge loss in the first period which it will never recover in future periods.

4 Conclusion and Directions for Future Work

This article extends a model for technological efficiency and organizational inertia. By the means of an agent-based computer simulation, virtual experiments have shown that the use of even simple forecasting techniques, applied to the positions of the entrant technology, allow the detection of threatening competitors. The creation of a new firm similar to the entrant assures the survival of the consolidated firm group, but leads to lower profits due to intense competition, and may cause severe cannibalization effects: when the incumbent has a technology which is less efficient than the entrant's, it vanishes from the market. The message of this finding is clear and has already been applied by leading high-tech firms (see, e.g., Brown and Eisenhardt (1998)): an incumbant under threat by disruptive technologies does not have to be overly innovative himself. Rather technology management is important in the sense that the development of entrants has to be closely watched and that a homogeneous, centrally controlled firm structure has to be given up. Managerial advice is thus, that the firm should organize as a patch work of small, independent units pursueing different technologies independently, also competing

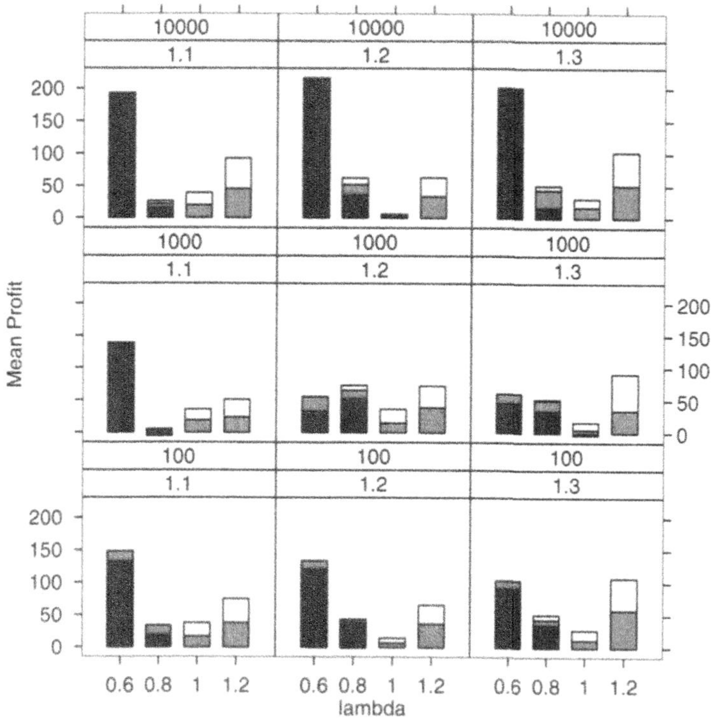

Fig. 4. Mean profit shares at the end of the simulations for all design settings. The incumbent firm is colored black, the entrant gray, and the clone white.

with each other. Strategy in such a framwork resembles to the close monitoring of technological developments in other market segments, the forecasting of technological positions to detect threats, and the making of appropriate portfolio decisions—that is, setup of new units, also including the acquisition of successfull entrants. However, while survivial can be secured in this way, it is the consumers who benefit from more intense competition and lower prices. Also, this finding only holds in the case of no uncertainty regarding the technological development: as Schivardi and Schneider (2001) show using a differential game approach, underperformance of the disruptive technology in the early periods can lead to a biased evaluation of the incumbent and disruption even in a perfectly rational setting. Thus, an interesting further development of the agent-based model would be to introduce randomness in the technological trajectories.

References

Adner, R. (2003). When are technologies disruptive? a demand-based view of the emergence of disruption. *Strategic Management Journal.* forthcoming.

Brown, S. L. and Eisenhardt, K. M. (1998). *Competing on the Edge : Strategy as Structured Chaos.* Harvard Business School Press.

Buchta, C., Meyer, D., Mild, A., Pfister, A., and Taudes, A. (2004). Technological efficiency and organizational inertia: A model of the emergence of disruption. *Computational and Mathematical Organization Theory.* Forthcoming.

Christensen, C. M. (1997). *The Innovator's Dilemma.* Harvard School Press, Boston, MA.

Schivardi, F. and Schneider, M. (2001). Strategic experimentation and disruptive technological change. Technical report, UCLA Department of Economics.

Risk Preference and Survival Dynamics

Shu-Heng Chen[1] and Ya-Chi Huang[2]

[1] AI-ECON Research Center
Department of Economics
National Chengchi University
Taipei, Taiwan
chchen@nccu.edu.tw

[2] AI-ECON Research Center
Department of Economics
National Chengchi University
Taipei, Taiwan
yachi@aiecon.org

Summary. Using an agent-based multi-asset artificial stock market, we simulate the survival dynamics of investors with different risk preferences. It is found that the survivability of investors is closely related to their risk preferences. Among the eight types of investors considered in this paper, only the CRRA investors with RRA coefficients close to one can survive in the long run. Other types of agents are eventually driven out of the market, including the famous CARA agents and agents who base their decision on the capital asset pricing model.

Key words: Market selection hypothesis, Agent-based artificial stock markets, Autonomous agents, Genetic algorithms

1 Introduction

The paper is concerned with a part of the debate on the *market selection hypothesis*. The debate, if we trace its origin, started with the establishment of what become known as the *Kelly criterion* ([8]), which basically says that a rational long-run investor ***should*** maximize the expected growth rate of his wealth share and, therefore, should behave as if he were endowed with a logarithmic utility function. Alternatively speaking, the Kelly criterion suggests that there is an optimal preference (rational preference) which a competitive market will select and that is logarithmic utility. The debate on the Kelly criterion has a long history, so not surprisingly, there is a long list of both pros and cons standing alongside the developments in the literature.[3]

[3] See [11] for a quite extensive review.

The Kelly criterion may further imply that an agent who maximizes his expected utility under the *correct* belief may be driven out by an agent who maximizes his expected utility under an *incorrect* belief, simply because the former does not maximize a logarithmic utility function, whereas the latter does. [1] were the first to show this implication of the Kelly criterion in a standard asset pricing model. As a result, the market selection hypothesis fails because agents with accurate beliefs are not selected. A consequence of this failure is that asset prices may not eventually reflect the beliefs of agents who make accurate predictions, and hence may persistently deviate from the *rational expectations equilibrium* and violate the *efficient market hypothesis.*

However, a series of recent studies indicates that the early analysis of [1] is not complete. [10] shows that, if the saving behavior is endogenously determined, then the market selection hypothesis is rescued, and in the long run, only those optimizing investors with *correct beliefs* survive. The surviving agents do not have to be log-utility maximizers, and they can have diverse risk preferences. [10]'s analysis is further confirmed by [2] in a connection of the market selection hypothesis to the *first theorem of welfare economics.* [2] show that in a dynamic and complete market *Pareto optimality* is the key to understanding selection either for or against traders with correct beliefs: in any optimal allocation the survival or disappearance of a trader is determined entirely by beliefs, and not by risk preferences.

Despite the rigorousness of these theoretical studies, there exists a fundamental limitation, which may make it difficult to grasp their empirical counterparts, namely, they are *non-constructive.*[4] Take [10] as an example. First, the analysis crucially depends on the appearance of agents who *eventually make accurate predictions* or *eventually make accurate next period predictions.* Nevertheless, the process that shows the emergence of these sages is unknown. It is, therefore, not clear how these agents emerge, or whether they will ever emerge.[5] Second, maximizing expected utility is equivalent to assuming that agents are able to solve any infinite-time stochastic dynamic optimization problem implied by their utility function. However, current dynamic optimization techniques, regardless of whether they include stochastic optimal control or stochastic dynamic programming, can only help us solve a very limited subset of the whole problem space. As for the rest of them, it is necessary to rely on numerical approximations, and their effectiveness to a large extent is also unknown.

Given these practical limitations, we are motivated to re-examine the issue from a more realistic perspective or, technically speaking, a computational perspective. By remaining in the general equilibrium analysis framework, we replace the rational agents with bounded-rational agents. More precisely, these agents are constructed in terms of what is known as *autonomous agents* in

[4] This kind of issue is generally shared in many general equilibrium analyses.

[5] Back to the real world, we have not been convinced that these agents have ever appeared in human history.

agent-based computational economics ([12]). Basically, these agents are able to learn to optimize and to forecast in an autonomous manner. So, they are not necessarily utility-maximizers. Instead, they use adaptive computing techniques to approximate the optimal solution. In this sense, they are Herbert Simon's ***satisfying*** agents. Similarly, they base their decisions upon beliefs which may not be and may never be correct, but are reviewed and revised continuously ([9]).

By introducing autonomous agents, we are getting closer to the world of flesh and blood, and enhancing the study of the empirical relevance of risk preference to survival dynamics.

2 A Simple Multi-Asset Model

The simulations presented in this paper are based on an agent-based version of the multi-asset market as per the studies of [1] and [10]. The market is complete in the sense that the number of states is equal to the number of assets, say M. At each date t, the outstanding volume of each asset is exogenously fixed at one unit. There are I investors in the market, with each being indexed by i. At time t asset m will pay dividends w_m if the corresponding state m occurs, and 0 otherwise. The behavior of these states follows a finite-state stochastic process, which does not have to be stationary. The dividends w_m will be distributed among the I investors proportionately according to their owned shares of the respective asset. The dividends can only be either re-invested or consumed. Hoarding is prohibited. If agent i chooses to consume c, her satisfaction is measured by her utility function $u(c)$. This simple multi-asset market clearly defines an optimization problem for each individual as follows:

$$\max_{\{\{\delta^i_{t+r}\}^{\infty}_{r=0},\{\alpha^i_{t+r}\}^{\infty}_{r=0}\}} E\{\sum_{r=0}^{\infty}(\beta^i)^r u^i(c^i_{t+r}) \mid B^i_{t-1}\} \tag{1}$$

subject to

$$c^i_{t+r} + \sum_{m=1}^{M} \alpha^{i,*}_{m,t+r} \cdot \delta^{i,*}_{t+r} \cdot W^i_{t+r-1} \leq W^i_{t+r-1} \quad \forall r \geq 0, \tag{2}$$

$$\sum_{m=1}^{M} \alpha^i_{m,t+r} = 1, \quad \alpha^i_{m,t+r} \geq 0 \quad \forall r \geq 0. \tag{3}$$

In equation (1), u^i is agent i's temporal utility function, and β^i, also called the discount factor, reveals agent i's time preference. The expectation $E(\;)$ is taken with respect to the most recent belief B^i_t, which is a probabilistic model used to represent agent i's subjective belief regarding the stochastic nature of the state. The maximization problem asks for two sequences of decisions, one related to saving, and the other to the portfolios, denoted by

$$\{\{\delta^i_{t+r}\}_{r=0}^{\infty}, \{\alpha^i_{t+r}\}_{r=0}^{\infty}\},$$

where δ^i_t is the saving rate at time t, and

$$\alpha^i_t = (\alpha^i_{1,t}, \alpha^i_{2,t}, ..., \alpha^i_{M,t})$$

is the portfolio comprising the M assets.

Equations (2) and (3) are the budget constraints. W^i_t is the wealth of agent i at time t, which is earned from the dividends paid at time t. Notice that these budget constraints do not allow agents to consume or invest by borrowing.

The equilibrium price $\rho_{m,t}$ is determined by equating the demand for asset m to the supply of asset m, i.e.

$$\sum_{i=1}^{I} \frac{\alpha^{i,*}_{m,t} \cdot \delta^{i,*}_t \cdot W^i_{t-1}}{\rho_{m,t}} = 1, \quad m = 1, 2, ..., M. \tag{4}$$

By rearranging Equation (4), we obtain the market equilibrium price of asset m:

$$\rho_{m,t} = \sum_{i=1}^{I} \alpha^{i,*}_{m,t} \cdot \delta^{i,*}_t \cdot W^i_{t-1}. \tag{5}$$

3 The Agent-Based Multi-Asset Artificial Stock Market

An agent-based version of the Blume-Easley-Sandroni standard multi-asset model is developed in [4]. There they ([4]) propose a sliding-window adaptation scheme to approximate the original infinite-time horizon optimization problem (Equations (1) – (3)) by a finite-time horizon optimization problem. The stochastic optimization problem (1) has two mainstays: first, finding an appropriate belief, and second, under that belief, searching for the best decisions regarding saving and portfolios. To distinguish the two, [3] calls the former "*learning how to forecast*," and the latter *learning how to optimize*. Genetic algorithms are then applied to evolve both beliefs and investment strategies.[6]

To simulate this agent-based multi-asset artificial stock market, a software called *AIE-ASM Version 5.0* is written using *Delphi, Version 6.0*. In each single run, we generate a series of artificial data. At the micro level, it includes the dynamics of agents' beliefs, investment behavior, and the associated wealth

$$\{B^{i,*}_t, \delta^i_t, \alpha^i_t, W^i_t\}_{t=1}^{100}, \quad i = 1, ..., I.$$

At the aggregate level, we observe the asset price dynamics

$$\{\rho_{m,t}\}_{t=1}^{100}, \quad m = 1, ..., M.$$

Figure 1 displays the time series plot of prices in a five-asset market. In this specific simulation, the state follows an *i.i.d.* process.

[6] Details can be found in [4].

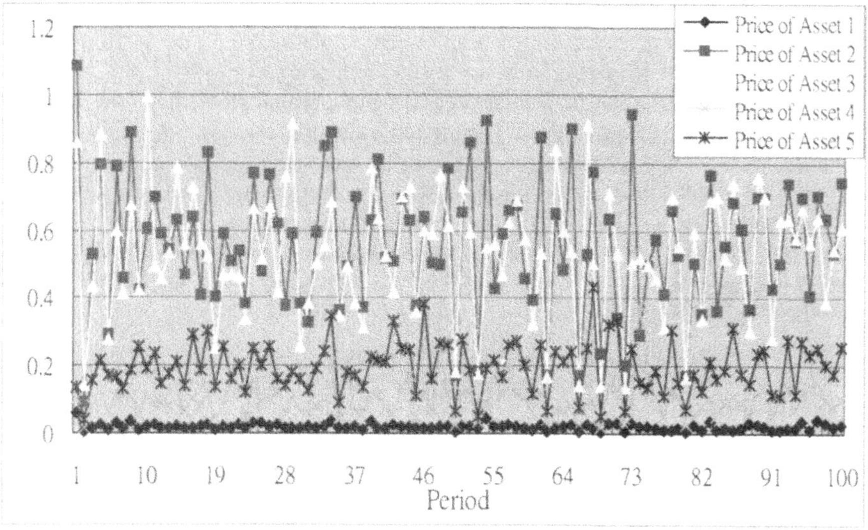

Fig. 1. Time Series Plot of the Prices of Assets; M =5.

By multiplying the dividends by the associated probabilities, we can obtain the expected dividends for each asset, and they are 0.004, 0.419, 0.373, 0.069 and 0.133 in this case. The mean prices taken over the entire sample periods are 0.0191, 0.558, 0.530, 0.099 and 0.196, respectively. It can then be clearly seen that the prices do reflect the underlying dividends.

4 Experimental Design

Since the main focus of this paper is to examine the relevance of risk preference to survivability, we shall assume that the autonomous agents are identical in all aspects except in terms of their preferences over risk. With this assumption, we run two series of experiments. These two experiments differ in their constituent agent types. In Experiment 1, the market is composed of eight types of agents, and they are distributed evenly among 40 market participants, i.e. five agents for each type. These eight types of agents are agents with the seven utility functions specified in Table 1 plus the CAPM (capital asset pricing model) believers.

The type-one agent has the logarithmic utility function. We are very much interested in knowing whether this type of agent has any advantage over others in the long-run wealth share. As to types two to six, they are also frequently used in economic analysis.[7] Among them, type four has the well-known *CARA* (constant absolute risk aversion) utility function. In addition to these six familiar types of utility functions, we also consider any arbitrary utility function. By using Taylor's expansion, an arbitrary analytical utility

[7] See, for example, [6], pp. 27-33.

function can be approximated by a finite-order polynomial function. Here, we consider the approximation only up to the sixth order.

Notice that types 3 to 7 refer to a class of parametric utility functions. Parameters of these types of utility functions, namely, $\alpha_1, ..., \alpha_4, \beta_1, ..., \beta_3$, and $a_0, a_1, ..., a_6$, can in principle be randomly or manually generated as long as they satisfy the regular first- and second-order conditions: $u^{'} > 0$ and $u^{''} < 0$. Since each type of utility function is assigned to five agents, parameter values are generated for each agent for each type separately. So, type 3 agents may have different values of (α_1, β_1), type 4 agents have different values of (α_2, β_2), and so on and so forth.

Table 1. Types of the Utility Function $u(c)$: Experiment 1

	Utility Type	Relative Risk Aversion (RRA)
Type 1	$u(c) = \log(c)$	1
Type 2	$u(c) = \sqrt{c}$	0.5
Type 3	$u(c) = \alpha_1 + \beta_1 c$	0
Type 4	$u(c) = \frac{\alpha_2}{\beta_2} \exp\{\beta_2 c\}$	$-\beta_2 c$
Type 5	$u(c) = \frac{1}{(\gamma_3+1)\beta_3}(\alpha_3 + \beta_3 c)^{\gamma_3+1}$	$-\frac{\beta_3 \gamma_3}{\frac{\alpha_3}{c}+\beta_3}$
Type 6	$u(c) = c - \frac{\alpha_4}{2}c^2$	$\frac{\alpha_4}{\frac{1}{c}-\alpha_4}$
Type 7	$u(c) = a_0 + \sum_{i=1}^{6} a_i c^i$	$-\frac{2a_2c+6a_3c^2+12a_4c^3+20a_5c^4+30a_6c^5}{a_1+2a_2c+3a_3c^2+4a_4c^3+5a_5c^4+6a_6c^5}$

In Experiment 2, all agents are restricted to the family of the CRRA (constant relative risk aversion) utility functions,

$$u(c) = \begin{cases} c^{\rho}/\rho, & if \quad -\infty < \rho < \infty, \\ \ln^{c}, & if \quad \rho = 0. \end{cases} \tag{6}$$

They, however, differ in terms of their RRA coefficients, i.e. $1-\rho$. The smaller the ρ, the larger the risk aversion coefficient. Eleven different ρs, starting from 0, 0.1., 0.2.,..., to 0.9, and 1.0, are distributed evenly to all 55 agents, with five agents for each ρ.

5 Experimental Results

Figure 2 shows the wealth-share dynamics of the eight types of investors in Experiment 1. Notice that each line is based on the average of 100 simulations. The results clearly indicate the strong dominance of the type-one investors, i.e. the agents who have a log utility function. While in some cases type-two investors are still hanging in there for the first 100 periods, their shares eventually decline toward zero. Maybe the most striking result is the extinction of the CARA type of agents (type-4 agents). It is striking because the CARA

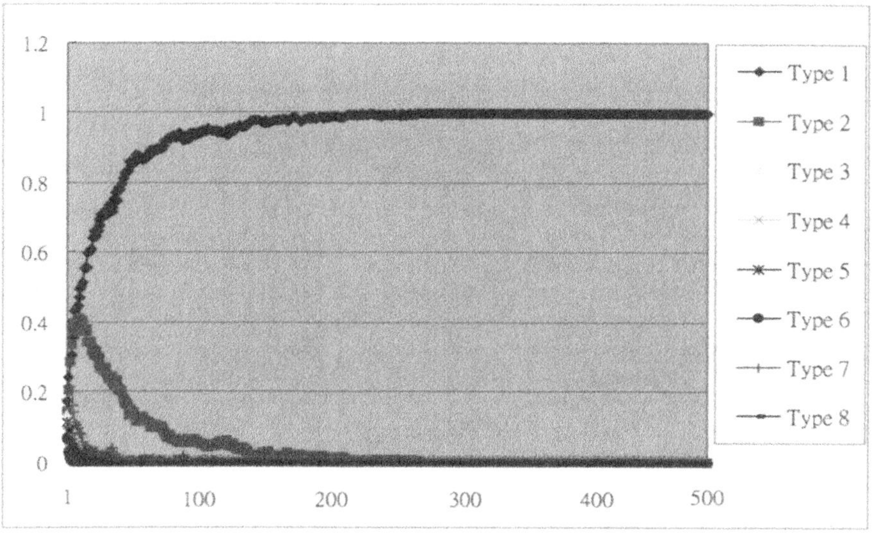

Fig. 2. Time Series Plot of the Wealth Share of Eight Types of Investors: Experiment 1

utility function has been used so extensively in the finance literature that one can hardly cast any doubt on its appropriateness.[8] Equally surprising is the fiding that CAPM believers also fail to survive. This result is consistent with an earlier finding by [11], who shows that a sufficient condition to drive CAPM traders to extinction is that an investor endowed with a logarithmic utility function enters the market.

Since the type-one investors have a constant relative risk aversion coefficient that is one, our experimental results also lend support to Blume and Easley's main argument: *the market selects those investors whose coefficient of relative risk aversion is nearly one.*[9] To further examine this claim, the wealth share dynamics of Experiment 2 is depicted in Figure 3.

As can be seen from Figure 3, the wealth share seems to be positively correlated with the RRA coefficient. Agents with very low values for their the RRA coefficients are driven out of the market at different speeds. The lower the RRA, the faster the evaporation. Towards the end of this 100-period simulation, all agents with RRA values of less than 0.6 are driven out of the market. However, when the RRA coefficient increases to 0.9, the respective

[8] For example, it was used to develop the standard asset pricing model ([5]), and was also used in agent-based artificial stock market simulations ([7]).

[9] See [1], Theorem 5.4, pp. 23-24. The words in italics shown in the main text are not quoted exactly from that theorem, which was originally made by controlling saving rates. Since saving rates are treated endogenously in our paper, our finding suggests that the theorem can still hold true even if the assumption of saving rates is relaxed.

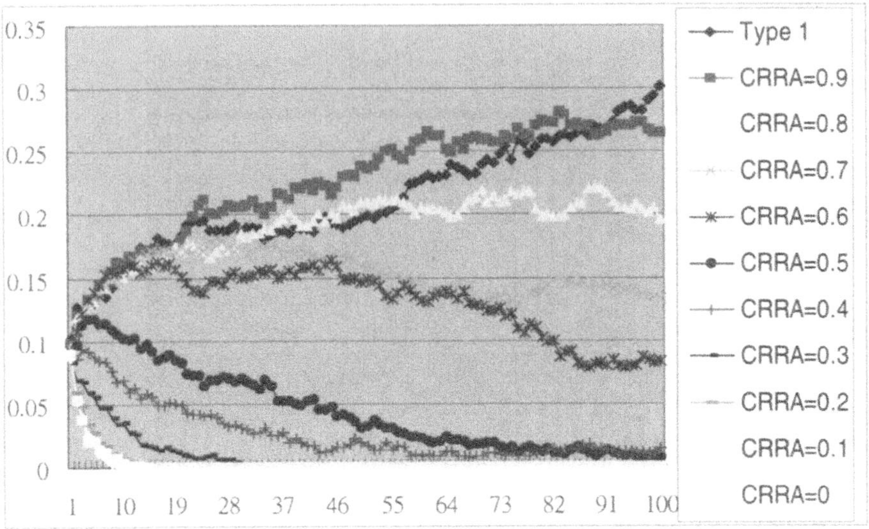

Fig. 3. Time Series Plot of the Wealth Shares of Eleven Types of Investors: Experiment 2

agents perform equally well, and sometimes even better, in terms of their wealth shares, as compared with the log-utility agents.

6 Concluding Remarks

The irrelevance of risk preference to the survivability of agents is dismissed in this paper. Our first experiment indicates that the only agents who survive in the long run (up to a 500-period simulation) are the log-utility agents. The rest are all driven out, including the CARA agents and the CAPM believers. In the second experiment, we further test for the significance of the RRA coefficient by assuming that all agents are CRRA types, and it is found that the agents' wealth share is affected by how close their RRA coefficients are to 1.

Acknowledgements

National Science Council (NSC) funding support NSC:91-2415-H-004-005 is greatly appreciated by the authors.

References

1. Blume E, Easley E (1992) Evolution and Market Behavior. Journal of Economic Theory 58: 9–40.

2. Blume E, Easley E (2003) If You're So Smart, Why Aren't You Rich? Belief Selection in Complete and Incomplete Markets. Working paper.
3. Bullard J, Duffy J (1999) Using Genetic Algorithms to Model the Evolution of Heterogeneous Beliefs. Computational Economics 13 (1): 41–60.
4. Chen S-H, Huang Y-C (2004) Risk Preference, Forecasting Accuracy and Survival Dynamics: Simulations Based on a Multi-Asset Agent-Based Artificial Stock Market. Working Paper Series 2004-1, AI-ECON Research Center, National Chengchi University.
5. Grossman SJ, Stiglitz J (1980) On the Impossibility of Informationally Efficienct Markets. American Economic Review 70: 393–408.
6. Huang C-F, Litzenberger RH (1988) Foundations for Financial Economics. Prentice Hall, North-Holland New York.
7. Izumi K, Nakamura S, Ueda K (2004) Development of an Artificial Market Model Based on a Field Study. Information Sciences, forthcoming.
8. Kelly JL (1956) A New Interpretatatin of Information Rate. Bell System Technical Journal 35: 917–926.
9. Lucas R (1986) Adaptive Behaviour and Economic Theory. In: Hogarth R, Reder M (eds) Rational Choice: The Contrast between Economics and Psychology. University of Chicago Press: 217–242.
10. Sandroni A (2000) Do Markets Favor Agents Able to Make Accurate Predictions? Econometrica 68: 1303–1341.
11. Sciubba E (1999) The Evolution of Portfolio Rules and the Capital Asset Pricing Model. DAE Working Paper No. 9909, University of Cambridge.
12. Tesfatsion L (2001) Introduction to the Special Issue on Agent-Based Computational Economics. Journal of Economic Dynamics and Control 25: 281–293.

Analysis Passive Investment Strategies and Asset Price Fluctuation in Financial Market Through Agent

Hiroshi TAKAHASHI[1], Satoru TAKAHASHI[1,2], Kazuhiko TSUDA[2] and Takao TERANO[2,3]

[1] Investment Engineering Group, Quantitative Investment Department, Mitsui Asset Trust and Banking,3-23-1,Shiba, Minato-ku, Tokyo 105-8574, Japan {Hiroshi_1_Takahashi,Satoru_1_Takahashi}@mitsuitrust-fg.co.jp
[2] University of Tsukuba,3-29-1,Otsuka,Bunkyo-ku,Tokyo,112-0012,Japan {satoru, tsuda, terano}@gssm.otsuka.tsukuba.ac.jp
[3] Tokyo Institute of Technology, 4232, Nagatsuta-cho, Midori-ku, Yokohama-shi, Kanagawa, 226-8502, Japan terano@dis.titech.ac.jp

Summary. In this paper, using agent-based models, we discuss the effects of Passive Investment Strategies in asset management business. Although the Passive Investment Strategy is an effective way in efficient markets, Behavioral Finance points out that markets aren't always efficient. We build a virtual financial market which consists of a thousand investors and allows them to trade two types of assets: a stock and a riskless asset. In this market, multiple types of investors exist and conduct trades based on the investment rules defined for each type. The experiments suggest that Passive Investment is valid in a realistic efficient market, yet it could have bad influences such as market instability and inadequate asset pricing deviation.

Key words: Financial Engineering, Behavioral Finance, Distributed Artificial Intelligence, Agent-Based Modeling, Passive Investment Strategy

1 INTRODUCTION

The role of financial systems is critical because of the rapid globalization of financial markets and the rigidity of economic systems. So far, a growing body of evidence has been published to understand the mechanisms of the asset price fluctuations and various kinds of investment methods, including Financial Engineering Techniques, have been proposed for dealing with the financial markets[5],[13],[14].

In the asset management business, although many kinds of method have been proposed, Active Management is the predominant model for investment strategy today. Active Management is an attempt to find "good deals" in the financial markets, and fund manager allocate assets based upon empirical research delineating probable asset class risks and returns within and across asset classes. Their objective is to make a profit better than they would have done if they simply accepted average market returns. However, they sometimes fail because of unpredictable phenomena in the financial markets.

On the other hand, making no attempt to distinguish attractive from unattractive securities, Passive Management tries to maintainan average return using benchmarks based on market indices. They invest their assets in company stock in proportion to market weight and maintain it throughout the investment period. The efficiency of the market is the central hypothesis in the world of traditional financial theory[11], [10],[24],[14],[7],[20]. Since it is very difficult for investors to get excess returns in an efficient market, Passive Investment Strategy is considered to be an effective investment method.

But recently Behavioral Finance has raised some doubts about the efficient market assumption, by arguing that an irrational trader could have an influence on asset prices[26],[28],[15],[16]. In the inefficient market, the Passive Investment Strategy might not be effective. Moreover other questions may arise such as what would happen at a macro level, when very large numbers of investors employ the Passive Strategy. To address these problems, we employ an agent-based simulation model [1], [2]. We have developed an artificial financial market model with decision-making agents. So far, we have reported on micro-macro links among agents and markets, investors' behaviors with various mental models, and portfolio risk management strategies[29], [30].

In this paper, enhancing the agent-based model we have developed, we discuss the effects of Passive Investment Strategies in a virtual financial market. Our simulation model is characterized by 1) fundamentalist and non-fundamentalist agents with decision-making strategies about trading the assets of either individual stock or riskless assets; 2) an artificial market, in which the profits will occur based on Brownian motion, and each agent trades its asset based on its profits and past pricing information [29]. The contributions of the paper include showing the effectiveness of agent-based modeling toward Behavioral Finance and to analyze the effects of Passive Investment Strategies from micro-macro links through the modeling methodology.

The paper is organized as follows. In the next section, we describe the studies related to this paper. Section 3 describes the model and Section 4 illustrates the experimental results. Section 5 concludes.

2 RELATED WORK

Recent developments in Behavioral Finance have causes great concern. A growing literature on Behavioral Finance points out that deviation from rationality in decision-making can be useful in uncovering the mechanisms of anomalies which cannot be explained by traditional financial theories [28], [27], [8]. While the traditional asset pricing theories are normative, the Behavioral

Financial theories appear to be more descriptive[19]. It is very important for both academic and business purposes to elucidate the mechanisms of price fluctuations in real markets.

In the areas of Complex Systems and Computer Science, much recent research reports that complex phenomena emerge from interactions between Micro-rules and Macro-behavior [1]. Lux [21] has analyzed the influences of heterogeneous investors with differential equation formulas, but the analyses lack constraints assumptions about investors. On the other hand, the agent-based model deals with various kinds of analysis difficult to analyze with differential equations. This is one of the advantages of applying our agent-based model to financial market analyses. In the context of financial markets, the micro-rules correspond to investors' behavior and the macro-behavior corresponds to the fluctuation of asset prices. The influences of investors' behavior on asset pricing are not necessarily derived with analytical methods so that complex macro-behavior may emerge in real markets. We need to introduce a different method to analyze the systems that show complex macro-behavior.

In the field of Computer Science, the agent-based model is proposed as an effective method to analyze the relation between Micro-rules and Macro-behavior [3], [23]. The Agent-based model is an attempt to explain the macro-behavior of systems by local rules. As a result of applying this model to Social Science, it is found that a variety of different macro-behaviors emerges bottom-up from local micro-rules [9], [19], [31], [32]. An artificial market is one of the good applications of agent-based model to financial markets [1], [33]. However, most research in artificial markets make the micro-rules as simple as possible in accordance with Axerlod's KISS (Keep It Simple, Stupid) principle [2], or sometimes the rules are too mechanical. These micro-rules are different from investors' behavior in real markets.

In this paper, we apply agent-based model to analyze the micro- and macro- structure in financial markets. The objective of the research is to investigate (1) the effects of Passive Investment Strategy at the micro- and macro-level, (2) the roles of the evaluation method, and (3) financial behaviors, when there are so many investors with different strategies.

3 Model

We build a virtual financial market on a personal computer using Pentium IV 2.8GHz CPU, 1GB of RAM. The market consists of a thousand investors and allows them to trade two types of assets: a stock and a riskless asset. In this market, multiple types of investors exist and conduct trades based on the investment rules defined for each type. The market operates in three steps: accrual of corporate profit, formation of the investors' predictions, and determination of the traded price. In the following sections, we explain in detail how the financial market operates. See the appendices at the end of this paper for the details of the rules of the Natural Selection Principle and the major parameters of the models used in this paper.

3.1 Assets Traded in the Market

This virtual market contains a riskless asset and a risky asset. Following Takahashi/Terano [29], the riskless asset pays a real dividend (r_f) in every period. On the other hand, the risky asset pays the entire profit(y_t) to the shareholders as a dividend for each period [1],[28]. The corporate profit (y_t) accrues according to the process of $y_t = y_{t-1} + \varepsilon_t$, where $\varepsilon_t \sim N(0, \sigma_y^2)$ [22], and the stock is traded after the profit of the current period is announced. The investors in the market can borrow or lend the riskless asset without limite in principle, and the initial asset amount for every investor is 1,000 in stock and 1,000 in riskless asset.

3.2 Modeling of Passive Investors

Passive investors of the simulation model invest their assets with the same ratio of market benchmarks. This means that (1) each Passive Investor keeps one volume stock during the investment periods, (2) the investment ratio to the stocks is automatically determined, and (3) the trade strategy follows buy-and-hold of initial interests.

3.3 Modeling of Active Investors

Active Investors make decisions based on Expected Utility Maximization[4]. Contrary to Passive Investors, Active Investors forecast the stock price. In the following section, we will explain the forecasting models of Active Investors.

Forecasting Models of Active Investors

1. **Fundamentalists** In this paper, we refer to the investors who make investment decisions based on fundamental values as "fundamentalists". We adopt the dividend discount model, which is the most basic derivation model for the fundamental value of stocks. The fundamentalists are assumed to know that the profit accrues according to Brownian Motion. They forecast the stock price (P_{t+1}^f) and the profit (y_{t+1}^f) from the profit of current period (y_t) and the discount rate of the stock (δ) as $P_{t+1}^f = y_t/\delta$ and $y_{t+1}^f = y_t$ respectively.
2. **Trend Predictors**
   We formulate a model of the investor who finds out the trends from randomly fluctuating stock prices. This type of investor predicts the stock

[4] For the details of the model, refer to Black/Litterman [6]

price of the next period by extrapolating the latest stock trends(10 days). The trend predictors forecast the stock price and the profit from the trend at period $t-1$ (a_{t-1}) as $P^f_{t+1} = P_{t-1}(1+a_{t-1})^2$ and $y^f_{t+1} = y_t(1+a_{t-1})$, where $a_{t-1} = (1/10)\sum_{i=1}^{10}(P_{t-i}/P_{t-i-1})$. Predicted price($P^f_{t+1}$) and profit($y^f_{t+1}$) are different when trend measurement period is different.

3. **Loss Over Estimation Investors**
   We formulate a model who doubles the loss estimates from the reference stock price. In this paper, reference stock price is the stock price 10 periods ago. When the most recent price (P_{t-1}) is lower than the price at the reference point (P_t^{ref}), the Loss Over Estimation investors forecast the stock price (P^f_{t+1}) by converting the original predicted price (P^{beff}_{t+1}) using the formula $P^f_{t+1} = 2.25P^{beff}_{t+1} - 1.25P_t^{ref}$[5]. As for the original predicted price (P^{beff}_{t+1}), we use the dividend discount model.
4. **Overconfident Investors**
   Bazerman reported that human being tends to be overconfident in his/her own ability [4]. In the area of Behavioral Finance, Kyle analyzed the influence of the overconfident investment behavior on the markets with the analytical method [18]. Also in real markets, we often find that each investor talks about different future prospects with confidence. It seems like all investors tend to have overconfidence in varying degrees.
   We formulate the model of investors who are overconfident in their own predictions by assuming that they underestimate the risk of the stock. The risk of the stock estimated by an overconfident investor (σ^s) is calculated from the historical volatility (σ^h) and the adjustment factor to determine the degree of overconfidence ($k = 0.6$) as $(\sigma^s)^2 = k(\sigma^h)^2$.

Calculation Method for Expected Rate of Return on Stock

The investors in this virtual market predict the stock price and the corporate profit at the term t+1 (P^f_{t+1} and y^f_{t+1}) based on the corporate profit at the term t (y_t) and the stock prices at and before the term t-1 ($P_{t-1}, P_{t-2}, P_{t-3}\cdots$). In this paper, we represent the predicted values of the stock price and the corporate profit by the investor i($i = 1,2,3\cdots$) as ($P^{int,i}_{t+1}$) and ($y^{f,i}_{t+1}$) respectively. The expected rate of return on the stock for the investor i ($r^{f,i}_{t+1}$) is calculated as $r^{int,i}_{t+1} = (r_t^{im}c^{-1}(\sigma^s_{t-1})^{-2} + r^{f,i}_{t+1}(\sigma^s_{t-1})^{-2})(c^{-1}(\sigma^s_{t-1})^{-2} + (\sigma^s_{t-1})^{-2})^{-1}$, where $r^{f,i}_{t+1} = ((P^{f,i}_{t+1} + y^{f,i}_{t+1})/P_t - 1)(1+\varepsilon^i_t)$ and $r_t^{im} = 2\lambda(\sigma^s_{t-1})^2W_{t-1} + r_f$ [25], [6].

3.4 Determination of Traded price

The traded price of the stock is determined at the price the demand meets the supply [1]. Both of the investment ratio (w^i_t) and the number of the stock held

[5] When the most recent price is higher than the price at the reference point, the original predicted price remains as the ultimate predicted price.

by investors ($\sum_{i=1}^{M} F_t^i w_i/P_t$) are the decreasing function of the stock price, and the total number of the stock issued in the market (N) is constant. We derive the traded price as ($\sum_{i=1}^{M} F_t^i w_i/P_t = N$) by calculating the price (P_t) where the total amount of the stock retained by investors ($F_t^i\, w_i/P_t$), which is the demand, meets the total market value of the stock, which is the supply.

4 EXPERIMENTS

The series of our experiments are divided into the two part: First, we have fundamentalist agents and Passive-Investment agents in the market to investigate the influences of the two strategies; Next, we introduce the other investors, such as trend chasers, loss over estimation investors, and overconfident investors to analyze the effects.

4.1 Trading with Fundamentalist and Passive Investors

Figures 1 and 2 illustrate the case where there exist the same 500 numbers of the two kinds of investors (Case 0). Figure 1 shows the histories of stock prices. The solid line in Figure 1 shows the traded price and the line with the mark shows the fundamental value. Figure 2 shows the histories of cumulative excess returns of each investors. This graph denotes that the fluctuation of the traded price agrees with the one of the fundamental value. The line with the mark in Figure 2 shows the performance of Passive Investment Strategy and the dotted line shows the ones of fundamentalists. The performances of fundamentalists are slightly different among them, because each of fundamentalists respectively has a predicting error. As the traditional asset pricing theory suggests, the trading prices are coincide with the fundamental values and fundamentalist and Passive Investors can get the same profit in average.

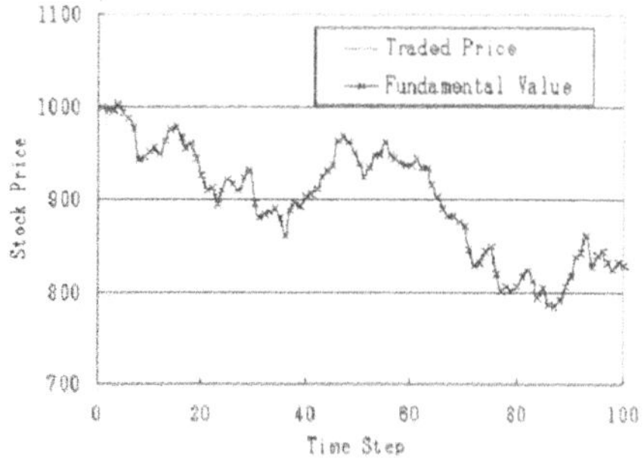

Fig. 1: Changes of Traded Price (Case 0)

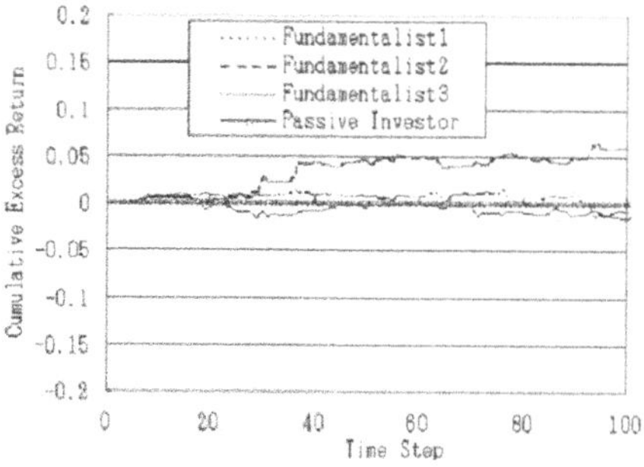

Fig. 2: Cumulative Excess Returns (Case 0)

Next, using natural selection principles of Genetic Algorithms, let the investor agents change their strategies when (1) the excess returns are under the target (e.g., over 10%), (2) the excess returns are under 0%, and (3) the excess returns are too bad (e.g., under 10%)[6].

The results of Case 1 are shown in Figures 3, 4, 5 and 6;and Case 2 are shown in Figures 7, 8, 9 and 10. Figures 5, 6, 9 and 10 are obtained by 100 experiments, each of which consists of 3000 simulation steps.

In Case 1, traded price changes in accordance with fundamental value and both of investors coexist in the market. On the other hand, in Case 2, traded price doesn't reflect the fundamental value and only Passive Investors can survive in the markets after around 1600 time step. This result is quite different from the ones in Case 1. In Case 3, similar results such as in Case 2 are obtained. These differences among each experiment are brought about by the difference of evaluation methods. In this sense, evaluation methods have a great influence on the financial markets.

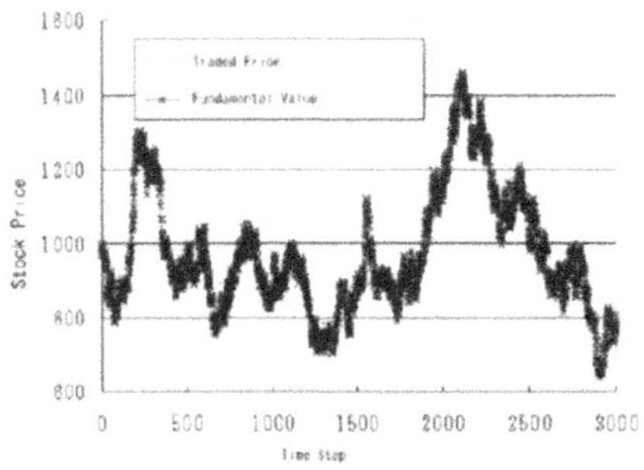

Fig. 3: Changes of Traded Price (Case 1)

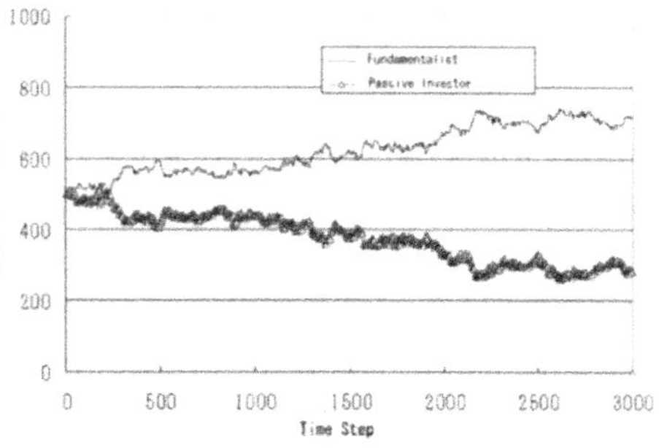

Fig. 4: Changes of Number of Investors (Case 1)

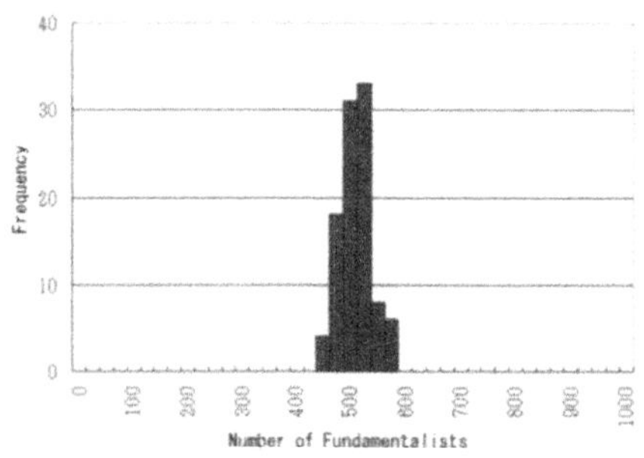

Fig. 5: Distribution of Fundamentalists (Case 1, 100 Steps)

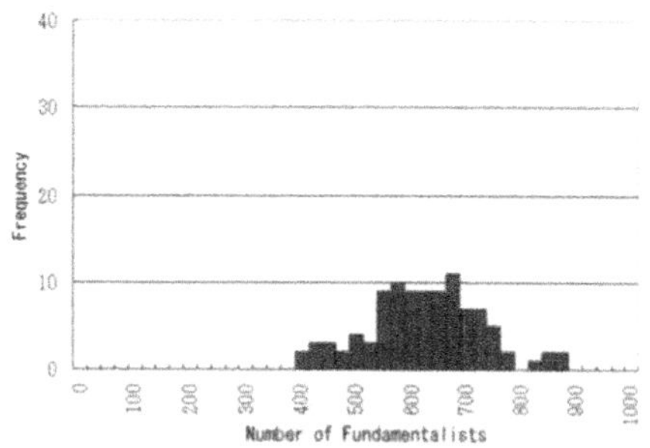

Fig. 6: Distribution of Fundamentalists (Case 1, 1500 Steps)

6 For the detail of the natural selection rule, refer to the appendices.

Figures 11 shows the result when a small number of trend chasers (10 investors) enter into the market at term 1000 in Figure 7. In this case, we can observe the large deviation of the traded price from the fundamental value. Figure 12 illustrates the result when investors need to pay costs for trading and investigation. In this case, Passive Investors can get relatively good performance because they don't have to pay both of costs.

Throughout the experiments shown above, we can confirm the effectiveness of Passive Investment Strategy. Especially the result in Figure 12 indicates the superiority of Passive Strategy in more actual situation. However as is shown in Case 2 and Figure 11, we are able to confirm the unfavorable influence of Passive Investment on the market.

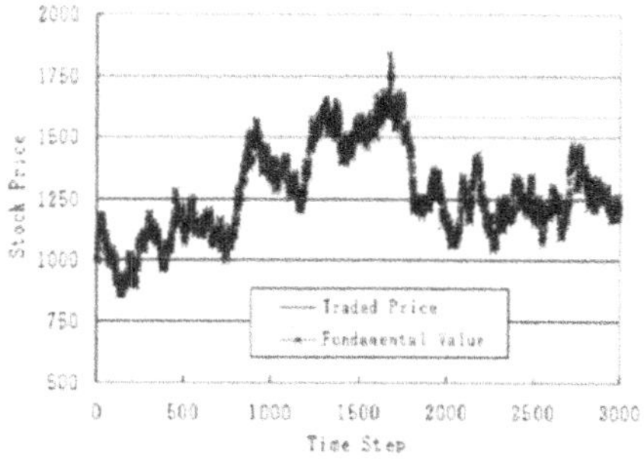

Fig. 7: Changes of Traded Price (Case 2)

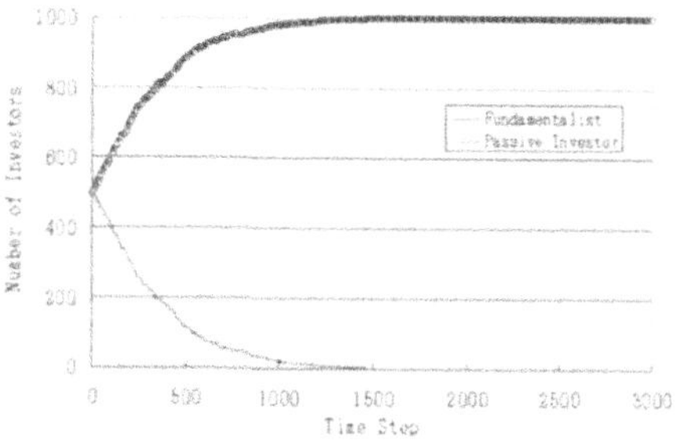

Fig. 8: Changes of Number of Investors (Case 2)

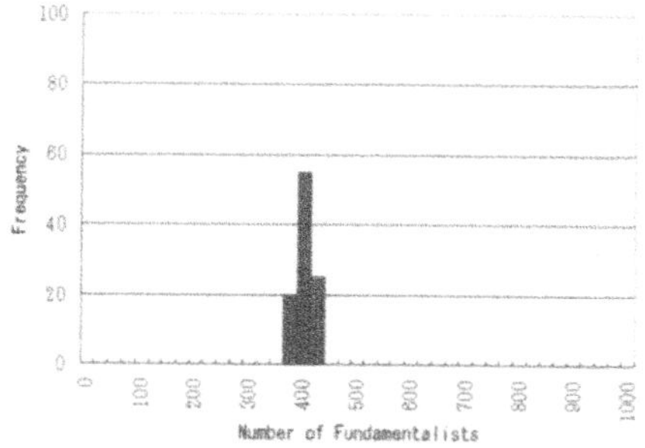

Fig. 9: Distribution of Fundamentalists (Case 2, 100 Steps)

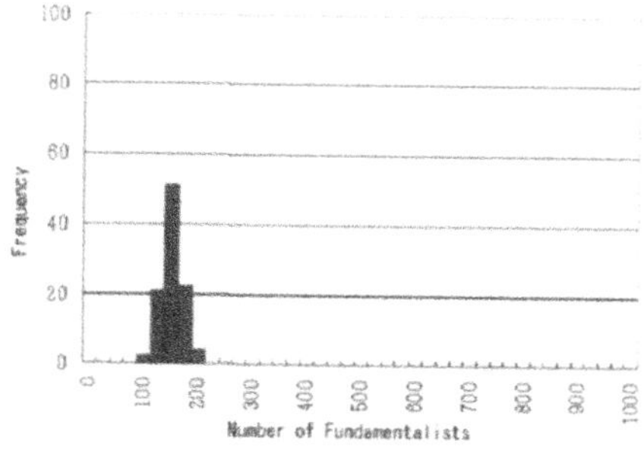

Fig. 10: Distribution of Fundamentalists (Case 2, 400 Steps)

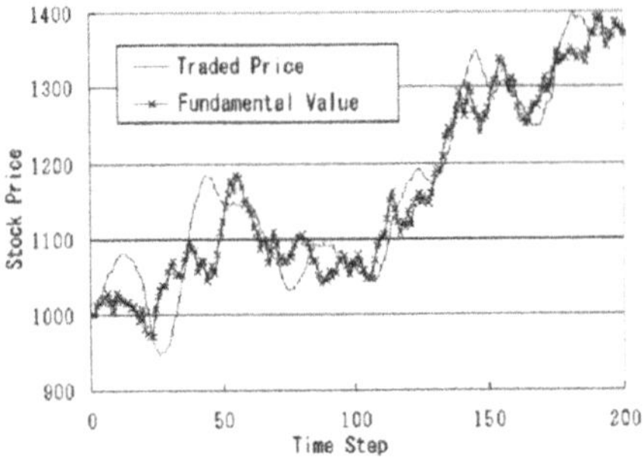

Fig. 11: Changes of Traded Price

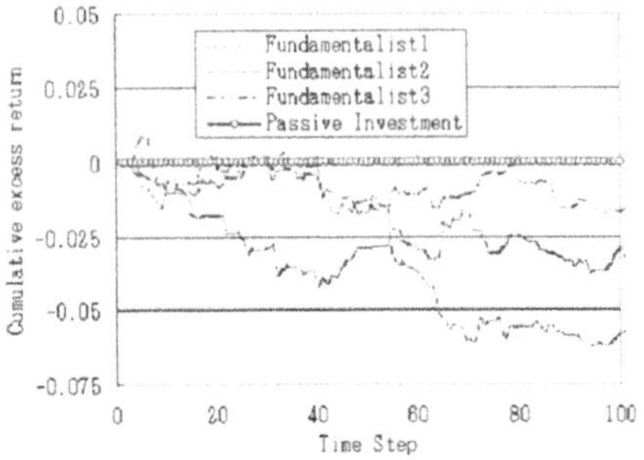

Fig. 12: Cumulative Excess Returns

4.2 Trading with Fundamentalists, Passive Investors, and Over Confident Investors, and Investors with Prospect Theory

This section describes the experimental results with the five different investor agents: Fundamentalists, Passive Investors, Trend Chaser, Investors with Prospect Theory, and Over Confident Investors. First, the results of Case 4 with 400 Fundamentalists, 400 trend chasers, and 200 Passive Investors are shown in Figures 13 and 14. Second, the results of Case 5 with 400 Fundamentalists, 400 Over Confident Investors, and 200 Passive Investors are shown in Figures 15 and 16. Third, the results of Case 6 with 400 Fundamentalists, 400 Investors with Prospect Theory, and 200 Passive Investors are shown in Figures 17 and 18.

In all cases, we have observed that Passive Investors keep their moderate positions, even when stock prices largely deviate from the fundamental value. In other words, Passive Investment Strategy is the most effective way if investors want not to get the worst result in any cases, even if they cannot get the best result. In asset management business, some investors adopt the Passive Investment to avoid getting the worst performance.

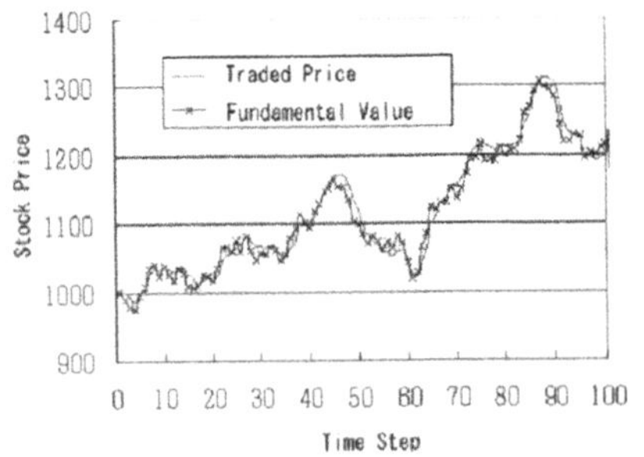

Fig. 13: Changes of Traded Price (Case 4)

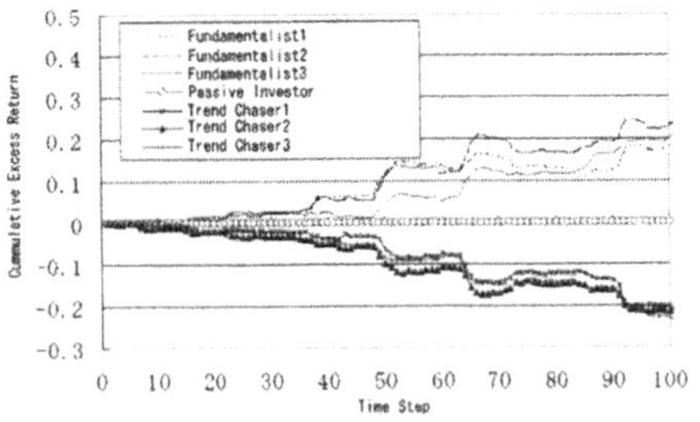

Fig. 14: Cumulative Excess Returns (Case 4)

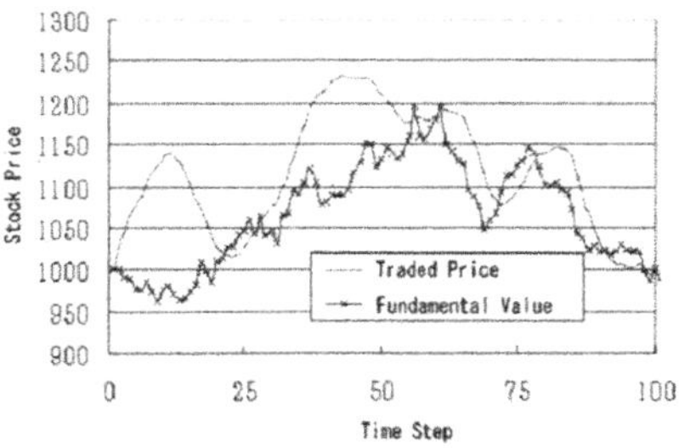

Fig. 15: Changes of Traded Price (Case 5)

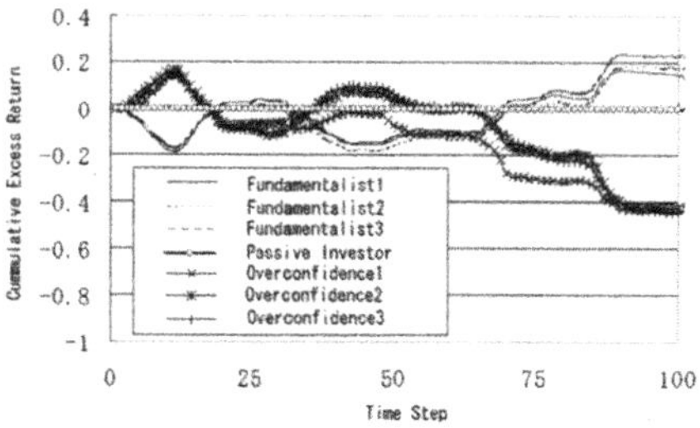

Fig. 16: Cumulative Excess Returns (Case 5)

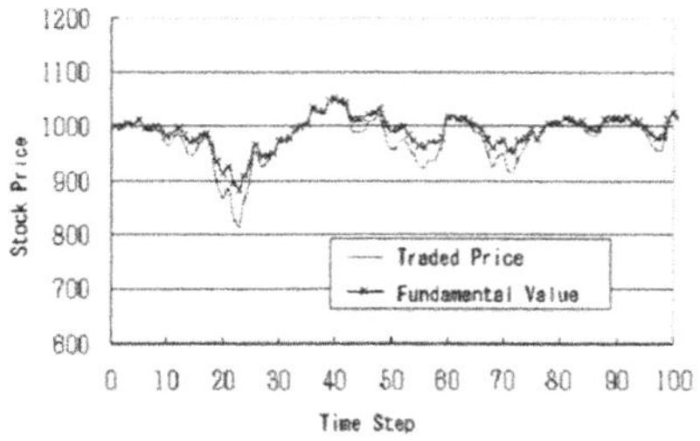

Fig. 17: Changes of Traded Price (Case 6)

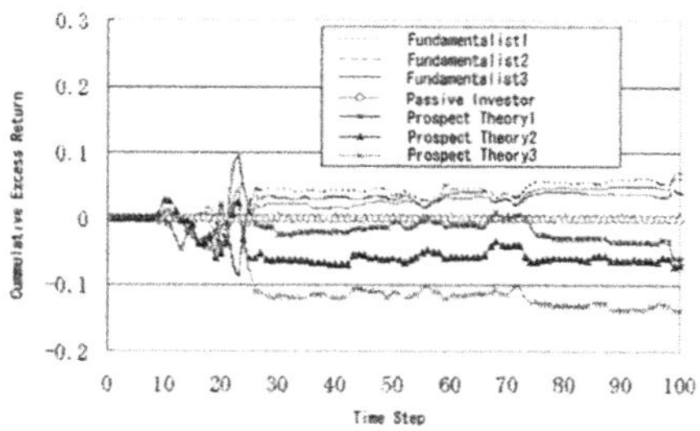

Fig. 18: Cumulative Excess Returns (Case 6)

Figures 19 and 20 shows the results where the agents can change their strategy when the excess returns are less than 0. In this experiments, we slightly change the natural selection rule as is described in previous section. In the following experiments, investors change their strategy depending on their recent performance as is the same way in previous section and after that, investors change their strategy randomly in a small possibility (0.01%) which is correspond to mutation in genetic algorithm. The result shown in Figure 20 suggests that there remain both fundamentalist and Passive Investors in the market and that they keep the market stable. The results shown in Figures 19 and 20 are quite different from the ones in Case 2. These results suggest that even slight differences in the market conditions and investors behavior could cause large changes in the markets. In this sense, these results are thought-provoking.

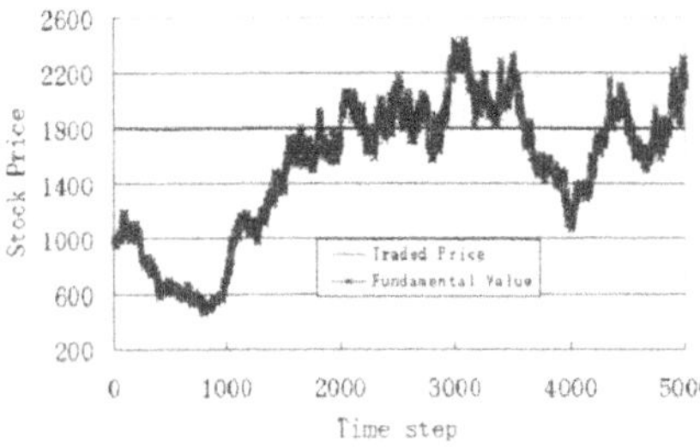

Fig. 19: Changes of Traded Price (Case 7)

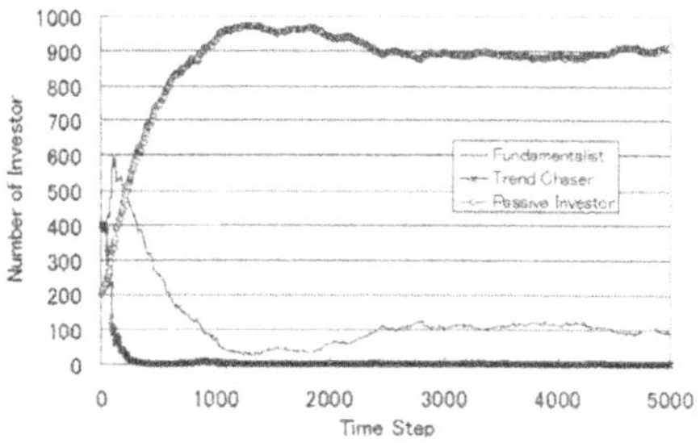

Fig. 20: Changes of Number of Investors (Case 7)

5 CONCLUDING REMARKS

In this paper, we have analyzed the influence of Passive Investment Strategies on financial markets through agent-based model. Our financial simulator is enough powerful to analyze such various kind of phenomena emerged in financial market. The experimental results suggest that (1) Passive Investment is usually effective, however, they have bad influence on the market such as the market prices do not reflect the fundamental values and become unstable, when the number of Passive Investors is too large, (2) the variety of investors is dramatically changed, according to the evaluation criteria of investment, and (3) there can remain both Active and Passive Investors, when there are so many investors with different strategies in the market. Future work includes to extend our simulator to be a tool kit for behavioral financial analyses.

Appendices

A List of Parameters

The parameters used in this paper are as follows:

M : the number of investors(1000)

N : the number of issued stocks(1000)

F_t^i : the total amount of assets of the investor i at the term t($F_0^i = 2000$: *common*)

W_t : the stock ratio in the market at the term t($W_0 = 0.5$)

w_t^i : the investment ratio of the stock of the investor i at the term t($w_0^i = 0.5$: *constant*)

y_t : the corporate profit at the term t
σ_y : the standard deviation of the profit fluctuation($0.2/\sqrt{200}$: *constant*)
δ : the discount rate of the stock($0.1/200$: *constant*)
r_t^{im} : implied stock return at the term t
λ : the degree of risk aversion of the investor(1.25 : *common*, *constant*)
c : the adjustment coefficient for variance(0.01)
σ_t^h : the historical volatility of the stock (for the recent 100 terms)
σ_t^s : the expected value of the standard deviation of the stock price fluctuation
P_t : the traded price at the term t
$P_t^{f(,i)}$: the predicted value of the traded price at the term t (of the investor i)
$y_t^{f(,i)}$: the predicted value of the corporate profit at the term t (of the investor i)
P_t^{beff} : the predicted value before conversion based on Prospect Theory
P^{ref} : the stock price used as the reference point
$r^{f(,i)}$: the short term expected rate of return on the stock (of the investor i)
σ_n : the standard deviation of the dispersion of the short term expected rate of return on the stock(0.01:common, except the one for rational investors, which is 0.)
p_i : the probability that the investor i change own strategy
r_i^{cum} : the cumulative excess return of the investor i during the recent five terms
k : the adjustment coefficient for confidence(0.6)

B Rules of Natural Selection Principle

This section explains the rules of natural selection principle. The principle used in this paper is composed of two steps: (1) selection of investors who change their investment strategies and (2) selection of new strategy. Each step is described in the following sections:

B.1 Selection of investors who change their investment strategies

After 25 terms pass since the market has started, each investor makes decision at regular interval (every five terms) whether he/she changes the strategy. The decision is made depending on the cumulative excess return during the recent five terms and the investor who obtain smaller return changes the strategy at higher probability. To be more precise, the investor who obtain negative cumulative excess return changes the strategy at the following probability:

$$p_i = max(0.3 - a \cdot e^{r_i^{cum}}, 0)$$

p_i : probability at which investor i changes own strategy
r_i^{cum} : cumulative return of investor i during recent 5 terms,
a : the coefficient for the evaluation criteria(0.2,0.3,0.4).

B.2 Selection of new strategy

We apply the method of genetic algorithm (Goldberg [12]) to the selection rule of new strategy. The investors who change the strategy tend to select the strategy that has brought positive cumulative excess return. The probability to select s_i as new strategy is given as:

$$p_i = \frac{e^{(r_i^{cum})}}{\sum_{j=1}^{M} e^{(r_j^{cum})}},$$

where r_i^{cum} is the cumulative excess return of each investor.

References

1. Arthur, W. B., Holland, J.H., Lebaron, B., .Palmer, R.G. and Taylor, P. [1997], "Asset Pricing under Endogenous Expectations in an Artificial Stock Market," *The Economy as an Evolving Complex System II*, Addison-Wesley, pp.15-44.
2. Axelrod, R. [1997], *The Complexity of Cooperation -Agent-Based Model of Competition and Collaboration*,Princeton Uniersity Press.
3. Axtell, R. [2000], "Why Agents? On the Varied Motivation For Agent Computing In the Social Sciences," *the Brookings Institution Center on Social and Economic Dynamics Working Paper*, November, No.17.
4. Bazerman, M. [1998], *Judgment in Managerial Decision Making*,John Wiley & Sons.
5. Bernstein, W. [2001], *The Intelligent Asset Allocator: How to Build your Portfolio to Maximize Returns and Minimize Risk*, McGraw-Hill.
6. Black, F. and Litterman, R. [1992],"Global Portfolio Optimization," *Financial Analysts Journal*, September-October, pp.28-43.
7. Bondarenko, O. [2003], "Statistical Arbitrage and Securities Prices," *Review of Financial Studies*, 16, pp.875-919.
8. Brunnermeier, M.K. [2001], *Asset Pricing under Asymmetric Information*, Oxford University Press.
9. Epstein, J.M. and Axtell, R. [1996], *Growing Artificial Societies Social Science From the The Bottom Up*, MIT Press.
10. Fama, E. [1970], "Efficient Capital Markets: A Review of Theory and Empirical Work," *Journal of Finance*, 25, pp.383-417.

11. Friedman, M. [1953], *Essays in Positive Economics*, University of Chicago Press.
12. Goldberg, D. [1989], *Genetic Algorithms in Search, Optimization, and Machine Learning*, Addison-Wesley.
13. Hull, J. [1989], *Options, Futures, and Other Derivative Securities*, Prentice Hall.
14. Ingersoll, J. E. [1987], *Theory of Financial Decision Making*, Rowman & Littlefield.
15. Kahneman, D. and Tversky, A. [1979], "Prospect Theory of Decisions under Risk," *Econometrica*, 47, pp.263-291.
16. Kahneman, D. and Tversky, A. [1992], "Advances in. prospect Theory : Cumulative representation of Uncertainty," *Journal of Risk and Uncertainty*, 5.
17. Kahneman, D. and Tversky, A. [2000], *Choices, Values, and Frames*, Cambridge University Press.
18. Kyle, A.S. and Wang, A. [1997], "Speculation Duoply with Agreement to Disagree:Can Overconfidence Survive the Market Test?," *Journal of Finance*, 52, pp.2073-2090.
19. Levy, M., Levy, H. and Solomon, S. [2000], *Microscopic Simulation of Financial Markets*, Academic Press.
20. Lo, A. [2004], "The Adaptive Markets Hypothesis," *The Journal of Portfolio Management*, The 30th Anniversary Issue, pp.15-29.
21. Lux, T. [1998], "The Socio-Economic Dynamics of Speculative Markets: Interacting Agents, Chaos, and the Fat Tails of Return Distributions," *Journal of Economic Behavior & Organization*, 33, pp.143-165.
22. O'Brien, P. [1988], "Analysts' Forecasts as Earnings Expectations," *Journal of Accounting and Economics*, January, pp.53-83.
23. Russell, S. and Norvig, P. [1995], *Artificial Intelligence*, Prentice-Hall.
24. Sharpe, W.F. [1964], "Capital Asset Prices:A Theory of Market Equilibrium under condition of Risk," *The Journal of Finance*, 19, pp.425-442.
25. Sharpe, W.F. [1987], "Integrated Asset Allocation," *Financial Analysts Journal*,September-October.
26. Shiller, R.J. [1981], "Do Stock Returns Move Too Much to Be Justified by Subsequent Changes in Dividend?," *American Economic Review*, 71, pp.421-436.
27. Shiller, R.J. [2000], *Irrational Exuberance*, Princeton University Press.
28. Shleifer, A. [2000], *Inefficient Markets*,Oxford University Press.
29. Takahashi, H. and Terano, T. [2003],"Agent-Based Approach to Investors' Behavior and Asset Price Fluctuation in Financial Markets," *Journal of Artificial Societies and Social Simulation*, 6, 3.
30. Takahashi, H. and Terano, T. [2004],"Analysis of Micro-Macro Structure of Financial Markets via Agent-Based Model: Risk Management and Dynamics of Asset Pricing, " *Electronics and Communications in Japan*, 87, 7, pp. 38-48.
31. Terano, T., Nishida, T., Namatame, A., Tsumoto, S., Ohsawa, Y. and Washio, T.(eds.) [2001], *New Frontiers in Artificial Intelligence*, Springer Verlag.
32. Terano, T., Deguchi, H. and Takadama, K.(eds.) [2003], *Meeting the Chalenge of Social Problems via Agent-Based Simulation: Post Proceedings of The Second International Workshop on Agent-Based Approaches in Economic and Social Complex Systems*, Springer Verlag.
33. Tesfatsion, L. [2002], "Agent-Based Computational Economics," *Economics Working Paper*, No.1, Iowa Sate University.

Report of UMIE 2004 and Summary of U-Mart experiments based on the classification of submitted machine agents

Yuhsuke Koyama[1], Hiroshi Sato[2], Hiroyuki Matsui[3], and Yoshihiro Nakajima[4]

[1] Tokyo Institute of Technology koyama@dis.titech.ac.jp
[2] National Defence Academy hsato@nda.go.jp
[3] Kyoto University hmatsui@econ.kyoto-u.ac.jp
[4] Osaka City University yoshi@econ.osaka-cu.ac.jp

Summary U-Mart is interdisciplinary education / research project of a virtual futures market on computer for engineering and economics. We have held the international open experiments UMIE 200x which is the competition for machine agents. This paper reports the result of UMIE 2004 and classify the machine agents submitted in UMIE 2002, 2003 2004 in six clssification criterion.

key words : U-Mart, UMIE, machine agents, artificial market, agent base simulation

1 Introduction

U-Mart is interdisciplinary education / research project of a virtual futures market on computer for engineering and economics. As for the market simulator, U-Mart is a hybrid system of the agent-based simulation and the gaming simulation, where both human trading agents and programmed trading agents (we call 'machine agents') can join simultaneously at the same simulation run. U-Mart system consists of gaming environments and trading agent developer's kit and is downloadable in our website[5].

In engineering faculties, U-Mart is used as educational material for programming. Assignments to program trading agents for U-Mart are challenging both for undergraduate students to study programming and for graduate students to challenge AI programming. In economics faculties, U-Mart system is used for undergraduate students to understand the market structure and pricing mechanisms through the gaming experience in U-Mart. In addition, it is also used as the training kit for programming.

U-Mart committee organizes the machine agent contest for four years. The aims of which are 1) to give incentives for students, and 2) to accumulate and brush up our understanding of market mechanism through collecting the trading algorithms. We have collected more than one-hundred agents through our experiments. The purpose of this article is to classify these agents according to the decision rules and to give basis for analyzing the market mechanism.

2 UMIE2004

2.1 Overview of UMIE2004

U-Mart project have held two types of open experiments. One is U-Mart 200x, which is the Japan-domestic conpetition among human agents. The other is UMIE 200x, which is the international competition for machine agents. UMIE2004 is the third international competiton.

The aims of UMIE are 1)to diffuse and share the U-Mart system as a common test bed, 2)to share variation of trading strategies and their development methodologies, and 3)to know complex behavior of the market consisting of agents having various strategies.

2.2 Rules and submitted agents

Rules and Expeliment Design

Competition rules and experiment settings are the same as those of UMIE2002 and UMIE2003[1, 3, 4] , excepting eight agents are added into standard agent sets. These added agents are submitted in UMIE2002 or/and UMIE2003 and showed good performance, and documents and source codes about these added agents are attached to UMIE2004 agent developper's kit.

Submitted agents

In UMIE2004, 12 teams are submitted and total number of submitted agents is 28. Applies from engeneering faculties and economics facalties are in the proportion 2:1. One of the characterisitc mark of UMIE2004 submitted agents is that all agents passed the qualifying round.

2.3 Best Agents in UMIE2004

Three agents took first place in all three experiments. Agents are: TriDiceP from Osaka Prefectural University, FuzzyStrategyB from Osaka Prefectural University, and ClassifierAgent from Tokyo Institute of Technology.

TriDiceP

This agent determines its action based on the approximation of the price by using the reinforcement learning techniques.The penalty is given to the agent according to the decrease of the property to decrease the corresponding occurrence probability of the action in the situation.

FuzzyStrategyB

This agent makes a decision by fuzzy if-then rules[5].The agent learn the fuzzy if-then rules online.

ClassifierAgent

This agent won the first prize in both UMIE2003 and UMIE2004. This agent divides the environment into 128 situations and learn the ratio $p(t)/p(t-1)$ in each situation. This agent trained its classifier in advance, and learn online in first five days. In addition to classifier mechanism, this agent order 500 units with $p(t-1)*1.25$ and $p(t-1)*0.75$ to hedge the risk of price spike[6].

2.4 Summary of UMIE2004

We sum up the result of UMIE2004 in three points:

Complexity of fitness landscape in multiagent enviromnent

One of the surprising is that STrendStrategy from standard agent kit took a 1st place in Exp.3. It indicates that combination of agents affects each agent's fitness landscape dracstically even if each submitted agent comfirmed to be able to beat the standard agent kit in the qualifying round.

Naive strategy cannot win and Top ranked agents seems to be fixed

In UMIE 2001, though online learning agent showed good performance,the best agent was written by the student at the faculty of economics. This agent employed a kind of arbitrager strategy which means it sell when $Spotprice > Marketprice$ and buy when $Spotprice > Marketprice$. Detail of pricing strategy is defined by one fixed paramater, this strategy is not so much as off-line earning. However,after UMIE2002, online learning agents such as FuzzyB and Classifier agents, using the AI methods, keep winning and gave a good performance.

[5] The example of fuzzy rule is: 'if x_1 is A_1 and x_2 is A_2 and x_3 is A_3 then Buy with q_1 and Sell with q_2'

[6] The behavior and performance of ClassifierAgent is analysed in Kitakubo et al[2]

Necessity of New approach

Major AI methods has already be implemented: GA, Fuzzy, Neural Nets, Classifier System, Reinforcement Learning, even though parameter must be tuned. For next break through, we need the new approach not only in the agent developping but also in the system of open experiment.

2.5 For the next step

To join the U-Mart Open experiment, applicants should disclose the document and the source code of submitted agent. We store more than 70 documents and source codes as common property for researcher and agent developper. We classified the agents library to clarify the actual agent developping situation and find the next challenge.

3 Overview of decision rules of agents: two triads

3.1 Multi level decicion making

Machine agents has to handle multi-level decision making about trading. First of all, machine agent has to decide whether to order or wait-and-see every market turn. If she decided to order, her decisions can be decomposed into three elements of partial decision makings. These elements are 1) sell or buy, 2) price to order, and 3) volume to order[7]. These three elements are classified of the short-term viewpoints.

In addition, for long-term and strategic viewpoints, agent decision can also be classified into three categories. These are 1) price forecasting, 2) risk management, and 3) profit management.

These two triads are closely related. One triad is the other's complement (See Figure1). Price forecasting is achieved by an agent to decide to buy (or to sell) and to settle the order price. Risk management is achieved to control the volume to order and the decision timing. Profit management is achieved to control the order price and order volume.

---

[7] Compared to other ordinary artificial market simulations, U-Mart is characterized by this complication in coding these decision rules. In most artificial market simulation, an agent has only to send their demand function, i.e., their portfolio function, which consists of the slope and the intersection of the linear function. Agents' demand functions are aggregated into the market demand function. Supply function is constant, because the volume of existing stock is fixed. Market price is determined as the intersection of demand and supply curves. Each agent's holdings are estimated by substituting market price for her portfolio function. Whether her bought or sold is revealed ex post analyzing the shift of her holdings.

Fig. 1. Two Triads

3.2 Decision making whether to buy or to sell

As 'when to buy (or to sell)?' is the core of the agent's algorithm, there are a lot of algorithms to be developed in the UMIE submitted agents.

Trend Chaser

Agents in this category adopt the moving average method to take occasion for ordering. Trend chaser can be classified into two sub categories; one is called 'normal-bid', which means that these agents order to buy when market price is on upward swinging. The other is called 'contrary-bid', which means that these agents order to sell when downward swinging.

Arbitrager

Some agents aggressively make positions when there is a wide divergence between spot price and U-Mart price. In a strict sense, there can be no arbitrager agent in U-Mart system because agents can only trade the futures. However, when there is a wide price divergence, U-Mart price would possibly return to the neighbor of the spot price in a few turns, so agents adopt fictitious repurchase trade as intertemporal arbitrage.

Price forecasting with machine learning

Some subscribers whose major is computer science adopt various kinds of machine learning techniques to forecast futures price. These techniques are: fuzzy inference system, classifier system, neural network, and so on. As these learning agents do not have enough opportunity to learn price fluctuation in one U-Mart simulation trial, which has only 240 itayoses, subscribers trained their agents and adjusted agents' parameters at their laboratory in advance of submitting.

Double ordering

This strategy is implemented with reference to the well-known strategy of day-traders. It ordered both the order to sell with a little higher than the last futures price and the order to buy a little cheaper than the last futures price.

Random (Tarot)

This strategy picks a Tarot card from the deck and act according to the oracle on the card.

Trend Chaser Killer

When agents' price forecasting in market is nearly one-sided, huge price fluctuation sometimes happens in U-Mart simulation because of uneven distribution of orders. As some orders from trend chaser are not the limit ones but market ones, this strategy tries orders the outrageous price compared to the current market price in order to entrap such silly trend chaser strategies.

Technilcal Treding

There are various kinds of rules which are used by the technical analysts in real market trade. Some participants used these rules for their machine agents. In addition, some of these strategies are used in the preliminary qualify in UMIE, and supplied to all participants as 'standard agents' in Agent Developer's Kit.

3.3 Decision making of the order price

There are not so many agents to order with limit price. One of the reasons is because decision making of the order price is more difficult than that of whether to buy or to sell. However, this is mainly because there is little possibility to succeed in trading futures with the exact ordered price as U-Mart system adopts the *itayose* method in price determination.

Instead of the price forecasting strategies, decision rules for pricing are only three rules.

Nariyuki(Market order)

This strategy does not decide the order price and entrust the result of the market.

Quasi-*Nariyuki*

This strategy is appeared at U-Mart 2001in which nariyuki pricing is inhibited. It orders the enough high (20% higher than last futures price) price to buy or low price to sell in place of the nariyuki pricing.

ΔP Method

This strategy set last futures price as a basic price and orders ΔP higher or lower price.

3.4 Decision Making for the order volume

As agents cannot access the market trading after their bankruptcy, risk management should have essential importance. However, because agents can trade only one kind of futures in U-Mart situation, agents cannot manage their portfolio and adopt some simple rules of position management. In addition, most agents take the strategy of risk aversion, the only exceptions are martingale.

Because decision for the order volume is more difficult than the other decisions, there is a room imporoving the strategy. One of the contrivances is the position adjust mechanism by ClassifierAgent. However, the efficiency of this mechanism has not been analized even in Kitakubo et al[2].

Setting the ceillings

This strategy does not take longer or shorter position over the fixed limit position.

Profit realization and loss cutting

This strategy set the target profit and limit loss line. If agents' unrealized profit achieve the profit line or limit loss line, they adopt the cross trade and cancel out the position in order to fix the profit (or loss).

Small size bidding

Most agents fixed their order volume small enough not to take risk of bankruptcy, and such agents need not to adopt any kind of decision making for order volume.

Position adjust mechanism

ClassifierAgent have implemented original position adjust mechanism. This agent decides position adjust volume at time t PA_t as $a_1 * (\hat{p}_{t+1} - p_t) - a_2 * PS_t$, where $\hat{p}_{t+1}$ is the forecasted next U-Mart price, p_t is the current U-Mart Price, and PS_t is the current position. a_1, a_2 are fixed paramaters, in UMIE2004, $a_1 = 4$ and $a_2 = 0.1$. Order volume is defined as $min(\mid PA_t \mid, maxQuant)$, where $maxQuant$ is the fixed paramator. In UMIE2004, $maxQuant = 200$. BuySell condition is that this agent decides to buy when $PA_t > 0$ and to sell when $PA_t < 0$.

ClassifierAgent makes larger order when $(\hat{p}_{t+1} - p_t) > 0, PS_t < 0$ or $(\hat{p}_{t+1} - p_t) < 0, PS_t > 0$ than $(\hat{p}_{t+1} - p_t) > 0, PS_t > 0$ or $(\hat{p}_{t+1} - p_t) < 0, PS_t < 0$. This condition indicates that ClassifierAgent make its position cautiously and settle its position agressively.

Martingale

Agents who adopt this strategy set the first bidding volume. If they lose profit in last trade, they order two times as much as last ordered volume. They continue this multiplying bidding until they win the profit or bankrupt.

3.5 Summary of Agent Strategy

Though new decision rules has been actively developed in rules of the trade timing, decision rules of pricing and order volume, especially rules of order volume, have not paid much attention by agents developers. Our next problem is promoting to develop the new decision rules, especially to develop fully integrated strategic packeage.

4 Conclusion

This paper reports the result of UMEI2004 and classification of submitted machine agents. Our agent libraly has great variety which cannot be brought forth by the individual researcher,however, it is difficult for reserchers to make use of our library because of the lack of standard of classification. This paper provides this classification and indicate that price decision and and order volume decision strategy is not matured and has room for the improvement.

References

1. Hiroshi Deguchi, Takao Terano, Hajime Kita, Yoshinori Shiozawa adn Robert Axtell, Katheleen Carley, Maksim Tsvetovat, Hiroshi Sato, Hiroyuki Matsui, Isao Ono, Yoshihiro Nakajima, and Naoki Mori. Report of umie 2002 – strategy and rank order of submitted machine agents –. In *NAACSOS2003 North American Association for Computational So-cial and Organizational Science Conference*, Carnegie Mellon University, 2003.
2. Takahiro Kitakubo, Yuhsuke Koyama, and Hiroshi Deguchi. The investigation of the agent in the artificial market. *AIS2004 postproceedings: Springer-Verlag's Lecture Note in Computer Science Series.*, 2004.
3. Y. Nakajima and T. Ueda. Analysis of submitted agents to umie2002 -influence of spot data and opponents on agents' rank orders -. In *NAACSOS2003 North American Association for Computational So-cial and Organizational Science Conference*, Carnegie Mellon University, 2003.

4. Y. Nakajima and T. Ueda. U-mart international experiment2003 (umie2003). In *NAACSOS2003 North American Association for Computational So-cial and Organizational Science Conference*, Carnegie Mellon University, 2003.
5. U-Mart Project Web Server. http://www.u-mart.econ.kyoto-u.ac.jp/index-e.html.

Grounded Theory and Multi-Agent Simulation for a Small Firm

Clinton J. Andrews, Ana I. Baptista, and Shawn L.W. Patton

Edward J. Bloustein School of Planning and Public Policy, Rutgers University, 33 Livingston Ave #302, New Brunswick, New Jersey, 08901, USA

Summary. There is a problematic disconnection in much research on organizational behavior between empirical evidence, mostly from case studies, and theorizing, most of which has been discursive rather than formal. This paper presents an empirically based, bottom-up view of organizational behavior, obtained by performing case studies of small firms in the New Jersey plastic injection molding industry, and then developing a multi-agent simulation model of such a firm. The model embodies a formal, explicit, and grounded (limited) theory of organizational behavior. Results suggest that a realistic account of corporate behavior depends in part on representing employees not as *homo economicus* but as agents having bounded rationality and subject to social influences.

Key words. Multi-agent simulation, grounded theory, organizational behavior, plastics

Introduction

The objective of this research is to test the efficacy of multi-agent simulation modeling for supporting grounded theorizing, that is, for developing theory by generalizing in a limited way from empirical evidence. This paper describes a research project that investigates organizational behavior through an iterative process of interviewing managers at small firms, developing narrative case studies of these firms, translating key elements of the case studies into a multi-agent simulation model, and then reviewing the modeling results with our original respondents.

Scientific understanding advances through the iterative actions of numerous individual researchers. Within a scientific community, deductive science connects theory to evidence with hypothesis testing (Popper, 1968), whereas inductive science connects evidence to theory with pattern matching (Tukey, 1970). And so the "wheel of science" spins forward, as evidence informs theory and theory guides the acquisition of new evidence (Wallace, 1971).

In the social scientific study of organizational behavior, where much data is qualitative, there are special challenges for making the wheel of science spin.

Hypothesis testing is notoriously difficult because variables are so interdependent that unidirectional assumptions of cause and effect are implausible. Pattern matching is equally difficult because many rival theories may equally well explain the typically very limited or even anecdotal data. As a result, there are many competing theories of organizational behavior and there is little convergence on empirically agreed "facts." Many of these explanatory theories have prescriptive counterparts that are championed by rival management gurus, resulting in continuing competition for mind-share rather than paradigmatic successions.

Grounded theory

One solution to this social scientific problem has been to define a humbler role for theory that recognizes severe limits to its generality. Grounded theory is such an approach. Like other inductive approaches, it means theory derived from data, systematically gathered and analyzed through the research process (Strauss and Corbin, 1998). In this particular method, data collection, analysis, and eventual theory stand in close relationship to one another (Glaser and Strauss, 1967). The researcher begins with an area of study and allows the theory to emerge from the data. One of the principal benefits of using the grounded theory approach is that it is closer to reality. Theories are drawn from data so they can offer insight, enhance understanding and provide a meaningful guide to action grounded in that same reality.

Thus grounded theory begins with a research situation. Within that situation, the task for the researcher is to understand what is happening there, and how the players manage their roles. A researcher will mostly do this through observation, conversation and interview. What most differentiates grounded theory from much other research is that it is explicitly emergent. It does not test a hypothesis. The aim, as its originator states it, is to discover the theory implicit in the data. This distinction between "emergence and forcing", as Glaser (1992) frames it, is fundamental to understanding how the methodology distinguishes itself from hypothesis testing. Constant comparison is the heart of the process. At first one compares interview (or other data) to interview (or other data). Theory emerges quickly in the form of crude classifications. When those have begun to emerge one compares further data to the theory. The researcher's task is to identify both categories (roughly equivalent to themes or variables) and their properties (in effect their sub-categories). In this way both methodology and theory develop gradually as data and interpretations accumulate. Eventually it becomes necessary to delimit the theory by ignoring categories deemed irrelevant to the inquiry. Finally, the theory must be written down, because the act of successfully communicating the theory greatly refines it. Grounded theory has its own sources of rigor (Glaser, 1992):

- It is responsive to the situation in which the research is done.

- There is a continuing search for evidence that disconfirms the emerging theory.
- It is driven by the data in such a way that the final shape of the theory is likely to provide a good fit to the situation.

Strauss and Corbin (1992) recommend that researchers develop grounded theory using a "memoing" technique that produces code notes, theoretical notes, operational notes. Lofland and Lofland (1995) advance the technique by recommending elemental analytical memos, sorting memos, and integrating memos. Babbie (2003; 379) urges researchers to write notes that "describe and define concepts, deal with methodological issues, or offer initial theoretical formulations." This paper takes the additional step of writing computer code to make the emerging theory even more highly explicit. The simulation model substantially extends the "memo."

Case study design and protocol

A case study research design was utilized to explore the questions of how social networks, both formal and informal, influence workplace behavior or business strategies of firms. A multiple case, replication design was used in which three cases or firms were studied (Yin, 2003). Firms were selected based on replication logic selecting three similar plastics processing firms in New Jersey of small to medium size. These particular firms were also selected because their manufacturing processes and organizational structure were simple relative to larger multinational firms and therefore would serve as a good starting point from which to begin to build a basic computer model.

The data collection protocol included several methods for each case:
(1) Elite, semi-structured interviews with firm executives or presidents
(2) Document analysis of financial, technical and environmental data
(3) Field visit, tours of plant operations

Access to each firm was garnered with the aid of an industry consultant familiar with many of the plastic injection molding and extruding firms in New Jersey. Confidential interviews with each firm were conducted, each was taped with the permission of the interviewee. The interview guide can be found on the project website shown at the end of this paper. Documents for analysis included company annual reports, company websites, industry wide websites, organizational charts, and U.S. EPA toxic release inventory website, newspaper and trade magazine articles. Individual case reports were created for each firm that included data from all three data collection methods. A cross case report was then developed with an overview of the project and analysis of cross case findings.

Case study findings

We expected to find that traditional family run firms would have more prominent social networks in which informal relationships hold great importance relative to more formal structures within a firm. Using company sponsored social activities as one indicator of the strength of social/informal networks within each company the cases revealed an interesting pattern. Company 1 and 2, both family run businesses that experienced a generational transition in leadership from fathers to sons, experienced a decrease in the number of company sponsored activities. These generational shifts also occurred at the same time as market shifts in the plastics industry with increased competitiveness resulting from new Asian competitors. Interestingly, Company 3, which is a similar establishment in size and technological terms but is not a family-run business, offers more company sponsored social activities than the family run companies. Company 3, unlike the other companies, is a subsidiary of a large multinational firm and has access to a wide variety of resources. This difference in the level of company-sponsored programs suggests that it is not just the familial nature of a company but rather the financial stability of the firm that matters a great deal in terms of supporting informal, social activities.

Another factor contributing to a change in the nature of social relationships within firms is the drive towards automation. Increased competition from Asia is pressuring firms to reduce costs, primarily labor costs. All three firms spoke about streamlining low skill jobs. At the same time, this streamlining process is putting increased emphasis on the quality of remaining employees. The interviews with all three companies revealed that the firms have a stable workforce characterized by low turnover and long-term employees. Loyalty to the firm, competence, and interest in the business are all highly sought after qualities in employees, which the firm in turn rewards with internal promotions. The importance of informal networks is also revealed in the "totem pole" hierarchy established by long-term employees. Within this informal hierarchy, seniority or tenure on the job is more important than professional or academic credentials. This accumulated job knowledge also forms the basis of internal promotional practices.

Another aspect of the business in which informal networks seem to play a key role is in the recruitment practices of all three firms. The majority of entry-level employees are of similar ethnic and cultural backgrounds; many are family members or reside in the same towns. These employees are mostly of Hispanic origin and they were brought into the firm via "word of mouth" practices with no formal recruitment practices in place. Company 3, unlike the firms, had a much stronger corporate culture in place than the family run firms, evidenced by their more stringent adherence to corporate principles, rules and regulations. Interestingly though, Company 3 still relied heavily on informal knowledge on the factory floor to improve its safety practices in particular. In order to improve safety, the company went beyond basic formal training and procedures and encouraged employees to make suggestions on the floor via a suggestion box and also as part of a committee. The head of the company also recognized the value of bringing knowledge from outside the firm to bear on the issue of workplace safety. Ultimately, the drive towards automation coupled with the market shift to Asian companies (away from traditional U.S.-based family run businesses) appears to mean a decrease in the overall importance of social networks within these firms.

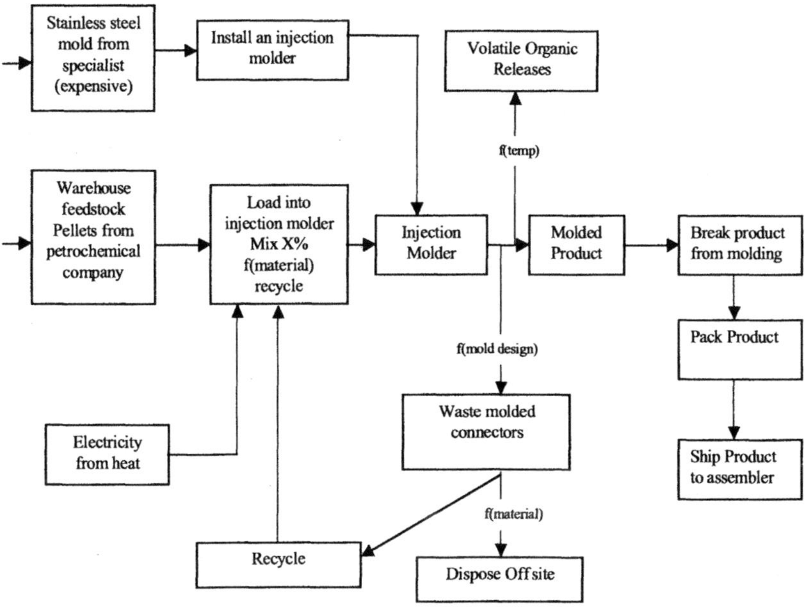

Fig. 1. Plastic injection molding process.

Model-building activity

Researchers often productively induct theory from case studies that, like good computer programs, are parsimonious and logically coherent (Eisenhardt, 1989). Parsimony was a goal of the modeling effort, and logical coherence was a handy byproduct of the debugging process. The dual challenges with any type of modeling are to simplify reality appropriately and to communicate the results effectively (Andrews, 2002). Both challenges proved significant during the modeling process.

Using the Brookings Institution's Ascape multi-agent simulation framework, a Java programmer created PolyModel, a simulation of operations at a plastic injection-molding firm. Approximately 100 employees interacted with the production technology and one another, subject to changes in the firm's external environment. The model included technology details, organizational structures, and parameter values taken from Firm 1 in the case study. The model tested alternative theoretical constructs explaining the behavior of employees, to be roughly validated against the evidence from case study Firms 2 and 3.

Version 1.0 of the model includes 22 classes, related as follows. Figures 2 through 8 provide additional details.

PolyModel contains People, the Factory, and the External Environment.

The Factory includes a Warehouse, Production Lines, and a Shipping Department.

Employee extends Person.

Owner, Plant Manager, Marketer, Engineer, Shift Supervisor, Shipping Clerk, Materials Mixer, Maintenance Technician, Machine Operator, and Janitor all extend Job. Each Employee has a Job.

Remaining Java classes serve as computational infrastructure.

The time step in the model is hourly, so the firm cycles through the work day and the work week over a period of years. Each employee assesses whether to go to work every morning, based on health, social pressures, and finances. The plant manager determines how many production lines and associated employees are needed based on pending orders for widgets. The marketer brings in orders and tries to keep ahead of production so that the capacity factor of the plant is high. The janitor keeps the factory clean, and other employees become unhappy if the factory gets dirty. The materials mixer ensures that raw materials reach the production lines, and the shipping clerk packages completed products and sends them out the door. The maintenance technician keeps the production lines in working order. The machine operators perform several sequential duties (load plastic pellets, set molder temperature, separate widgets from scrap plastic). The shift supervisor encourages machine operators to work more carefully and reports on employee performance to the plant manager.

All employees are subject to worker error that affects the quality of their performance, and the probability that error will occur is a function of aptitude, experience, tiredness, and happiness. Worker Error impacts most stages of the production line. Higher worker error results in mistakes that cost the factory profits and increased waste which contributes to greater pollution.

Happiness, the lack of which contributes to worker error, is a weighted additive function of wealth and social embeddedness. Moneygrubbers like wealth (90, 10), Socialanimals like their friends (10/90), and TheRestofUs are more balanced (50, 50). Wealth increases by getting paid at work, social embeddedness increases by making more friends at work and elsewhere. Friendship depends on affinity (similar intrinsic characteristics) and frequency of interaction.

The dynamics of these employee interactions provide realistic drama and aggregate up to firm-level performance measures of interest to management.

Parameters are adjustable on the fly, and various diagnostic tools allow the user to investigate the causes of particular dynamic behaviors.

Developing the model required intense interaction between the programmer and the qualitative researchers. Much conversation centered on eliciting precisely what was the theory being formalized in the model. As the researchers played with the resulting simulations, the theoretical framework evolved.

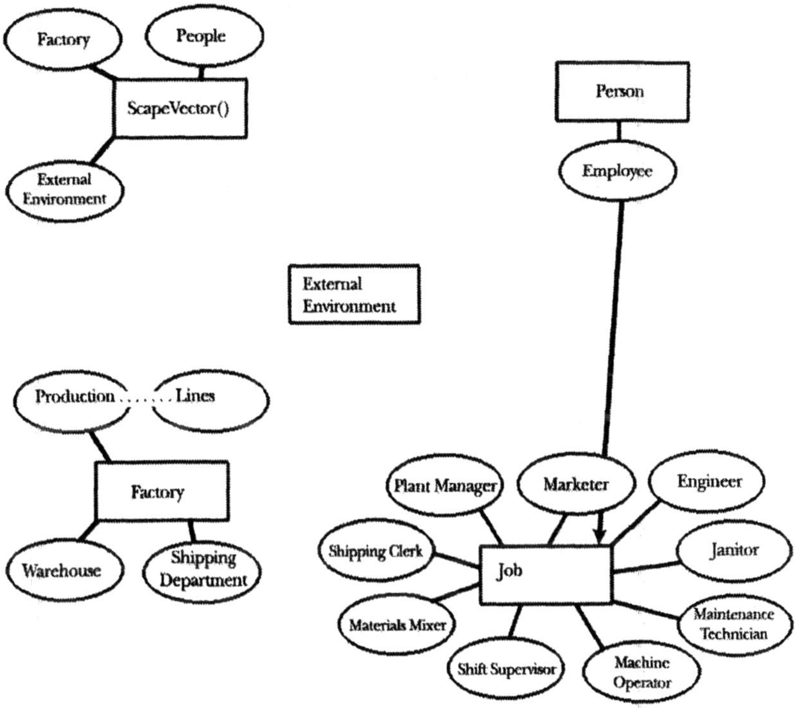

Fig. 2. PolyModel structures and agents.

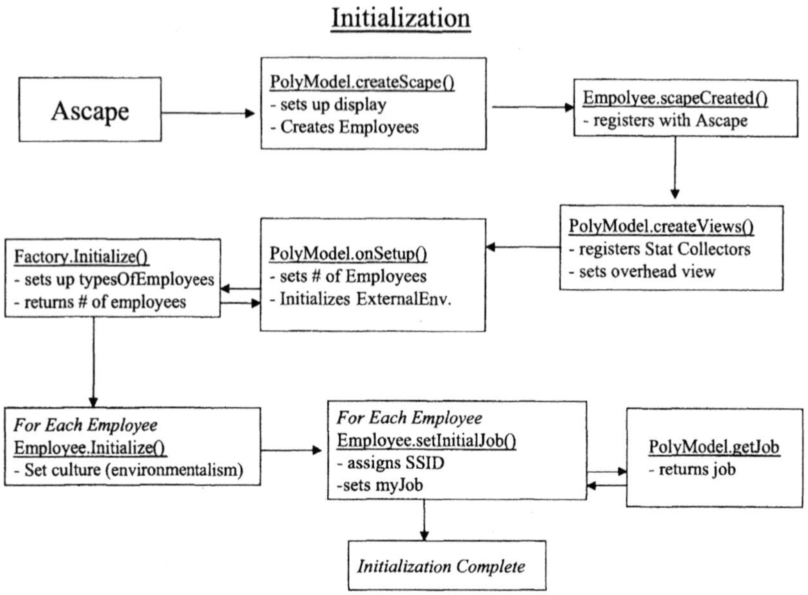

Fig. 3. PolyModel initialization logic.

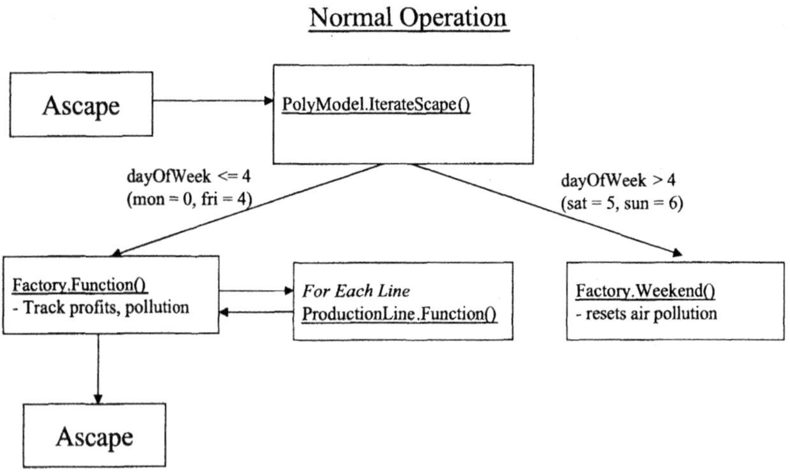

Fig. 4. PolyModel normal operation logic.

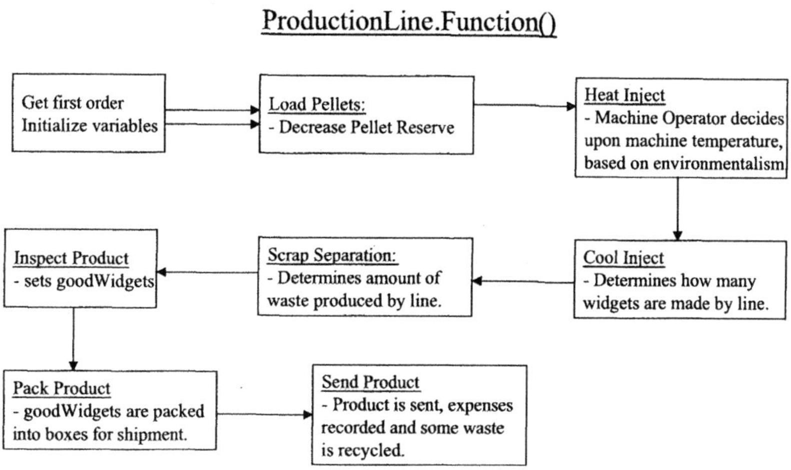

Fig. 5. PolyModel production technology logic. It mirrors that described in Figure 1.

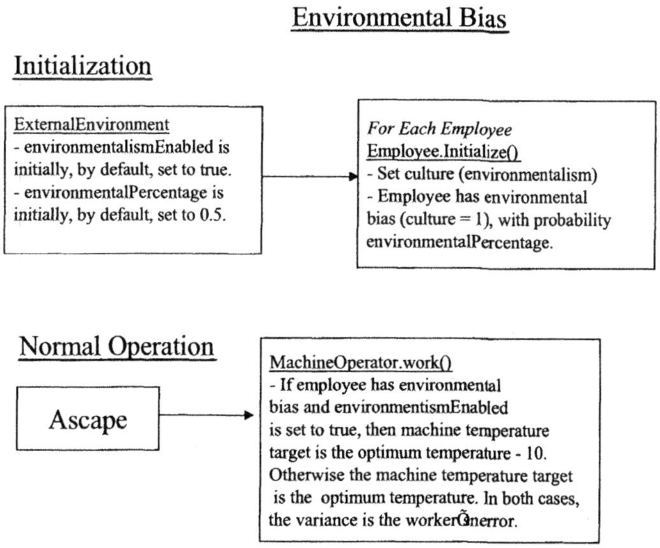

Fig. 6. How an environmentalist bias was implemented in PolyModel.

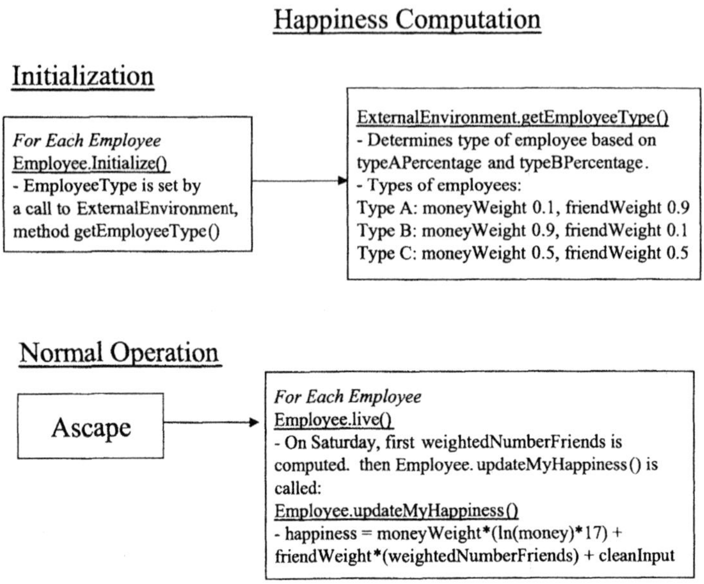

Fig. 7. Employee utility functions implemented in PolyModel.

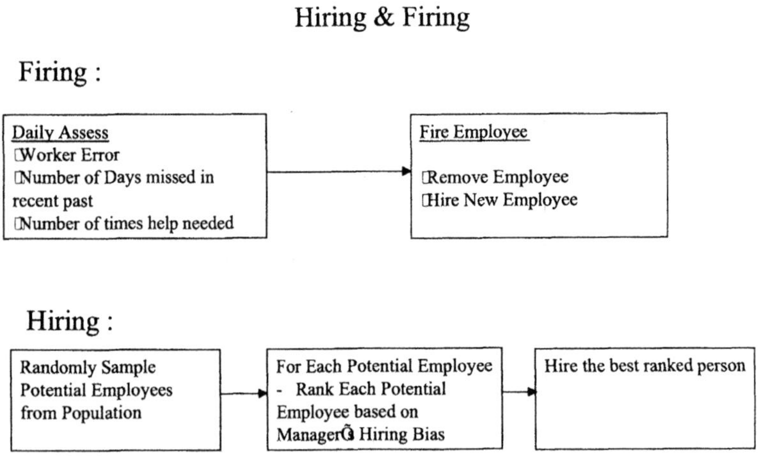

Fig. 8. PolyModel's hiring and firing logic, executed by the plant manager.

Illustrative results

This paper briefly discusses one set of illustrative results. The project continues as of this writing, so that the model, underlying theories, and empirical evidence are evolving. The goal is to make the model robust enough to serve as a management-training simulator for the plastic injection molding industry.

Figures 9 and 10 compare profitability and environmental performance of the firm over a multi-year period under two representations of bounded rationality among employees. Under standard *homo economicus* assumptions, the firm is much more profitable and less polluting than when the model is populated with more realistic employees who commit worker errors.

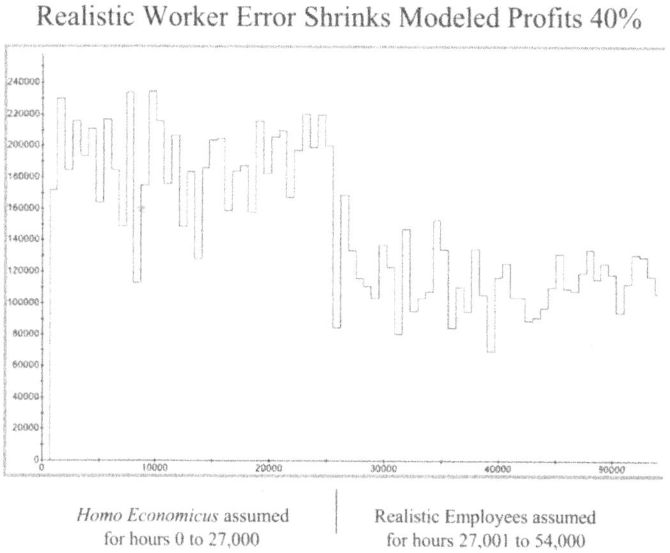

Fig. 9. Monthly profits under two sets of assumptions regarding worker error.

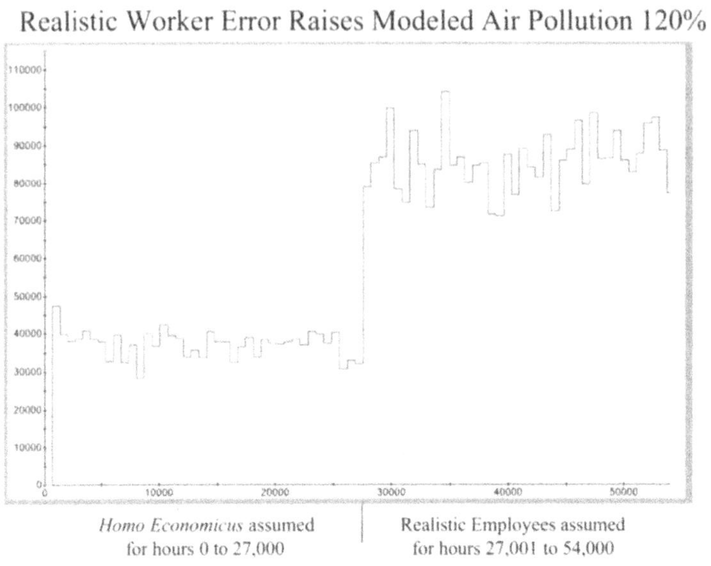

Fig. 10. Monthly air pollution under two sets of assumptions regarding worker error.

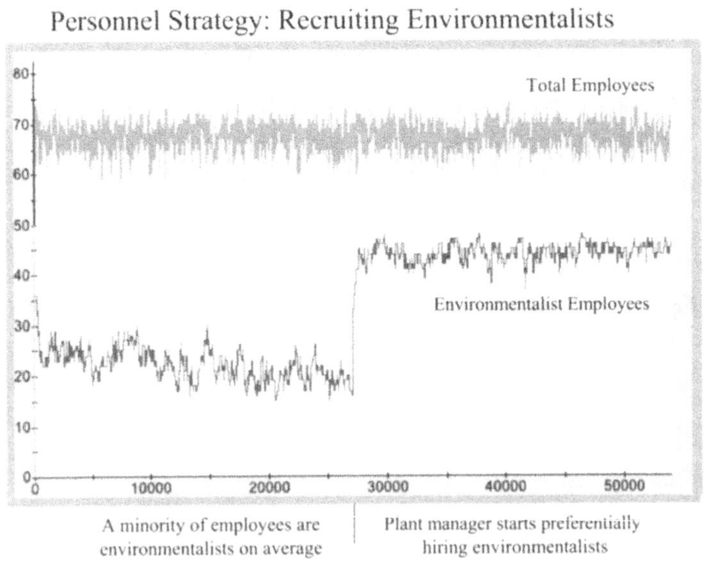

Fig. 11. Employees and employee composition under two hiring scenarios.

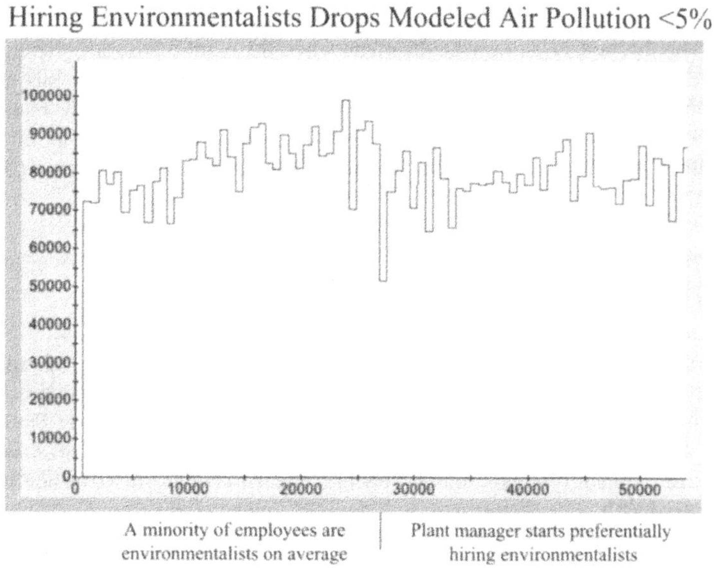

Fig. 12. Monthly air pollution under two hiring scenarios.

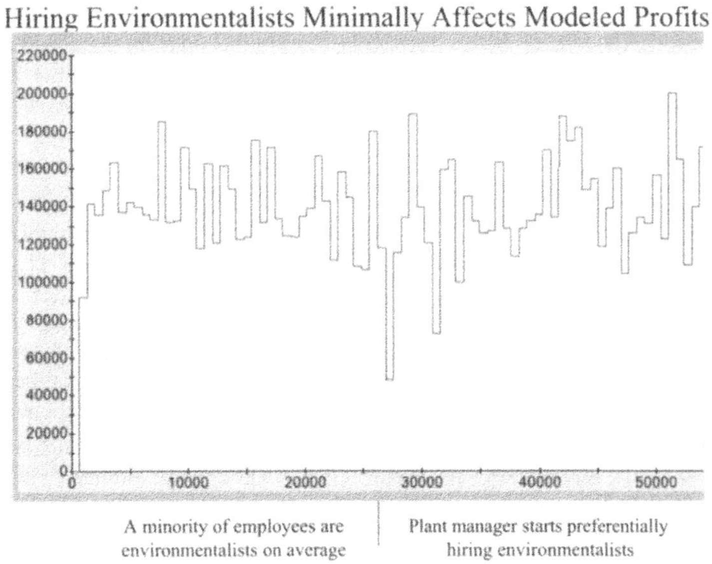

Fig. 13. Monthly profits under two hiring scenarios.

Figures 11, 12, and 13 show what happens when the plant manager preferentially hires environmentalists. The environmental benefit is minimal, but luckily so are the impacts on profits. A quality management strategy (suggested by Figures 9 and 10) seems more likely than an environmentalist hiring bias to improve corporate environmental performance, while simultaneously improving financial performance.

Theory building

Regarding the motivating question for this project—can multi-agent simulation advance organizational behavior research by better linking evidence with theorizing?—the results are promising. The set of simulations shown in Figures 9 through 13 illustrates how both frictionless neoclassical theories (that miss worker error) and human relations/social network theories (that miss technological factors) are incomplete. The former will never help managers discover the benefits of total quality management strategies. The latter will never help managers discover the benefits of technological improvements. The multi-agent simulation illuminates both, plus other insights.

In addition to what has been shown in the figures, the modeling and case study evidence support two more insights to date. First, informal networks are very important for hiring new employees and for helping employees to decide to take job actions like strikes and sick day protests. Second, formal structures are hugely important for explaining almost everything else. In this industry there also appears to be a substantial amount of technological determinism. In other words, the type and economics of the technology explain much of the firm's overall behavior.

Lessons learned

There are two major lessons learned for researchers interested in using multi-agent simulation models in a grounded theory-building context. First, this project shows that highly diverse skill sets are needed. In fact, it is unlikely that a single individual will have the requisite range of skills, necessitating recruitment of a multidisciplinary team consisting of an interviewer, case study developer, and Java programmer. Second, iterative modeling and interviewing is crucial because new questions arise, and alternative theories need to be explored and elaborated.

A benefit of developing multi-agent simulations in this inductive, evidence-based way is that they appear to inform action more directly than might deductive, theory-based models. Organizational behavior becomes a humbler but perhaps more valuable type of social science—less general but more applicable.

Acknowledgements

The authors gratefully acknowledge financial support from the U.S. Environmental Protection Agency's Science To Achieve Results grant program in Corporate Environmental Behavior. They also acknowledge Robert Axtell's collegiality and profusely thank the plastics manufacturers who allowed case study visits.

References

Project website with case study and model details and is at http://policy.rutgers.edu/andrews/projects/abm.

Andrews, C.J. (2002) Humble Analysis, Praeger, Westport, CT.

Babbie, E. (2003) The Practice of Social Research, 10th ed., Wadsworth, Belmont, CA.

Eisenhardt, K.M. (1989) "Building theories from case study research," Academy of Management Review 14(4): 532-550.

Glaser, B.G. (1992) Basics of grounded theory analysis: Emergence vs. forcing, Sociology Press, Mill Valley, CA.

Glaser, B.G., and A.L. Strauss (1967) The Discovery of Grounded Theory: Strategies for Qualitative Research, Aldine, Chicago.

Lofland, J., and L.H. Lofland (1995) Analyzing Social Settings: A Guide to Qualitative Observation and Analysis, 3rd ed., Wadsworth, Belmont, CA.

Popper, K.R. (1968) The Logic of Scientific Discovery, 3rd ed. rev., Hutchinson, London.

Strauss, A., and J. Corbin (1998) Basics of Qualitative Research: Techniques and Procedures for developing Grounded Theory, 2nd ed., Sage Publications, Thousand Oaks, CA.

Tukey, J.W. (1970) Exploratory Data Analysis, Princeton University Press, Princeton, NJ.

Wallace, W. (1971) The Logic of Science in Sociology, Aldine-Atherton, Chicago.

Yin, R.K. (2003) Case Study Research: Design and Methods, Sage Publications, Thousand Oaks, CA, pp. 44-51.

The Use of Hybrid Agent Based Systems to Model Petrol Markets

Alison J. Heppenstall[1], Andrew J. Evans[1], Mark H. Birkin[1], and David O'Sullivan[2]

[1] School of Geography, University of Leeds, Leeds, UK, LS2 9JT
`www.geog.leeds.ac.uk`

[2] School of Geography and Environmental Science, The University of Auckland, Private Bag 92019, Auckland, NZ `www.geog.auckland.ac.nz`

Summary. The petrol price market is a highly sensitive and competitive market with many processes combining at different temporal and spatial scales to affect each petrol station's prices. Previous models developed to represent the relationship between petrol and a variable are empirical and mathematical. These suffer from a number of problems, chiefly: the parameters are all on the same scale (behaviours executed at the 'micro' level are not tied to 'global' level variables like oil prices); the parameters are often difficult to estimate and lack realism; very little, if any, account of any geographical effects is taken, and, finally, mathematical models by their nature only consider quantitative parameters and therefore miss out on qualitative, behavioural information.

The work within this paper presents a series of three multi-agent and hybrid models that seek to rectify some of these problems. The models are behavioural and work at the scale of the individual. The results show that this is a promising method for modelling dynamic, geographical systems.

Key words: Multi-agent models, spatial interaction model, network, petrol.

1 Introduction

Petrol is one of the most valuable oil derived commodities, valued by retailers and customers alike. Despite pressures on natural resources there is a rising demand for petrol associated with an ever increasing individual mobility. At the end of 2002, there were 11707 sites retailing over 36 billion litres of motor fuel per annum in the UK. This equates to an average of approximately 1,350 litres of fuel consumed by each vehicle per year. Consumers are becoming ever more aware of petrol prices; internet sites in the UK, such as the Automobile Association site, enable consumers to have an almost perfect knowledge of prices within their area. Consumer sensitivity to petrol prices was clearly demonstrated in the UK during August and September 2000 when there was a "Petrol Crisis", consisting of consumer blockages of refineries and protests in reaction to soaring fuel taxes. This sensitivity and knowledge has created both a highly competitive and rapidly responding market, with organisations employing various strategies to maximise profits.

Many processes combine at different temporal and spatial scales to affect each petrol stations' prices. For example: internal costs (cost of production; fixed costs like staff pay), external influences (price of crude oil and levels of taxation) and effects of locality (rural versus urban areas). More importantly, in the UK, competition within the local neighbourhood exerts a great influence on the setting of prices. For example, ESSO have explicitly stated they use a price-watching scheme whereby individual petrol stations attempt to undercut local competitors.

The literature concerned with the examination of petrol prices and its relationship with other variables is vast. These studies generally differ in one or more of the following aspects: the variables considered; the country under scrutiny; the time frequency and period of data used; the focus on wholesale or retail prices and, finally, the model employed [7]. Examples include [1], [9], [14], [13] and [10]. High frequency price cycles have been thoroughly investigated by [4], [11] and [5] [6].

Typically, the models developed by researchers to represent the relationship between petrol and a variable are empirical and mathematical. They suffer from a number of problems, chiefly: the parameters are all on the same scale (behaviours executed at the "micro" level are not tied to "global" level variables like oil prices); the parameters are often difficult to estimate and lack realism; very little, if any, account of any geographical effects is taken, and, finally, mathematical models by their nature only consider quantitative parameters and therefore miss out on qualitative, behavioural information.

Within this paper, we present a series of three multi-agent and hybrid models that seek to rectify some of these problems. The models are behavioural and work at the scale of individual customers and petrol stations, but take into account quantitative and global parameters.

2 Petrol Stations as Agents

The three systems were developed in Java. Each has a similar model for the petrol stations. Individual petrol stations are created as agent-objects and supplied with knowledge of their initial starting price, production costs, and the prices of those stations within their neighbourhood. The prices are either set with real data or idealised data depending on whether the systems are being used to examine real or abstract dynamics. Each agent views the prices of neighbouring stations and applies a series of rules to adjust its own prices. The geographical distribution of the stations can, again, be either real or idealised. In this paper we present the results of real data experiments modelling the West Yorkshire region of the UK (Figure 1).

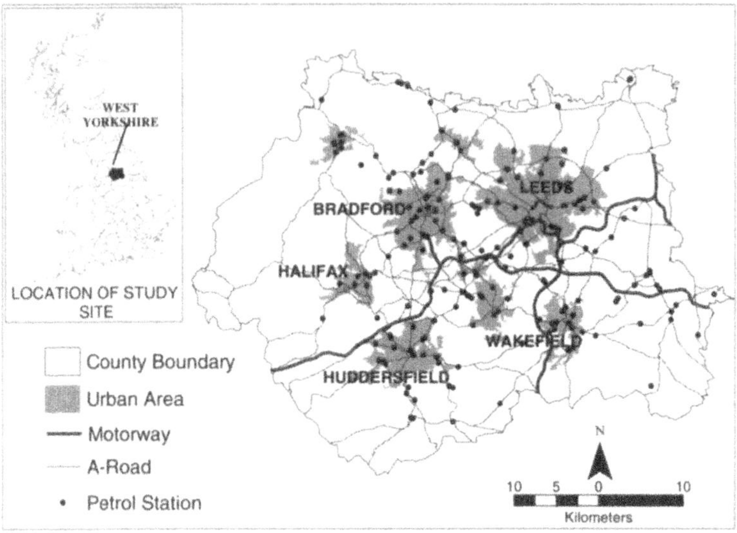

Fig. 1. Maps showing the location of West Yorkshire within the UK and the distribution of petrol stations and extent of urban areas within West Yorkshire.

The rules can be assigned to stations on the basis of the company running them, geographically, or simply given identically to all the stations. They are based on industry knowledge and implemented after experimentation with differing parameters. The interplay of different rule sets allows the stations to compete and implement behaviour with the aim of profit maximisation. The stations update their prices synchronously once per day. The parameters that form the basis of the rules are:

- The allowable minimum and maximum price.
- The amount each station might try to undercut its competitors by.
- The amount each station can be priced above its competitors before it takes action.
- The neighbourhood size in which stations are regarded as competitors.
- The station profitability compared with the last time iteration.

These parameters can be built into rules or strategies such as: 'Am I more expensive by X amount than the competition in my neighbourhood (Ykm)? If yes, drop my price by Z'. Such rules are utilised under the following conditions:

1. If the profit is increasing then agents carry on with the current price change strategy.

2. If the profit is falling, agents pick a strategy to either:
   a) Increase the price.
   b) Decrease the price.
3. If the profit between the last two iterations hasn't changed much, then keep the price constant until the profit falls again.

The petrol stations are designed to be only interested in their own profit. Secondary aims, such as attaining market share or behaviours such as inter-station collusion are currently ignored. Future research will investigate these areas.

3 Consumer Models

The models vary chiefly in how profitability is assessed. The three systems have an increasing complexity of customer model. Plainly, an individual-level agent based model of each potential customer would be a vast computational and behavioural modelling effort, so the three systems utilise simplified models of customers. The systems are:

1. A pure agent based model in which the profitability is decided by simple price comparison. Stations attempt to undercut competitors while maximising price.
2. A hybrid SI-Agent system (henceforth referred to as the hybrid model). Here, consumers travel to petrol stations depending on the distance to them and their prices. Stations aim to maximize their profit based on customer numbers, price, and a fixed volume of fuel that is sold to each customer. Where real data is used, the customers' initial locations are based on population and car ownership data from the UK census
3. A hybrid Network-SI-Agent system (henceforth referred to as the network hybrid model). This is the same as the hybrid model, except that the customers are initially distributed on the basis of journey to work data along potential routes prior to the SI model running. This introduces an "intervening opportunities" style component.

4 Pure Agent Model

In the experiments conducted with the basic Agent model, all the petrol stations within West Yorkshire were initialised with the real data for one day and the same rule set. The simulations were run to equilibrium (defined as the stage when all the prices within the area remained static for 3 days). The predicted days data was then compared with the real data for those days (Figure 2).

Figure 2 shows the mean per-station price difference (in UK pence) between the real and agent data over the course of the data set. The model

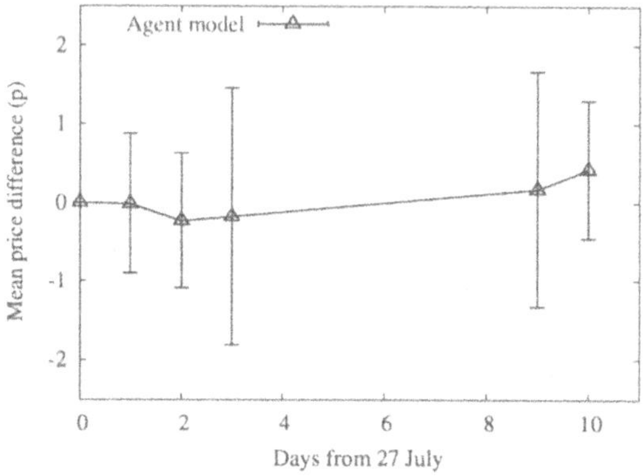

Fig. 2. Comparison of mean price per day between the agent model and real data over time within West Yorkshire. The SD is indicated by the vertical bars.

under-predicts the prices, a difference that increases over time. However, the model only took two days (iterations) to reach equilibrium. This is clearly not enough time for the model to operate the rule set effectively. Any variations in the difference between the real and model data after equilibrium were entirely due to changes within the real data. To examine whether the model could generate observed geographical variations, for example different price levels between rural and urban areas, the model was run with all the stations' prices initially set to the average level from day one of the real dataset. As can be seen by comparing Figure 3(a) and Figure 3 (b), the model does not capture the system dynamics adequately enough to replicate these variations.

5 Hybrid Model

Spatial Interaction (SI) models essentially calculate the amount of people travelling to multiple locations, based on levels of attractiveness and distance-costs. Traditionally, they are used for 'what-if?' scenarios [3], for example, what will happen to the sales of supermarket X if supermarket Y locates nearby? Within the petrol models discussed here, they are used to calculate customer numbers and, hence, volume of sales information by assuming a constant, average, customer fuel requirement. This information is then used to calculate the amount of profit that is being made. Each petrol station implements profit maximising strategies based on this information.

The SI model is in two parts (a detailed description of both the pure agent and hybrid models can be found in Heppenstall et al. [8]). Equation 1 calculates the relative amounts of fuel sold by each station to the population of each ward (UK Census area of 400 to 35,000 people). The amount sold decays

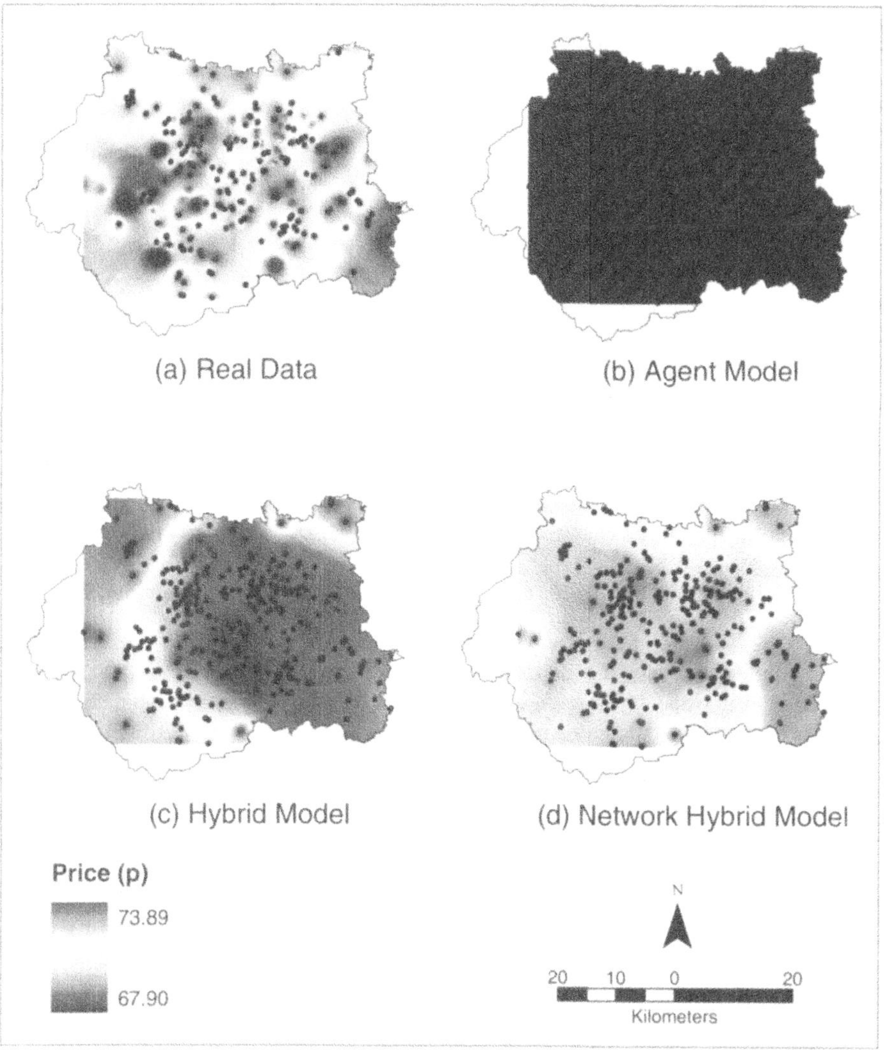

Fig. 3. Price distributions for the various models ten days after runs started with all stations initialised at 71 pence: (b) agent model, (c) hybrid model and (d) network hybrid model. Data from day ten of the real dataset (a) is included for comparison. Price surfaces are interpolated from point station prices for ease of visualisation.

exponentially with the distance between the ward centroid and the station, and also with price. The exponential fall off is traditional in SI models and well matched by many retailing examples [2]. Equation (2) ensures that the total volume of each fuel sold to each ward equals the demand H_iF^m (the amount of fuel type m required by car owners in ward i per day). This gives the actual amount sold in each ward. β and λ are two coefficients which are usually determined by calibrating the model to real data.

$$\hat{S}_{ij}^{m} = \delta_{j}^{m} \exp\left[-\beta d_{ij} - \lambda p_{j}^{m}\right] \tag{1}$$

$$S_{ij}^{m} = \frac{\hat{S}_{ij}^{m}}{\Sigma_{j}\hat{S}_{ij}^{m}} H_{i} F^{m} \tag{2}$$

where:

- S_{ij}^{m} is the amount of fuel m sold by station j to ward i.
- δ_{j}^{m} is 1 where station j sells fuel m and 0 otherwise.
- d_{ij} is the distance between ward i and station j.
- p_{j}^{m} is the price of fuel m at station j.
- H_{i} is the number of households within the ward i.
- F^{m} is the amount of fuel of type m required per car per day.

This model assumes that the monetary costs of collecting the fuel are of no significance to the customer - this is reasonable as people are rarely driving just to get petrol.

Interactions between the agent model and SI model can be summarised as:

- The agent model and population are initialised with the real data.
- The fuel price and station location data is passed to the SI model.
- The SI model calculates fuel sales for each station and passes the information to them.
- The stations use this information to choose the rules to implement based on their profitability.
- Each agent calculates its new price and the simulation returns to step 3 until equilibrium or a set time limit is reached.

Figure 4 shows that the hybrid model performs slightly better than naive agent model after the latter has reached equilibrium. Given a constant price surface, this model can generate the known geographical variations and patterns within the real data better than the agent model (Figure 3(c) and (b)). Additionally, this model has a sounder theoretical basis than the agent model with each station reacting competitively to consumer actions.

6 Network-Hybrid Model

The SI model clearly models the dynamics of the system well, but suffers from having an over-simplified notion of when people buy fuel. Most people tend to buy fuel on the way to somewhere [12] and, in most cases, this will be on the way to work. The hybrid model, however, represents people who travel directly from home to the nearest petrol station where fuel is cheap. To rectify

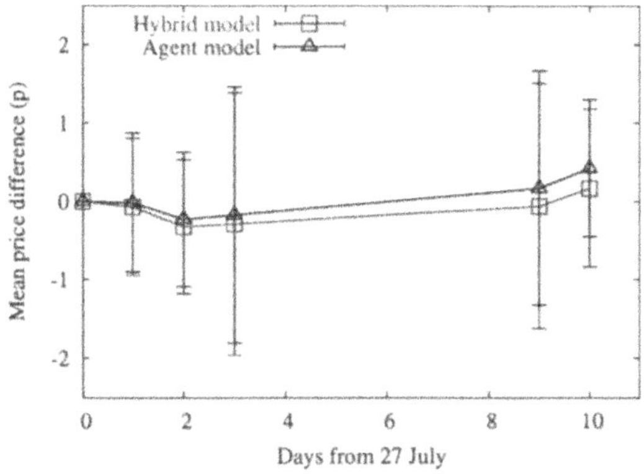

Fig. 4. Comparison of the mean price difference over time (SD is indicated by the vertical bars) for the agent and hybrid model for West Yorkshire (Model initiated on July 27th).

this disparity, a network model was added. The purpose of this model was to reallocate people to wards on the basis of non-cascading travel to work data (derived from UK Census data). An algorithm was required to calculate an optimal route between the origin and destination of the consumer. This classic shortest path problem was solved using Dijkstra's Algorithm. In this example, the shortest distance through the intervening network of wards for each set of ward-to-ward movements was calculated. Car users were then redistributed to the home, destination and intervening wards evenly.

In order to re-distribute the population around West Yorkshire using Dijkstra's algorithm and simple graph theory, nodes and edges have to be established. The nodes can be represented by the population weighted centroids and connections between neighbouring wards can be represented by weighted edges (Figure 5). The weights represent the distance between neighbouring nodes.

The basic network model is run before any of the interactions between the agent and spatial interaction model take place. The shortest path between each pair of wards is calculated. Each route in the journey to work data is taken as the shortest path between the start and end wards. The model takes each route in the journey to work data and redistributes the people from the origin ward equally amongst each ward the route passes through. This creates a redistributed population surface that is fed to the spatial interaction model. The network model is not used again during the course of the simulation.

What effect has running this network model had on the performance of the hybrid model? The distribution of consumers before and after the application of the networking was calculated (Figure 6). Figure 6 (a) clearly shows that before the networking was applied, high densities of consumers were found

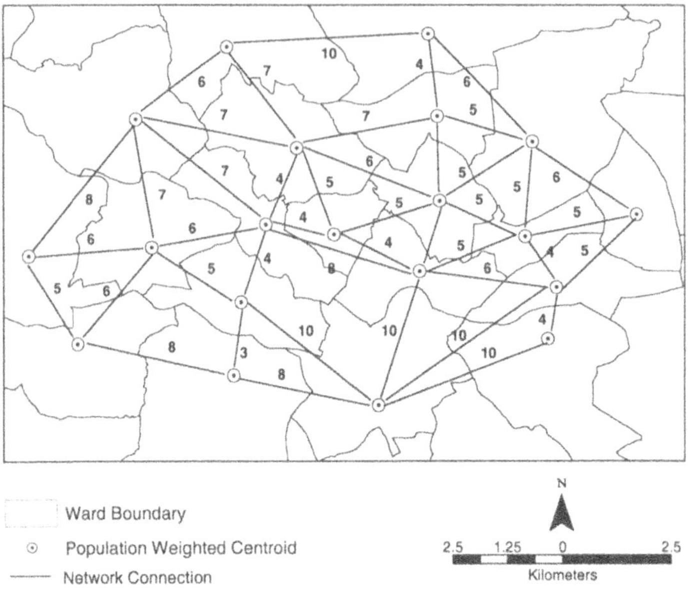

Fig. 5. Example of a weighted graph network.

predominately in the centre of the study area. This area covers the West Yorkshire conurbation of Leeds, Bradford, Wakefield, Huddersfield and Halifax. In the suburban areas of Leeds and Bradford, the density of consumers is at its highest. After the networking has been applied (Figure 6 (b)), all of the city areas, not just the suburbs are characterised by having an even higher density of consumers. This increase in population within the city centres is simply a reflection of the number of people who live within the suburbs, but work in the cities.

This new population is fed into the SI model. Future work will use petrol journey data to weight the home populations of the simple hybrid model against these new travelling populations appropriately. For now we present the initial results of a purely travelling population.

The averaged results using the network hybrid model (Figure 7) are almost identical to that of the hybrid model. However, the network hybrid model is much better than either of the other models at generating the geographical variation in the data, convincingly generating the observed rural-urban differences in price (see Figure 3 (c) and (d)).

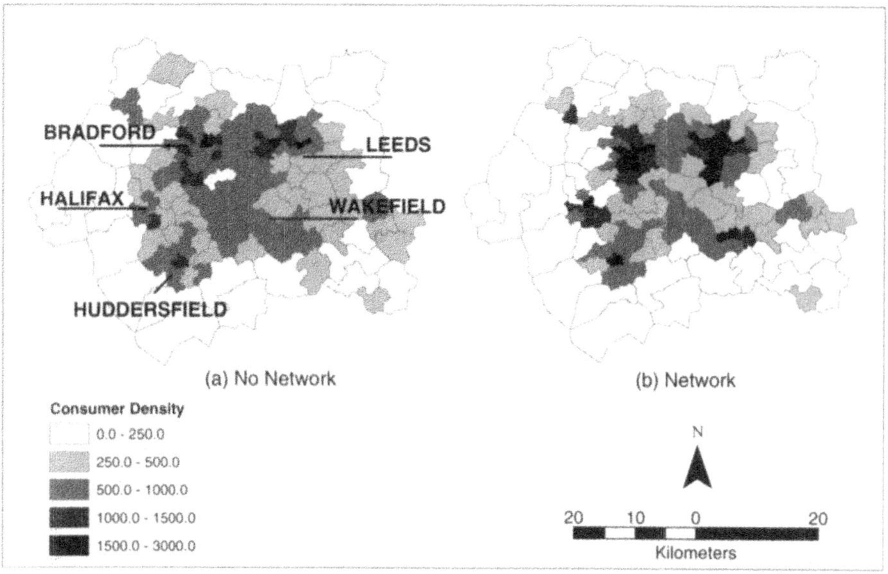

Fig. 6. Distribution of consumer density before (a) and after (b) application of the networking.

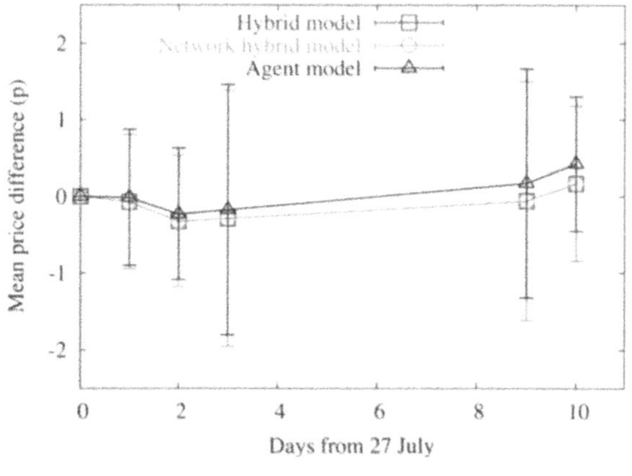

Fig. 7. Comparison of (a) the mean price difference over time (SD is indicated by the vertical bars) for the agent, hybrid and network hybrid model for West Yorkshire (Model initiated on July 27th).

7 Conclusions

In this paper we have presented two hybrid agent based models of a petrol market. These models were found to outperform a naive agent model that did not account for important customer movement behaviour. Despite the good performance of the hybrid models, further experimentation with the assignment of different rules to individual brands is required to reproduce the interactions that occur within real markets. Multi-agent systems provide an ideal framework in which a retail market can be accurately described. Individual agents (petrol stations) can be successfully supplied with detailed knowledge of the market by the attachment of more specialised models, such as spatial interaction models. This type of model can be extremely valuable when modelling trends at a regional level. The outcome of local interactions can be easily seen at a global level and behavioural and quantitative data can be easily combined. This flexibility, coupled with the upsurge in readily available computing power makes agent based modelling a valuable tool for studying market forces and dynamics.

8 Acknowledgements

The work reported within this paper is funded by the Economic and Social Research Council and GMap. All digitised boundary data are UK Crown and ED-Line Copyright. The Network Model components were developed during an exchange visit to The GeoVista Center funded by the Worldwide Universities Network.

References

[1] R.W. Bacon. Rockets and feathers: the asymmetrical speed of adjustment of UK retail gasoline prices to cost changes. *Energy Econ*, 1:211 - 218, 1991.

[2] M. Birkin and G. Clarke, editors. *Intelligent GIS.* Geoinformation International, Cambridge, 1st edition, 1996.

[3] M. Birkin, G. Clarke, and M. Clarke, editors. *Retail Geography and Intelligent Network Planning.* Wiley, 1st edition, 2002.

[4] R. Castanias and H. Johnson. Gas wars: Retail gasoline price fluctuations. *The Review of Economics and Statistics*, 75:171 - 174, 1993.

[5] A. Eckert. Retail price cycles and response asymmetry. *Canadian Journal of Economics*, 35:52 - 77, 2002.

[6] A. Eckert. Retail price cycles and the presence of small firms. *International Journal of Industrial Organisation*, 21:151 - 170, 2003.

[7] M. Galoetti, A. Lanza, and M. Manera. Rockets and feathers revisited: an international comparison on european gasoline markets. *Energy Economics*, 25:175 - 190, 2003.

[8] A.J. Heppenstall, A.J. Evans, and M.H. Birkin. A hybrid multi-agent/spatial interaction model system for petrol price setting. *Transactions in GIS*, 9(1):35–51, 2005.

[9] D. N. Manning. Petrol prices, oil price rises and oil price falls: Evidence for the UK since 1972. *Applied Economics*, 23:1535 – 1541, 1991.

[10] J. D. Mitchell, L. L. Ong, and H. Y. Izan. Idiosyncrasies in Australian petrol price behaviour: Evidence of seasonalities. *Energy Economics*, 28: 243 – 258, 2000.

[11] M. Noel. *Edgeworth Price Cycles in Retail Gas Markets*. PhD thesis, MIT, 2002.

[12] P. S. Plummer, E. Sheppard, and R. P. Haining. Modeling spatial price competition: Marxian versus neoclassical approaches. *Annals of the American Association of Geographers*, 88(4):575 – 594, 1998.

[13] B. Reilly and R. Witt. Petrol price asymmetries revisted. *Energy Economics*, 20:297 – 308, 1998.

[14] D. Shin. Do petrol prices respond symmetrically to changes in crude oil prices? *OPEC Review*, 18:137 – 157, 1994.

A Study on Pareto Optimality of Walrasian Virtual Market

Toshiya Kaihara and Susumu Fujii

Department of Computer and Systems Engineering, Kobe University, 1-1, Rokko-dai, Nada, Kobe, 657-8501, Japan, **{kaihara, fujii}@cs.kobe-u.ac.jp**

Summary. Conventional supply chain management (SCM) is not always concerned with optimal solutions in terms of product allocation. Virtual market based supply chain operation solves the product allocation problem by distributing the scheduled resources according to the market prices, which define common scale of value across the various products. We formulate supply chain model as a discrete resource allocation problem, and demonstrate the applicability of the Walrasian virtual market concept with multi-agent paradigm to this framework. In this paper we demonstrate the proposed algorithm successfully calculates Pareto optimal solutions in the supply chain product allocation problem by comparing our method with conventional analytic approaches, such as ε constraint method and fixed point algorithm.

Key words. Supply chain management, Market-oriented programming, Walrasian general equilibrium theory, Multi-Agent programming, Microeconomics

1. Introduction

Market price systems constitute a well-understood class of mechanisms that provide effective decentralisation of decision making with minimal communication overhead. In a market-oriented programming approach to distributed problem solving, the resource allocation for a set of computational agents is derived by computing competitive equilibrium of an artificial economy [1][2]. Market mechanism can provide several advantages on resource allocation as follows:

- Markets are naturally distributed and agents make their own decisions about how to bid based on the prices and their own utilities of the goods.
- Communication is limited to the exchange of bids and process between agents and the market mechanism.

In this paper we formulate agent strategies in resource allocation problem, based on virtual market concept, and demonstrate the proposed virtual market successfully calculates Pareto optimal solutions in resource allocation problem by comparing our method with conventional analytic approaches, such as ε constraint method and fixed point algorithm.

2. Walrasian Virtual Market

2.1 Walrasian Market

There are several types of market defined in Economics, and Walrasian market, which was originally proposed in Microeconomics [3], is one of the most well-known markets. In the Walrasian market of general equilibrium, where it is assumed that the relevant supply and demand conditions are known and all markets are cleared at equilibrium prices, it superficially appears as if a "market" outcome and a "planned" outcome are interchangeable with each other. In the Walrasian market, the following fundamental theorem of welfare economics has been proved:

- In a market economy, any competitive equilibrium is Pareto optimal
- Any Pareto optimal allocation can be implemented as a competitive equilibrium for some set of initial endowments

According to the theorem, the resource allocation in the Walrasian market is Pareto optimal. If we can apply this characteristic into resource allocation problem, optimised resource allocation could be realised, and that looks quite attractive.

2.2 Virtual Market (VM)

There exists a market-oriented programming to construct a computational market (i. e. virtual market), which consists of several heterogeneous agents [1]. Agent activities in terms of products required and supplied are defined so as to reduce an agent's decision problem to evaluate the tradeoffs of acquiring different products in the market-oriented programming. These tradeoffs are represented in terms of market prices, which define common scale of value across the various products. The problem for designers of computational markets is to specify the mechanism by which agent interactions determine prices.

Market-oriented programming is the general approach of deriving solutions to distributed resource allocation problems by computing the competitive equilibrium of an artificial economy. It involves an iterative adjustment of prices based on the reactions of the agent in the market. Definitions of the virtual market are based on general equilibrium concept in perfect competitive market, and that means it satisfies a necessary condition of Walrasian type virtual market. The algorithm of the proposed market-oriented programming is shown as follows:

Step1: A demand agent sends bids to a market to indicate its willingness to buy the resource according to its current price. The demand agent willingness is defined as a demand function in the bid message. The agent can send bids to the market within the limits of its domestic budget. Each resource has its own market, and they construct a competitive market mechanism as a whole.

Step2: A supply agent sends bids to the market to indicate its willingness to sell the resource according to its current price. The supply agent willingness is defined as a supply function in the bid message. The agent can send bids to the market within the limits of its current inventory level.

Step3: The market in resource sums up supply functions and demand functions, then revises balanced price of the resource. All the market must revise their balanced price via the same process.

Step4: Check the balanced prices of all the resources and if all the prices are fully converged, the acquired set of the prices is regarded as equilibrium price, then go to Step5. If not, go to Step1.

Step5: If dealing time is up, then stop. And if not, go to Step1.

3. Agent Definition

We describe consumers (i.e. demanders) as c_m ($m = 1,2,\ldots,M$), and producers (i.e. supplier) as s_n ($n = 1,2,\ldots,N$). The number of kind of goods is assumed as I in our Walrasian VM.

3.1 Demand Agent

Suppose demand agent c_m has utility function u^{c_m}, which is described with in equation (1). In this equation $x_i^{c_m}$ represents the demand quantity for resource i:

$$u^{c_m} = a^{c_m} \prod_{i=1}^{I} (x_i^{c_m})^{b_i^{c_m}} \quad \text{where} \quad \sum_{i=1}^{I} b_i^{c_m} = 1 \qquad (0 < a^{c_m}, b_i^{c_m}) \tag{1}$$

In this paper we adopt Cobb-Douglas function [3] as a demand function described in equation (1), because the Cobb-Douglas function is one of the primitive functions in microeconomics, which handles economical scale in the market by index constant b.

Budget of demand agent c_m is formulated by initial quantity of resource (i) : $e_i^{c_m}$, and their price: p_i as follows:

$$B^{c_m} = \sum_{i=1}^{I} p_i e_i^{c_m} + r^{c_m} \tag{2}$$

In this equation r^{c_m} represents supplier's profit, which suppliers return to demanders under zero-profit conditions in the general equilibrium theory.

Demand agents send their bid to their target resources in the market, and the bid is formulated as demand function. The function is obtained as the optimal solution as maximising problem of equation (1) under the constraints described in (2) (i.e. nonlinear programming). The following demand function is calculated by Lagrange's method of (indeterminate) multiplier in this research.

$$x_i^{c_m}(p_i) = \frac{b_i^{c_m} B^{c_m}}{p_i} \qquad (i = 1,\ldots,I) \tag{3}$$

We assume demander c_m supplies all the initial resources into the market according to the principle of microeconomics, and demander's supply function of resource j is defined as follows:

$$y_j^{c_m} = e_j^{c_m} \tag{4}$$

3.2 Supply Agent

As described in demand agent definitions, Cobb-Douglas function is a basic function which handles economical scale in the market easily. In micro-economics production function is assumed to be convex function, and that means market prices are established at a predictable level in the general equilibrium theory in convex shape production function.

We also formulate production function of supply agent s_n to resource j as Cobb-Douglas function to satisfy the assumption, shown as equation (5). Cobb-Douglas function is defined as a convex function in 0< β <1 in this equation.

$$y_j^{s_n} = \alpha^{s_n}(x_j^{s_n})^{\beta^{s_n}} \qquad (0 < \alpha^{s_n}, 0 < \beta^{s_n} < 1) \tag{5}$$

According to microeconomics assumption, supply agents have no initial resources. They can earn their profit π^{s_n} by producing value added resources from purchased resources. The profit function is defined as follows:

$$\pi^{s_n} = p_j y_j^{s_n} - p_i x_i^{s_n} \tag{6}$$

Supply agents send supply functions to production resources, and demand functions to purchase resources, respectively. They maximise their profit by solving maximising problem of equation (6) under the constraint in equation (5) (i.e. nonlinear programming). We also solve the problem by Lagrange's method of multiplier in this research, and obtain the following demand function and supply function in equation (7) and (8), respectively:

$$x_i^{s_n}(p_i) = \left(\frac{p_i}{\alpha^{s_n}\beta^{s_n}p_j}\right)^{\frac{1}{\beta^{s_n}-1}} \tag{7}$$

$$y_j^{s_n}(p_j) = \left(\frac{p_i^{\beta^{s_n}}}{\alpha^{s_n}(\beta^{s_n})^{\beta^{s_n}}p_j^{\beta^{s_n}}}\right)^{\frac{1}{\beta^{s_n}-1}} \tag{8}$$

4. Analytical Method

We demonstrate the proposed algorithm successfully calculates Pareto optimal solutions by comparing VM solutions with analytic approaches, such as ε constraint method and fixed-point algorithm. We will explain these approaches briefly below.

4.1 ε Constraint Method

The ε constraint method transforms the multi-objective problem into a single-objective optimisation problem by replace objective functions into scalarised inequality constraints.

Suppose there are multiple objective functions $f_1,\ldots,f_q$, and it has been proved that the solution of the following problem satisfies Pareto optimality by ε constraint method:

$$\begin{aligned} &\max\ f_q(x) \\ &s.t. \quad f_i(x) \le \varepsilon_i \qquad i = 1,\ldots,q-1 \\ &\qquad\quad x \in X = \{x \in R^n \mid g(x) \le 0\} \end{aligned} \tag{9}$$

where $\varepsilon = (\varepsilon_1,\ldots,\varepsilon_{q-1}) \in R^{q-1}$

We can use this method to validate the optimality of the equilibrium solution in Walrasian VM.

4.2 Fixed Point Algorithm

Scarf showed that how to compute an approximate Walras equilibrium and proposed a general algorithm for the calculation of a fixed point of a correspondence. This algorithm, named Scarf's algorithm, has been surprisingly efficient to find a general equilibrium that was guaranteed to converge, though does not permit a gradual improvement in the degree of approximation of the solution [4]. In equilibrium point the desired net trades of the two individuals at the equilibrium price ratio balance and the market excess demand functions for the two goods are zero. Computing general equilibria thus implies finding a set of prices corresponding to zero market excess demands for both goods. Although this procedure may work for simple two-commodity markets, difficulties can easily arise for higher-dimensional cases. There are no guarantees that such procedures will converge because the excess demand functions may have local inflection points, changing in slope, or both. Thus, determining prices corresponding to zero excess demands is usually complex.

The Scarf's algorithm applies a procedure to the problem of computing a fixed point of mapping of the unit simples into itself, a mapping whose existence is established by fixed point theorem. In using Scarf's algorithm to find such a fixed point, the unit simplex is divided into a finite number of smaller simplices, each defined by I vertices that are each associated with a label. Each vertex is labelled with the index number of goods, which has the maximum value in market excess demand. The market excess demand of goods i at the vertex is defined as the next equation.

$$E_i = \left(\sum_{m=1}^{M} x_i^{c_m} + \sum_{n=1}^{N} x_i^{s_n}\right) - \left(\sum_{m=1}^{M} y_i^{c_m} + \sum_{n=1}^{N} y_i^{s_n}\right) \tag{10}$$

The algorithm operates by moving through adjacent simplices, deleting and adding vertices. The starting point and each continuation step in the algorithm are such that, prior to finding an approximate equilibria, the algorithm always considers simplices whose verticles have all but one label present, with one label appearing as a duplicate. The procedure involves deleting a vertex with a duplicate label and replacing it with a new vertex, and it then moves to an adjacent simplex. The replacement procedure is such that no simplex once examined can ever be returned to. Because of the finiteness of the number of simplices, and the inability to terminate the procedure other than at a close approximation to an equilibrium, the procedure is guaranteed to find an approximation to an equilibrium. In the limiting process where the number of simplices considered becomes infinite, this approximation will be exact. A point-to-point mapping corresponds to the case in which the Brower fixed point theorem applies [5].

5. Experimental Results

We consider 3 types of basic market models with 2 kinds of goods so as to clarify the Pareto optimality of Walrasian VM.

1) 2-consumer market
2) 2-producer market
3) 2-consumer, 2-producer market

We construct the Walrasian VM models in computer and analyse its dynamic characteristics by computer simulation experiments. We also try to validate our methodology by comparing VM solutions with analytic approaches in converged prices of market goods. Finally we clarify the effectiveness of the proposed approach in terms of Pareto optimality and calculation time.

5.1 2-Consumer Market

Experimental 2-consumer-2-goods market (model 1) is illustrated in figure 1. There exist 2 consumers with 2 kinds of goods in this market model. Consumer agents send their bids to each goods based on their utilities defined in equation (3) and (4).

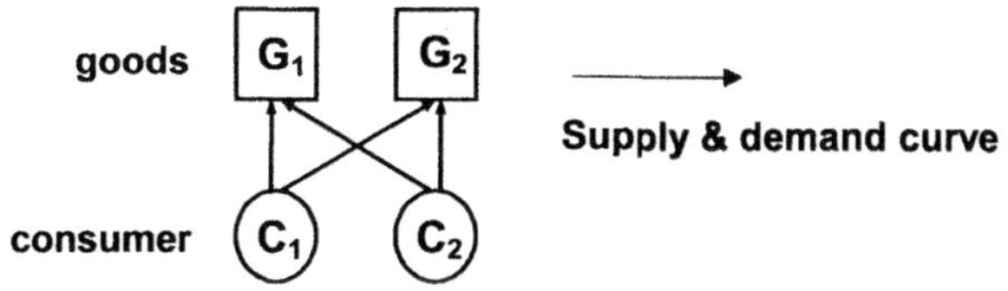

Fig. 1. 2-consumer market

Experimental values of each parameter (i.e. initial value set) in the model are shown in table 1. According to utility functions in the table, it is obvious that consumer agent 1 has the preference to goods 2 despite its smaller endowment at initial state in this example. Agent 2 has no preference to both goods in unbalanced initial endowment. That is why the initial utility of Agent 1 is lower than the one of the other.

Table 1. Parameters in model 1

Agent	Utility function (u^{c_m})	Initial endowment ($e_1^{c_m}, e_2^{c_m}$)	Initial utility
1	$1.0(x_1^{c_1})^{0.3}(x_2^{c_1})^{0.7}$	(30.0, 10.0)	13.90
2	$1.0(x_1^{c_2})^{0.5}(x_2^{c_2})^{0.5}$	(20.0, 40.0)	28.28

Simulation results on price and trade changes of goods 1 in this 2-consumers Walrasian VM are shown in Fig. 2 (a) and 2 (b), respectively. Horizontal axis represents the iteration number of calculation (i.e. step) to acquire equilibrium point.

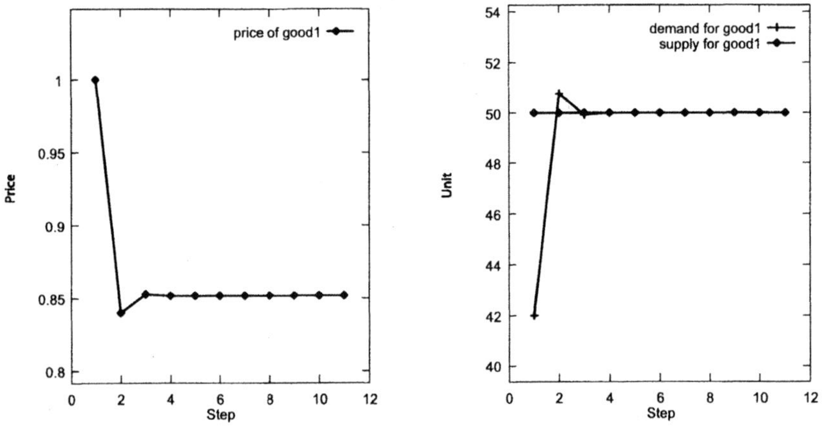

Fig. 2. Price and trade convergence

In Fig. 2 (a) it is shown that goods 1 is in excess supply at step 1, and that causes sharp price down at the next step (step 2) in Fig. 2 (a). Then goods 1 faces small excess demand situation at step 2 as a rebound of step 1, and price recovers accordingly. In a few step supply gradually meets demand, and price is converged into equilibrium by such an adjustment mechanism. We obtained equilibrium price vector $\hat{p} = (\hat{p}_1, \hat{p}_2)$ as follows:

Equilibrium price vector	$\hat{p} = (0.85185, 1.14815)$
Normalised equilibrium price vector	$\hat{p} = (0.42593, 0.57407)$

And final resource allocation in this experiment is illustrated in table 2. It has been observed that the total utility of agents increases in the equilibrium price from the comparison of table 1 and 2.

Table 2. Resource allocation in model 1

Agent	Consumption $(x_1^{c_m}, x_2^{c_m})$	Utility
c_1	(13.04, 22.58)	19.15
c_2	(36.96, 27.42)	31.83

We applied ε constraint method in this market model to confirm Pareto optimality of the VM solutions. Suppose the utility of consumer 2 has upper limit at $\overline{u}^{c_2}$, and replace utility function of consumer 2 into inequality constraint. Then the original problem is transformed into the maximise problem of utility of consumer 1 as follows:

$$\begin{aligned} &\max \quad u^{c_1} \\ &s.t. \quad u^{c_2} \le \overline{u}^{c_2} \\ &x_i^{c_1} + x_i^{c_2} = e_i^{c_1} + e_i^{c_2} \qquad i = 1,2 \end{aligned} \tag{11}$$

When we solve the problem, then we have the following equation:

$$\frac{b_1^{c_1} x_2^{c_1}}{b_2^{c_1} x_1^{c_1}} = \frac{b_1^{c_2} x_2^{c_2}}{b_2^{c_2} x_1^{c_2}} \tag{12}$$

If we input the acquired value in table 2 into equation (12), the left side and the right side are completely equivalent as 0.7419, and that means the acquired values from Walrasian VM satisfy the equation successfully. Then it has been confirmed that the equilibrium solution in Walrasian VM is a Pareto optimal in resource allocation problem.

Table 3. Final consumption

$(e_1^{c_1}, e_2^{c_1})$	$(e_1^{c_2}, e_2^{c_2})$	$(x_1^{c_1}, x_2^{c_1})$	$(x_1^{c_2}, x_2^{c_2})$
(0, 0)	(50, 50)	(0.0, 0.0)	(50.0, 50.0)
(10, 10)	(40, 40)	(6.5, 13.0)	(43.5, 37.0)
(0, 20)	(50, 30)	(7.1, 14.0)	(42.9, 36.0)
(20, 10)	(30, 40)	(9.8, 18.1)	(40.2, 31.9)
(40, 0)	(10, 50)	(12.0, 21.2)	(38.0, 27.8)
(30, 20)	(20, 30)	(17.9, 28.2)	(32.1, 21.8)
(10, 40)	(40, 10)	(22.1, 32.4)	(27.9, 17.6)
(40, 30)	(10, 20)	(27.6, 37.1)	(22.4, 12.9)
(30, 40)	(20, 10)	(30.9, 39.5)	(19.1, 10.5)
(50, 30)	(0, 20)	(31.6, 40.0)	(18.4, 10.0)
(20, 50)	(30, 0)	(35.0, 42.2)	(15.0, 7.8)
(50, 50)	(0, 0)	(50.0, 50.0)	(0.0, 0.0)

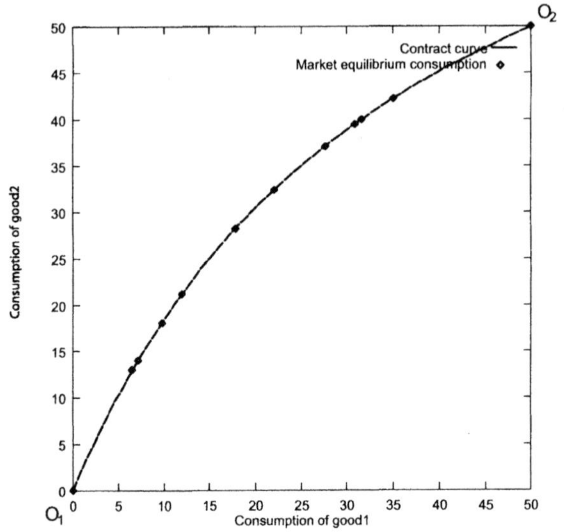

Fig. 3. Edgeworth box diagram-1

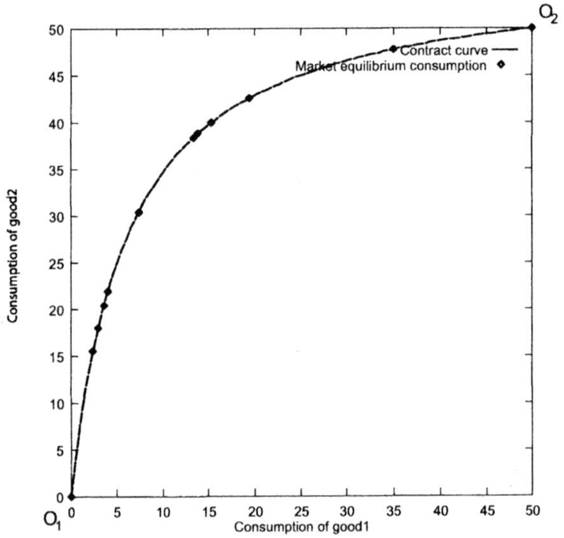

Fig. 4. Edgeworth box diagram-2

We investigate the relationship between initial endowment and final consumption under constant total resource amount for each goods, (50, 50), in our VM. Simulation results are shown in table 3. We plot each point of consumption in table 3 into Fig. 3. Contract curve in Fig. 3 is drawn as the solution set attained by ε constraint method in this experiment, and this figure is named as Edgeworth box diagram in microeconomics. It has been confirmed that the equilibrium solutions by VM are completely plotted on the contract curve, and they are Pareto optimal solutions perfectly.

Finally we investigated the influence of utility change into equilibrium solution in the next experiment. Utility function of consumer agent c_1 is modified to $u^{c_1} = 1.0(x_1^{c_1})^{0.1}(x_2^{c_1})^{0.9}$, and the agent has stronger preference to goods 2 then. Fig.4 shows the simulation results on final consumption correspond to Fig.3 in the original parameter.

Contract curve is sharper in Fig.4, because the goods 2 consumption of agent 1 increased according to the stronger preference to the goods. This result perfectly satisfies the theoretical trends in microeconomics.

5.2 2-producer market

Experimental 2-producer-2-goods market (model 2) is illustrated in Fig. 5 Because there is no resource supplement and consumption in 2-producer market, we introduced external supply & demand functions in this model. The parameters in the external functions are listed in table 4. Suppose both the producers, S1 and S2, transform resource 1 into resource 2 in this model. Initial parameter set in the model is shown in table 5.

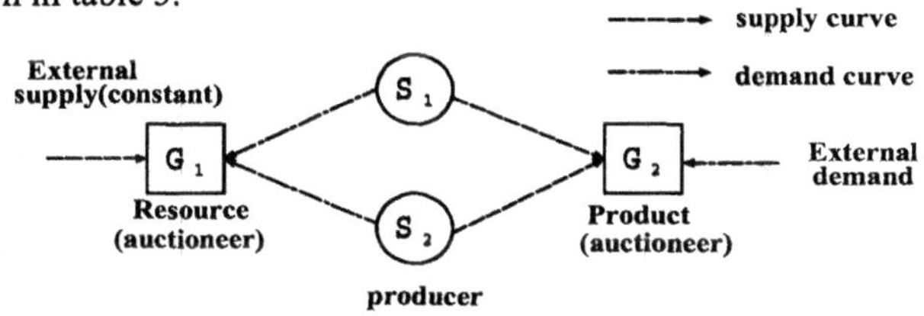

Fig. 5. 2-producer market

Table 4. External functions

External supply function	External demand function
$y_1^{ext} = 500\ (const.)$	$x_2^{ext} = 1.0 p_2^{-2.0}$

Table 5. Parameters in model 2

Agent	Input	Output	Production function
1	goods 1	goods 2	$y_2^{s_1} = 2.0(x_1^{s_1})^{0.7}$
2	goods 1	goods 2	$y_2^{s_2} = 3.0(x_1^{s_2})^{0.5}$

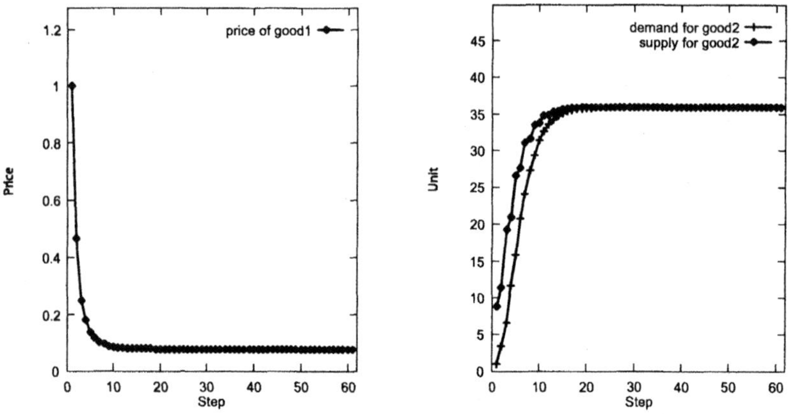

Fig. 6. Price and trade convergence

In this model we obtained equilibrium price vector $\hat{p} = (\hat{p}_1, \hat{p}_2)$ as follows:

Equilibrium price vector $\hat{p} = (0.07747, 0.16680)$

Normalised equilibrium price vector $\hat{p} = (0.31714, 0.68286)$

And final resource allocation in this experiment is illustrated in table 6.

Table 6. Resource allocation in model 2

Agent	Consumption	Production	Profit
s_1	39.57	26.25	1.31
s_2	10.43	9.69	0.81

Since the optimal production in this 2-producer market must maximise its yields, we consider the following maximising problem:

$$max \qquad y_2^{s_1} + y_2^{s_2} \tag{13}$$

It is obvious that the production function of each producer agent is convex in table 5, and the yields should be maximised at the inflection point. Then we obtain the following equation at the maximised point.

$$\frac{dy_2^{s_1}}{dx_1^{s_1}} = \frac{dy_2^{s_2}}{dx_1^{s_2}} \tag{14}$$

If we input the acquired value in table 6 into equation (14), the left side and the right side are completely equivalent as 0.4644, and that means the acquired values from Walrasian VM satisfy the equation successfully. Then it has been confirmed that the equilibrium solution is optimal in resource allocation problem in 2-producer Walrasian market model.

5.2 2-consumer 2-producer market

Experimental 2-producer-2-consumer market (model 3) is illustrated in Fig. 7. In this market 2 kinds of goods, goods 1 and goods 2, are also traded.
Consumer agents send their bids as supply & demand functions to both the goods homogeneously. Producer agents send their demand & supply function to goods 1 & goods 2, respectively. That means they both produce goods 2 from goods 1 in this market. This market has the equivalent initial set of experimental parameters to table 1 and 5. Simulation results on price and trade changes of goods 1 in the 2-consumer-2-producer Walrasian VM are shown in Fig. 8(a) and 8(b), respectively.

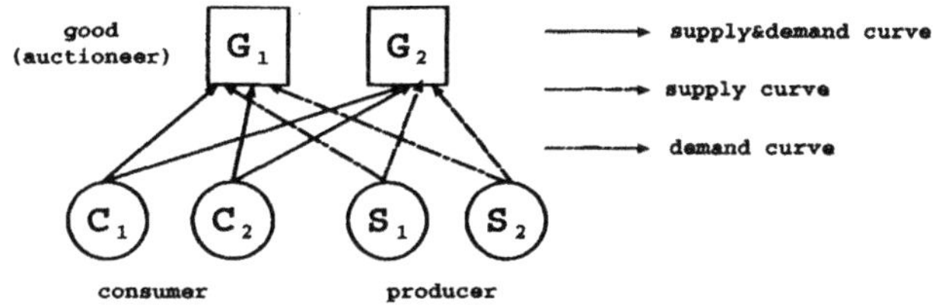

Fig. 7. 2-producer 2-consumer market

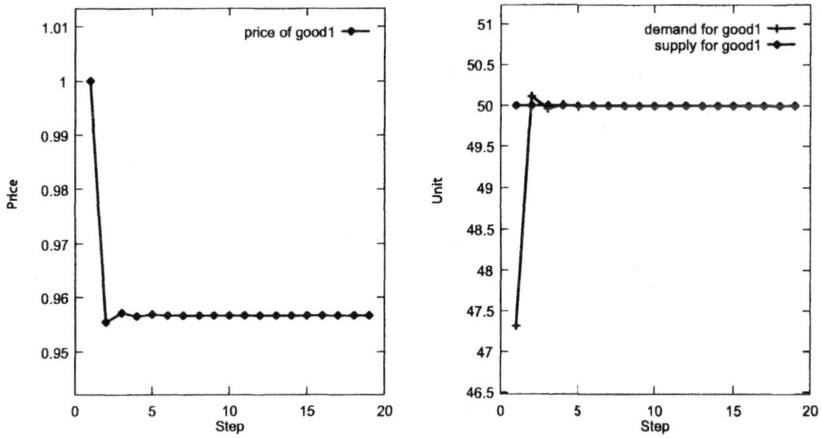

Fig. 8. Price and trade convergence

In this model we obtained equilibrium price vector $\hat{p} = (\hat{p}_1, \hat{p}_2)$ as follows:

Equilibrium price vector $\hat{p} = (0.95673, 0.98543)$

Normalised equilibrium price vector $\hat{p} = (0.49261, 0.50739)$

And final resource allocation in consumer agent and producer agent are shown in table 7 and 8, respectively. It is observed that the total consumer's utility is increased in table 7 compared with table 2, because the producer's profit is returned to consumer agents in this market under the zero-profit conditions in the general equilibrium theory. The utility of agent c_1 is increased by 17.2 % especially. That is because of the agent's preference to goods 2 as well as the zero-profit conditions. In this market all the producer agents supply goods 2, and that increases the utility of agent c_1. On the other hand, the utility of agent c_2 is slightly decreased, because it becomes slightly difficult to get both goods due to the stronger supply flow from producer agents to agent c_1.

Table 7 Resource allocation in model 3

Agent	Consumption $(x_1^{c_m}, x_2^{c_m})$	Utility
c_1	(12.67, 28.69)	22.45
c_2	(31.56, 30.64)	31.10

Table 8 Resource allocation in model 3

Agent	Consumption	Production	Profit
s_1	3.39	4.70	1.39
s_2	2.39	4.63	2.28

We applied fixed point algorithm in this market model to confirm Pareto optimality of the VM solutions. We calculated a fixed point of mapping of the unit simples into itself, a mapping whose existence is established by fixed point theorem. In using Scarf's algorithm to find such a fixed point, the unit simplex is divided into a finite number of smaller simplices (i.e. grid size). In this paper the grid size is set to 100,000 for the precise comparison.

We obtained equilibrium price vector $\hat{p} = (\hat{p}_1, \hat{p}_2)$ by the fixed point algorithm as follows:

Equilibrium price vector $\hat{p} = (0.49262, 0.50739)$

It is obvious that the equilibrium price set obtained by Walrasian VM is almost equivalent to the one from the fixed point algorithm, and that means VM solutions have been confirmed to be converged into Pareto optimal. The small difference is caused by the grid size of the fixed point algorithm.

We compared the calculation time between VM approach and fixed point algorithm. CPU consumption time (second) for each approach in this market model is as follows:

VM	: 0.0017 (sec.)
Fixed point algorithm	: 12.025 (sec.)

VM approach is obviously more than 7,000 times as fast as the analytic approach in this model. It has also been proved that the proposed VM based approach is much more practical in terms of calculation time to obtain Pareto optimal solutions in resource allocation problems.

6. Conclusions

We newly proposed a Walrasian Virtual Market (VM) approach for supply chain management (SCM) in this paper. Firstly we mentioned our general concept to apply resource allocation problems, and explained general idea of Walrasian market model in economics. Then one of multi-agent programming, named market-oriented programming, was focused and explained its negotiation process in the Walrasian market. After a brief explanation of several analytical approaches, we defined agent behaviour based on Walrasian market-oriented programming. As a basic study, we classified market model into 3 primitive types, and analysed each of them by computer simulation experiments. We obtained the following results:

- Walrasian VM successfully conducts Pareto optimal solutions in each market model
- The careful constructions of the decision process in our VM according to economic principles can lead to efficient resource allocations, and the behaviour of the VM can be analysed in economic terms
- Walrasian VM can take advantage of the market analogy into resource allocation problem, and that can lead to effective solution search mechanism both in optimality and calculation time

The contribution of the paper lies in the idea of resource allocation problems based on Walrasian market-oriented programming, an algorithm for distributed computation of competitive equilibria of computational economics, and an initial illustration of the approach on a simple market model. Effective resource allocationin global environment, such as manufacturing scheduling, supply chain and so on, is expected by this research.

References

1. Wellman M. P., A Market-Oriented Program-ming Environment and its Application to Distributed Multi- commodity Flow Problems, *ICMAS-96*, 1996, pp385-392.
2. Kaihara T., Supply Chain Management with Market Economics, *International Journal of Production Economics*, Elsevier Science, Vol. 73, Issue 1, 2001, pp.5-14.
3. Shoven J. B. and Whalley J., *Applying General Equilibrium*, Cambridge University Press, 1992.
4. Scarf, H. E., *The computing of Economics Equilibria*, New Heaven, Yale University Press, 1973.
5. Brouwer, L.E.J., *Collected Works 1. Philosophy and Foundations of Mathematics*, A. Heyting (ed.), North-Holland, 1975.

Coordination in rapidly evolving disaster response systems: the role of information

Louise K. Comfort [1], Kilkon Ko [1], and Adam Zagorecki [2]

[1]Graduate School of Public Administration, 3221 Wesley W. Posvar Hall, University of Pittsburgh, Pittsburgh, PA 15260, USA
[2]School of Information Sciences, IS Building B212, University of Pittsburgh, Pittsburgh, PA 15260, USA

Summary. Assessing the changing dynamic between the demand that is placed upon a community by cumulative exposure to hazards and the capacity of the community to mitigate or respond to that risk represents a central problem in estimating the community's resilience to disaster. We present an initial effort to simulate the dynamic between increasing demand and decreasing capacity in an actual disaster response system to determine the fragility of the system, or the point at which the system fails. The results show that access to core information enhances efficiency of response actions and increases coordination throughout the network of responding organizations

Keywords. Disaster management, networks, fragility, core information, multi-organizational response

Policy problem

The shock of severe disaster in a major city creates a cascade of disruption among interdependent operating systems that shatters the existing functional capacity of the wider metropolitan region (Comfort, 1999; Quarantelli, 1998). Failure in one operational system triggers failure in other interdependent systems of electrical power, communications, transportation, water, gas, and sewage distribution. Under severe threat, the operational capacity of a complex region staggers under spreading dysfunction, compounding failure and creating new dangers for the population.

In disaster response and recovery operations, the ratio of demand for assistance to capacity to provide resources varies over time. In the initial stages of disaster, immediate demands involve actions to protect lives and provide assistance to injured persons. First response organizations such as fire departments, emergency medical services, and police departments seek to meet urgent demands of disaster victims under tight time constraints. During the recovery period, issues of unemployment, sustainable business operations, housing, and medical care for

victims and their families emerge that require long-term consideration. Households and community organizations need appropriate resources to meet different needs in the distinct phases of disaster management: mitigation, preparedness, response, and recovery.
Theoretically, constructing a formal model to describe the dynamic relationship of demand to capacity in disaster operations is not easy. Different environments generate different types of demands that lead to the formation of different types of response patterns based upon different levels of capacity in the system. These variable conditions increase the complexity of the model. Complexity theory, based on discrete dynamics, reveals the power of self-organization embedded in complex systems. The interactions among agents who participate in response operations form a disaster response system that reveals a spontaneous order. Agent-based simulation enables us to model those interactions and to study the dynamics of a complex system (Prietula, Carley, and Gasser, 1998). Agent-based simulation is a technique that models a system based on agents' behavior and their interaction. While the initial definition of the system focuses on identifying the individual agents and their roles, the scope and order of the system emerges from the interactions among the participating agents. It is the interaction among the agents that defines the overall system properties. In this research, we test the applicability of a discrete dynamic modeling method, agent-based simulation, in a simulated disaster environment. We also emphasize the importance of identifying core information rather than the amount of information to be exchanged. Both social (Wasserman & Faust, 1994) and evolving network theories (Barabasi, 2002; Watts, 1999, 2003; Watts and Strogatz, 1998) are used to identify the structure of a disaster response network among organizations and the core information.

Disaster response and fragility

Model

When a major disaster occurs, it threatens the potential collapse of the interconnected sociotechnical system that provides technical, social, economic, and cultural services to a specific region or community. The disaster threatens not only the destruction of technical infrastructure such as power lines, roads, and communication lines, but also the social, organizational, and economic structures that support the daily operations of the community. The sociotechnical infrastructure in most communities is not a robust system, but rather a fragile, interdependent system that is sensitive to shocks and disruptions. In such systems, disruption triggers unexpected consequences and cascading failure. The actual environment of disaster is extraordinarily complex. In this preliminary research, we make four basic assumptions regarding the disaster environment and the relationships among agents participating in the disaster response system. These assumptions allow us to reduce the complexity of the disaster environment and explore a simple model between demand and capacity in a dynamic environment.

First, we develop our model for a discrete geographical space and legal jurisdiction exposed to risk. In an actual disaster, geographic and jurisdictional boundaries are not necessarily congruent. In our model, we introduce geographical and jurisdictional regions within a two-dimensional space, which could be expanded. Second, the interaction among agents engaged in disaster response operations and the patterns of communication among their internal components and between the agents and other external systems create the dynamics of the response process. We assume that the demand flow of disaster response actions depends on the initial magnitude of disaster, the degree of "cascade effect" or interdependence among potential or actual damaged parts, and the capacity flow among the participating agents based on their initial conditions of resources, knowledge, skills, and equipment. The initial magnitude of disaster is measured by factors such as physical severity, geographic location, and preparedness for disaster. Assessing the initial magnitude of disaster is necessarily a preliminary effort in uncertain conditions, and this estimate is likely to be revised repeatedly as more accurate information becomes available.

Estimating the cascade effect in any given disaster becomes a critical factor in assessing the demand for housing, sanitation, economic activities, telecommunication, psychological counseling, or other services. In routine operations, the components of the sociotechnical system are highly interconnected. Assessing the interdependence among organizations and systems in disaster operations makes the analysis of actual events very complex. In this simulation, we limit the number of interactions among the agents to two steps.

Third, the degree of coordination developed among agents also affects disaster operations. Disaster may shatter the existing socio-technical system, and rebuilding activities that reconnect components of the social and economic systems to the relevant technical systems through coordination are often more important than acquiring resources for the separate systems.

Finally, the type and quality of the initial disaster relief actions also affect the scope of demand over the period of recovery. Response to demand depends on the initial capacity of response agents, the inflow of additional resources from outside areas, and the burn-out rate of personnel engaged in disaster operations, or the rate at which individuals drop out of service voluntarily. By definition, disaster is an unexpected event that exceeds the normal capacity of a community to respond to adverse events. Each of these indicators can be measured and included in a dynamic computational model.

Within the above framework, individuals seek ways to assist victims and lessen damage. Their behavior depends heavily on the type and amount of information available, the degree of planning and preparedness in place prior to the event, the specific time, location, and magnitude of the incident, and the existing organizational resources or constraints. In theory, if responders have perfect information, they find victims and assist them immediately. However, in practice, rescue agents don't know exactly who needs what kinds of help in which locations. Thus, we initiate the simulation in a state of high uncertainty and observe the pattern of changes in the interaction among the agents by increasing the amounts of information and rationality available to the agents.

To test the model, we developed a simulation platform using an agent-based approach to describe the relation between demand for assistance and a community's capacity to provide disaster services. Agent-based simulation is not only easy to model, using discrete spatial dynamics, but it is also expandable, allowing the developer to include various types of behavior. It produces a complex pattern of interactions among multiple agents and allows researchers to observe the emergence of patterns. The cooperation process (Axelrod, 1997), description of demand and supply functions (Epstein & Axtell, 1996), and other models of complex systems use this method (Flake, 1998; Gaylord & D'Andria, 1998; Langton, 1994).

To construct the model, we simplified the problem situation of a disaster environment as follows:

First, we built a discrete two-dimensional, N by N, space which is divided by jurisdiction. The initial magnitude of the simulated disaster is annotated as C, and the number of damaged sites is N_d. We assign the initial demand to N_d randomly within the disaster space. The amount of resources required to meet demands at a damaged site is annotated as $D^t{}_{ij}$ which means that site i,j requires the amount of D resources at time t.

Second, a cascade effect is introduced to increase the demand for disaster services which, in turn, affects the capacity of the agents to reduce the demand. The relationship is formalized as:

$D^{t+1}{}_{ij} = (1+r)(D^t{}_{ij} - S^t{}_{ij})$, where r is the growth rate of demand coming from the cascade effect, and $S^t{}_{ij}$ is the supply of resources available to responding agents who are on site i,j at time t. Demand does not increase infinitely. For instance, the cost of rescuing injured victims does not exceed the cost of human life. Thus, we set a constraint for the maximum demand level.

Third, each agent occupies one cell and moves around the space looking for damaged sites. When agents find damaged sites, they allocate their resource capacity to restore the site. Based on these assumptions, the capacity of the agent on the site i,j at time t, $S^t{}_{ij}$, is defined as follows: $S^{t+1}{}_{ij} = (1+R)(S^t{}_{ij} - D^t{}_{ij})$, where R is the growth rate of capacity coming from outside help. If the agent's supply is smaller than the demand, $S^t{}_{ij} < D^t{}_{ij}$, we set $S^{t+1}{}_{ij} = 0$, and additionally introduce a time lag for an agent, which means that the agent is "frozen" for certain constant period of time (given as a constant beforehand).

Fourth, we follow the behavior rules for information search and movement defined by traditional agent-based simulation. We use the method attributed to Von Neumann and used by others in the simulation of complex systems (Epstein & Axtell, 1996; Gaylord & D'Andria, 1998; Wolfram, 1994) for designating movement of the agents among their near neighbors in the system. The search method is heuristic and assumes high uncertainty. No command and control mechanism is used to control agents.

Finally, we introduce a weak type of voluntary coordination. We assume that the jurisdiction with the highest surplus capacity dispatches its agent to the location that has the greatest need, or demand for services (Rawls, 1999). This process continues until either there are no surplus resources available or the demand is filled.

Findings

The graphs below present a simplified version of demand and capacity over time, interpreting capacity as available resources. In practice, capacity includes a dimension of organizational learning, but for this initial model, we simplify the term capacity to mean available resources. The initial magnitude of disaster is given 1,000 units, which implies that the disaster requires 1000 units of resources to relieve the damage at time t=1. These demands are randomly allocated to 40% of the region. The agents only have a capacity of 30% of the initial demand at time t=1. If agents determine the need and location of demand for damaged sites, they allocate their capacity for those sites and expend their resources but replenish their capacity at the rate R=0.02 at the beginning of each time period. In the real world, the amount of time from the identification of demand to replenishing the agents' capacity after aid is given differs according to region, organizations, and disaster types. In this paper, we assume 8 hours to be the unit of time for the simulation. The demand level decreases due to the agents' rescue activities, but also increases due to the cascade effect, estimated at the rate of r=0.01. The burn-out rate of agents is given a value of 5. Thus, agents who expend all resources will take a break and reactivate 40 hours later[1]. Using these assumptions, the basic patterns of demand and capacity are shown below.

Figure 1 shows that the demand and capacity levels are changed by the agents' response activities after disaster. The graph could be divided into three periods: Phase I, Phase II and Phase III. Phase I is the period from the starting point of disaster to the point where demand starts to decrease. In the initial period, from the first day to the 6th day, capacity gradually decreases as demand increases. This phenomenon occurs as agents expend their limited available resources to meet increasing demand from the event. Within our model, after a specific period of time, t=39 days, capacity exceeds demand.

[1] The sensitivity of the parameter affects the level of demand and capacity but it does not significantly change the pattern. Also we assume a unit of simulation time = 8 hours, but it could vary according to disaster types, organization types and geographical characteristics.

Fig. 1. Demand and capacity changes over time[2]

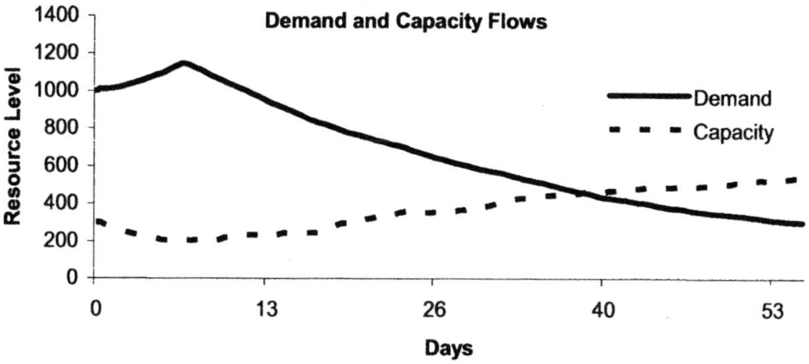

Phase II is the period from the end of Phase I to the threshold point of change in the response system. At this stage, new resources enter disaster operations from outside the area, and other organizations join to help victims. The entrance of new organizations increases the difficulty of coordination in managing disaster response tasks as the operational relationships among first response organizations and new organizations need to be defined. As response operations evolve, these interactions need to be redefined for each succeeding situation. New types of demand that are not anticipated in planned response procedures are likely to emerge, and respondents need to redefine the situation and assess their activities within their changed environment. Collective learning and action are essential to facilitate coordinated action.

The spatial size of the disaster area (N) also influences the demand and capacity flow. If the disaster affects a wide geographical area, it will require more time for recovery. To check this hypothesis, we increased the size of disaster area, N, and observed that the length of time required to terminate demand also increased. We assume that one unit of geographical area = 1 km^2. Termination time is defined as the time when the demand level decreases to 10% of initial demand, and it is used in this model as a measure of the efficiency of response activities.

[2] We rescaled 3 units of simulation time, 24 hours, to one day in the figure.

Fig. 2. The effect of spatial size on duration of disaster response activities[3]

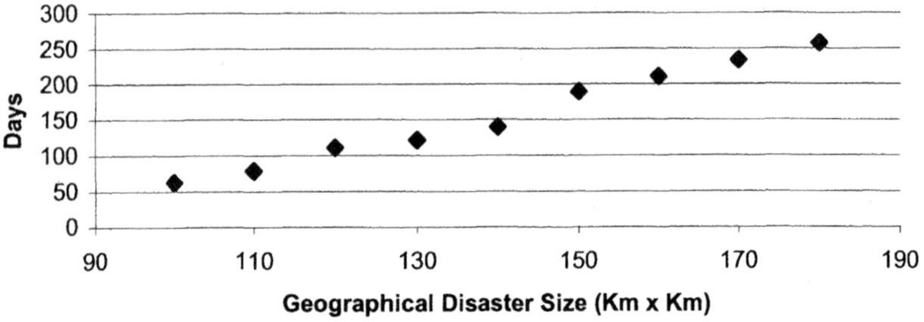

The above figure shows that as the size of the disaster area increases, the time needed to meet the demand also increases. If we divide the same spatial disaster area into multiple jurisdictions, it increases the efficiency of response activities. If relief teams affiliated with different jurisdictions have different command and control procedures, they may respond only to demands within their respective jurisdictions. We assume that each agent's activities are confined to his or her own region. We controlled the initial conditions such as scope of demand and capacity, area of disaster space, urgency of need, and divided the N by N disaster space according to the number of jurisdictions. Under a simulated disaster context, we calculated the termination time by increasing the number of jurisdictions participating in response operations.

Fig. 3. Duration of disaster response operations by number of jurisdictions[4]

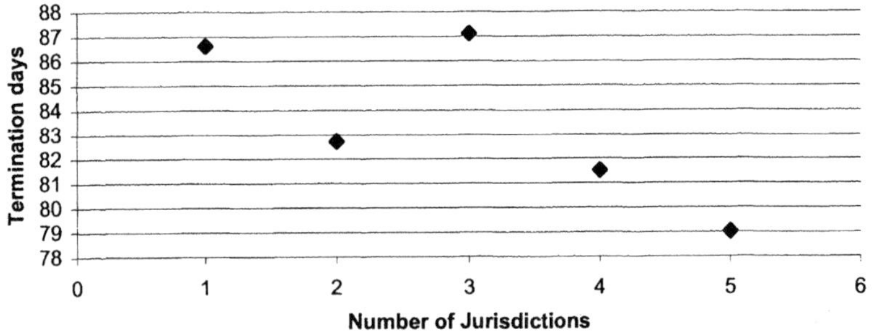

[3] We rescaled hours to days so that one day means three units of simulation time, 24hours. The numbers on X-axis represent square Km.; for instance 140 means 140 Km^2.
[4] Like figure 1 and figure 3, we rescale 3 units of simulation time to a day.

ANOVA analysis shows that the number of jurisdictions influences the termination time (F=169.9, p-value=0.0001). It implies a negative correlation between the number of jurisdictions and termination time. This finding suggests that smaller jurisdictions, operating as self organizing units, are more effective in managing recovery operations than a single, centralized authority for the region. The weak form of voluntary coordination among agents revealed no difference in increasing efficiency in allocating resources. The function of coordination will be explored further using more explicit conditions for action.

The role of core information in disaster response systems

Core information

Cooperation without information is not sufficient to increase response effectiveness. This argument raises two basic questions: 1) what kind of information is critical in response operations, and 2) how is the core information shared among agents or organizations? In this section, we show the importance of identifying and exchanging core information by means of simulation, network theory, and assumptions based on empirical data.

A common assumption in disaster management is that lack of information is the basic factor in limiting the efficiency of response among organizations, and significant efforts are being made to improve this capacity. The first scenario represents the absence of information about time and severity available to emergency responders, in which agents search for cells that need assistance and expend their resources when they find a demand. This strategy is called 'blind response.' The second scenario represents information available to agents based on time of demand, in which agents respond to demand on a "first come, first served' basis. This strategy is termed a time-based response and represents the general pattern of dispatching first responders immediately to emergency calls in practice.

In the third scenario, agents have access to information based on knowledge of time plus severity of the incident, but where severity is the dominant factor in determining action and allocating resources. This strategy is called 'severity-based response'. The three scenarios represent the relative importance of different strategies of action based on access to information regarding time and severity of the incident. These three scenarios are modeled with the following steps in an agent-based simulation.

This simulation framework is similar to the one previously discussed (see pp. 2-3), but differs in the following respects. First, we limited our second simulation to a single jurisdiction, so that the possible influence of cooperation would not interfere with the results. Second, we introduced demand throughout the whole period of the simulation rather than introducing all of the demand at the beginning. These conditions created a situation where the responding agents are operating in a simulated world in which they are unable to predict where or what future demand will be. Therefore, they can build their action plans only on the basis of information available at a given time. To make our simulation more realistic, the distribution of demand over time was sampled from an exponential distribution, based on an empirical analysis of the PEMA Morning Reports, June 1 – October 9, 2003[5]. The severity of the incidents was sampled from a uniform distribution.

As the first step in the simulation, we created a sequence of incidents (defined by time and severity) that would happen in the simulated world. The responding agents do not have access to this information, until an incident actually happens (at an earlier defined time). To model the influence of the information available to the responding agents, we learned that the amount of the information available to the agents should have been increased relative to the previous simulation setting. We achieved that effect by increasing the 'sight range' of the responding agents. In our simulations we used the fixed range of metro distance 2, which is equivalent to the square 5 by 5 (with the agent in the middle).

To identify the importance of the various types of information in the process of emergency response, we designed three different frameworks according to which the agents acted. The frameworks were defined as follows:

- Blind response. In this strategy, agents randomly select one demand site from the list of those available in their range. This behavior is exactly the same as that used in the previous simulation.
- Time-based search. A responding agent in this framework always selects the demand site that appears earliest on the list of sites within the agent's sight range. This framework corresponds to the strategy, 'first come, first served'.
- Severity-based search. In this framework, an agent selects a site from the available demand sites that has the greatest severity. This selection also includes knowledge of time.

Each of the three frameworks was placed in the same simulation setting and simulated multiple times to achieve meaningful results. For each simulation, we first created a series of incidents and assigned initial positions and amounts of resources for the responding agents. Then we used three copies of this setting to run simulations with the three different frameworks, ensuring that the initial conditions and the demand sequence was the same for each framework. This method allowed us to run what-if type of predictions.

We add one caveat regarding the interpretation of our findings. Because we placed a re-grow ratio in our simulation (which corresponds to increasing the scope of the accident over time if the demand has not been adequately met), such a framework most likely magnifies the differences between the three frameworks. Even though our intent was to build a model for an emergency response system, the results of the simulation should not be interpreted literally. That is, it should not be assumed that the information on severity is more important than the

---

[5] Pennsylvania Emergency Management Agency, "Morning Reports Summary", June 1 – Oct. 09, 2003, Harrisburg, PA.

information on time, but rather that there is an additive effect when information is available to agents on both time and severity.

As a measure of the efficiency of response, we used average demand for the time unit over the whole period of the simulation. We adjusted the parameters of the simulation in such way that the demand amount over time stayed on a flat level (with slight fluctuations). In other words, we wanted to have a system in which responding agents are constantly busy, but the global situation is under their control. Each of the three frameworks was run multiple times to make the results statistically significant. The findings show that the combination of information on time plus information on severity represents the "core information" for emergency managers. In Step 4, we repeated 300 simulations for each scenario to confirm the reliability of the results. The most effective scenario will maintain lower average demands during the disaster response period. The following table shows the simulation results for each scenario[6].

Table 1. Effectiveness of response actions by type of information strategy

Scenario Type	$\Lambda=0.14$	$\lambda=0.24$	$\Lambda=0.34$	$\lambda=0.44$	$\lambda=0.54$	Overall sample
Blind Response	8.36	8.5	8.33	8.46	8.19	8.37
Time-based Response	7.86	7.95	7.88	7.86	7.89	7.89
Severity-based Response	7.67	7.64	7.62	7.62	7.68	7.65

As observed, blind response in which agents have no information regarding time and severity is less effective than either time-based or severity-based response[7]. However, multiple comparisons of the three strategies using the Tukey-Kramer method[8] shows that the difference between time-based response and severity-based response is not statistically significant regardless of λ, although the paired t-test between time-based and severity-based response is statistically significant. These results indicate that blind search is the least effective strategy in comparison to the other two strategies. Further, severity-based response that includes information on time of incident is at least equally or more effective than time-based response alone. In practice, first responders are dispatched immediately to an incident based on the time-based rule, 'first come first served.' However, if coordinating organizations have access to information regarding the severity of the incident in addition to time, the allocation of scarce resources is more efficient.

Reviewing the simulation results, it is apparent that the relatively small size of the map used for the simulation may influence the efficiency of the outcome. If

[6] The initial size of two dimension map was given as a 20 by 20 lattice.

[7] The difference of means among three scenarios is statistically significant under the confidence level 95%.

[8] We used SAS V. 8e to perform Tukey-Kramer's multiple comparison.

agents have to search a wider area, it will likely affect their choice of desirable strategies and information. To test this possibility, we changed the map size to make the agents search in broader ranges for cells that have demand, and re-ran the simulation. We increased the map size from 20 by 20 to 30 by 30, 40 by 40, and 50 by 50.

One noticeable change is that severity-based response is far more effective than other two strategies over all ranges of sizes. In contrast, the blind search and time-based strategies do not show any differences in either the paired t-test or multiple comparison results. The differences come from the risk of time-based response. If agents have to search wider ranges for demand, a time-based response strategy does not enable them to reallocate resources flexibly to newly emerging damage. Even if agents have sufficient resources to respond to other heavily damaged sites, they are usually locked-in to a small area of damage.

The simulation results suggest two important conclusions. First, information contributes to increasing the efficiency of response activities. Utilizing the two basic types of information, time and severity, yields far better results than blind response. However, the actual contribution of information depends on the situation. Even though knowledge of the time of occurrence for incidents provides valuable cues for response operations, these cues may misguide the agents' response under successive incidents within a wider geographic area. Thus, the essential factor in increasing coordination in disaster management is not only to provide information to response agents, but also to identify the core information, including severity and time of incident, and share it with others.

Conclusions and further discussion

Based on our agent-based simulation, we developed a preliminary model of the dynamics of disaster response operations. We argue that different phases of disaster response require different types of information, equipment, and management skills. The interesting finding is the positive relation between the number of jurisdictions involved and the efficiency of disaster response operations. This finding is counterintuitive to the general observation from practice that efficiency drops as the number of jurisdictions involved in response operations increases. The intervening factor appears to be identifying the critical nodes through which core information is exchanged; that is, verifying the small number of links that are used to communicate critical information under urgent conditions. This finding is consistent with the small world analytic framework(Milgram, 1967). The degree of change and the direction of influence in this process need to be studied further in a more fully developed simulation of this pattern.

Finally, we explored different strategies of seeking coordination among agents. When we simulated different strategies of response based on types of information available to the agents, the factors of access, timeliness, and severity of incident demonstrated increasing efficiency in the agents' response.

This research represents an initial phase in the construction of a computational model of rapidly evolving disaster response systems. The structure and content of information exchange, communication, and timeliness in coordination processes will be further analyzed to explore the dynamics of evolving networks. Acknowledging its limitations, computational simulation nonetheless is an invaluable tool for analyzing the complex activities of disaster response. This simulation method can fill an important gap between qualitative and empirical studies of rapidly evolving response systems.

Acknowledgements

We acknowledge, with thanks and appreciation, the support of our colleagues, John R. Harrald, Julie Ryan and their research staff at the Institute of Crisis, Disaster, and Risk Management at George Washington University, Washington, DC in the conduct of this research. This research was supported in part by National Science Foundation grant #CMS0219953, "Terrorism and Corporate Crisis Management: The Strategic Effect of the September 11 Attacks." An earlier version of this paper was published as "Coordination in Rapidly Evolving Systems: The Role of Information." 2004. *American Behavioral Scientist*. Vol. 48, No. 3 (November): pp. 295-313.

A simulation analysis for pedestrian flow management

Toshiyuki Kaneda[1], Tomohiko Suzuki[1]

[1]Nagoya Institute of Technology, Gokiso, Showa, Nagoya 466-8555, Japan

Summary. An agent simulation test model for pedestrian flow has already been developed, but an experimental simulation that incorporates actual data about an accident has not been designed. In our research, we have reconstructed this accident by improving an existing test model. Based on the accident report and using data gained through spatial research we have revised a pedestrian flow simulator. Through a simulation analysis including rows of standing people and the confrontation of the ascent and descent flows, we have explored measures to prevent a pedestrian accident. The ASPF is to assess measures for managing pedestrian flows by focusing on the domino risk rather than a reconstruction of crowd collapse as in the overpass accident. The simulation results show that a two-way flow, combined with stationary people can trigger an accident even on an overpass that satisfies present design standards. Moreover, we have confirmed that even simple traffic regulations such as partitions can be an effective measure to prevent a pedestrian accident.

Key words. Agent-Based Simulation, Pedestrian Flow, Accident Analysis

1. Introduction

An agent simulation test model for pedestrian flow has already been developed (Kaneda, et.al, (2002)), but an experimental simulation that incorporates actual data about an accident has not been designed. On 21 July 2001, 11 people were killed and 247 injured on the Asagiri Station Pedestrian Overpass. The overpass was near the venue for a fireworks display and this tragic disaster occurred when visitors gathering to view the fireworks were caught up in an uncontrollable rush and the crowd collapsed. In January 2002, the official Accident Investigation Report (Akashi City, (2002)) was released and detailed accident information was revealed.

In our research, we have reconstructed this accident by improving an existing test model. Based on the accident report and using data gained through academic spatial researches we have revised a pedestrian flow simulator, and through a simulation analysis including rows of standing people and the flow coefficients of the ascent and descent flows we have explored measures to manage pedestrian flows confrontation.

2. The design principles of a simulation model to examine a pedestrian accident

In an agent simulation model of a cell automata type, discrete approximation restrictions relate to each cell space. In order to choose suitable protocols for the model, we selected relevant data from the accident report as follows (See Appendix).

The accident report concluded the cause of the accident was a phenomenon known as crowd collapse which occurred when the maximum crowd density on the pedestrian overpass reached 13 to 15 person/m^2 (C. ②). In contrast domino phenomena occur with a density of only 3 to 5 (F. ①, ②) and many such accidents have been reported in the past. In our research we assumed a density of 4 as the danger value representing congestion (D. ①). We then reconstructed the incident in our model and examined measures to manage pedestrian flows safely.

Next, we shall focus attention on ways of dealing with the flow coefficient. The Asagiri Pedestrian Overpass was designed with an evacuation plan standard of 1.5 person/m · sec, which is far higher than the design standard of 0.33 person/m · sec (A. ③④). However, both values assume a one-way flow. The flow coefficient value at the time of the accident was estimated as only 0.48 at the peak time; only about one third of the maximum capacity (D. ①) and in spite of this low value, the accident still occurred.

The accident report states contributory factors to the accident were: 1) two counter flows meeting and becoming tangled up (F. ④), and 2) fireworks spectators blocking the area around the stairs of the pedestrian overpass (J). Our research model is therefore designed to examine the effects of these factors.

The accident report also states that effective crowd management measures were not carried out. (J. II). Our simulation experiment examines the effect of placing a partition in the middle of the pedestrian overpass.

3. The development of ASPF with an agent based approach

3.1 Revision of ASPF

It is known that existing pedestrian simulations on the cell-space adopt cellular automata (CA) models (Muramtatsu et.al (1999), Fukui, Ishibashi (1999)) or CA-derived agent models (Burstedde et.al (2001), Blue, Adler (2001)). In this study we have revised The ASPF (Agent Simulation of Pedestrian Flow, Kaneda et.al (2002)) that was implemented on a multi agent simulation software, kk-MAS.

In the ASPF spatial scale, walking spaces are represented by 40 square cm cells and the time scale is set at one step per 0.5 seconds. An L-shaped section of the accident area was modeled as follows: a space 6.8m (17 cells) wide and 40m long represents the overpass and the stairs are 3.6m (9 cells) wide and 25.6m long giving a total modeled area of 386.6m^2 (2,416 cells). This model covers approximately 50% of the usable area of the actual overpass, however, the difference between stairs has been eliminated. The basic rule is only one person may enter a cell, but in areas of high density walking, with a surrounding density of 2 or more, two persons may enter a cell at the bend of the L-shaped space, giving a possible maximum theoretical density of 12.5.

3.2 A summary of agent walking behavior rules

In our research, based on the selective report data mentioned in the previous section, we added or changed the walking behavior rules, so as to conform to this data. Fig. 1 shows the simulation algorithm of ASPF determined as a result of trial and error.

The behavior rules for each agent are applied in the following order: ① a cornering rule, ② a direction change rule and ③ a walking behavior rule (Fig. 1). There are a total of 22 walking behavior rules applied to the agents: 6 basic behavior rules, 8 rules for slowing down in response to agents, 4 rules for avoiding agents, 3 rules for high density walking and 1 reading flow rule (Fig. 2)

We will now explain the walking behavior rules in more detail.

The basic behavior rules are applied when an agent is walking in a low density situation (density 2 or less). In rules ⑤ and ⑥ the number of cells to move forward is determined by a random number.

When slowing down in response to other agents, in a low density walking situation, the agent keeps a distance from agents behind and in front. The agent is forced to slow down in response to other agents, however, in rules ⑦ to ⑪, random numbers are used to decide forward movement.

When avoiding agents, in a low density walking situation, the rules maintain a distance between agents on the left and right sides.

In a high density walking situation (density 2 or more), the rules decrease the distance between agents in front and behind, but maintain the same distance to other agents on the left and right sides.

The flow reading rule regulates whether agents follow or avoid other agents by looking at the cells to the right of the direction of flow.

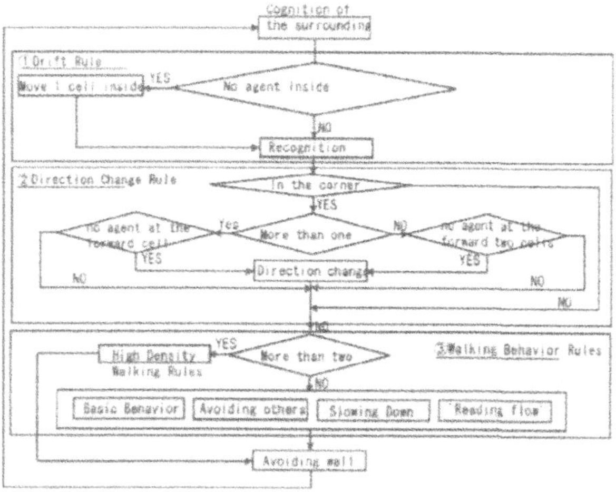

Fig. 1. Algorithm of Pedestrian Agent in ASPF

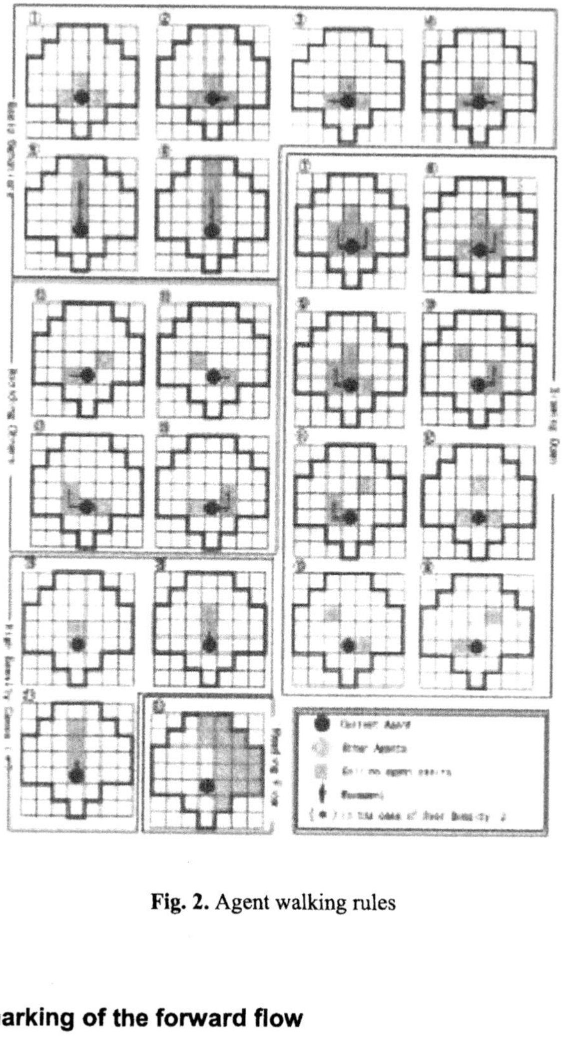

Fig. 2. Agent walking rules

3.3 Benchmarking of the forward flow

Many academic spatial researchers have examined the direction of flow and the relation between density and flow speed. Fig. 3 is a graph to show this relation (Architectural Institute of Japan (2003)). At this point we added the simulation performances of the forward flow given in ASPF to Fig. 3. The relation between density and flow speed in the revised simulation model revised gave a good approximation of the actual walking flow.

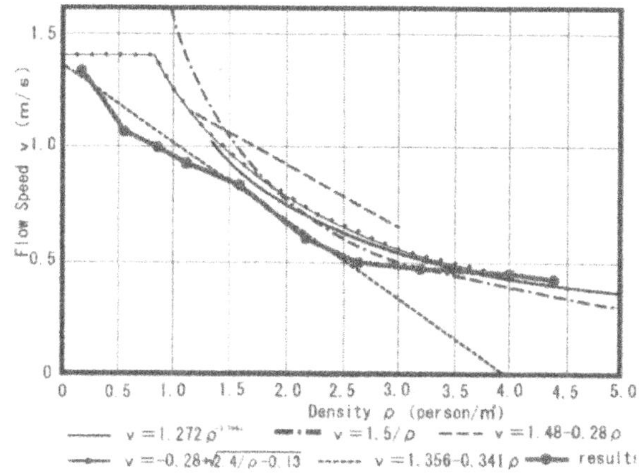

Fig. 3. Benchmarking of agent speed (forward flow)

3.4 About pedestrian's cornering behavior: 'ascent' and 'descent'

According to the accident report, the flow on the overpass from the venue to the station ('ascent' flow) shown in Fig. 4 (b) met and conflicted with the flow from the station to the venue ('descent' flow) shown in Fig. 4 (a) when moving round from the stairs to the east side of the overpass (Fig. 4 (c)). The descent flow was then pushed over to the west side and compressed. The report mentions both flows experienced friction on the north-east diagonal line from the corner between the overpass and the stairs and this situation was partly responsible for the accident (F. ④).

The micro-motive of pedestrians relating to cornering behavior can best be explained by comparing their behavior to car driving techniques. In other words, agents in the southern descent flow tend to move towards the inside (the right side of the direction of movement) and after turning right, swing over towards the outside (the left side). In this case, since there is a clear view of the south side of the stairs, this tendency naturally increases. In the same way, the ascent flow is to the east and inside (the left side), and when moving to the north, swing over towards the outside (the right side) (Fig. 4).

In order to include this cornering behavior in the simulation model, we introduced a cornering rule. This rule is applied before the direction change rule and under this rule an agent moves inside when the inside adjacent cells are vacant.

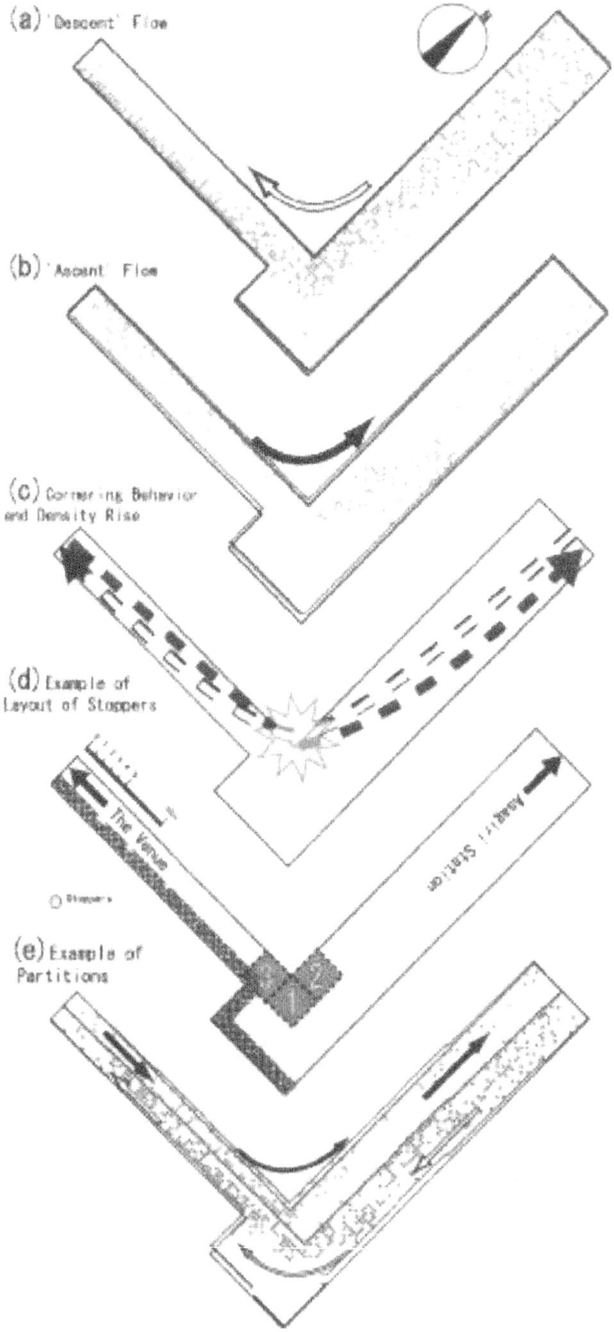

Fig. 4. Spatial model and density distributions

4. A simulation analysis by using the ASPF

4.1 Summary of the simulation experiment

The accident report mentioned the existence of these two counter flows and the occupation of space by standing people, however, it did not estimate any figures for either situation. In our research we conducted a simulation experiment to determine both the numbers standing and also those involved in the counter flows.

For this simulation, we combined five flow coefficients 0, 0.5, 1.0, 1.5, 2.0 for each ascent and descent flow, and 6 layouts for standing people (hereinafter referred to as 'stoppers'), a baseline case (no 'stopper'), 2, 3, 4, 5 rows and traffic regulations (Fig. 4 (d), (e)).

(Earlier some coefficients even with no stoppers gave an extremely high density increase and after stoppers were included, we decided not to use these coefficients).

Fig. 4 (d) shows three areas of high density measurements that correspond to areas on the accident report map, where there was a high concentration of fallen people. Area 2 is mentioned in the report as the place where the crowd collapse occurred.

In the simulation experiment we used a step value of 200 (100 seconds) and this gave a constant number of agents and density for each area. Experimental results were obtained by calculating the average of 5 or 10 simulations.

The traffic regulation shown in Fig. 4 (e) is a spatial model where ascent and descent flows are separated by installing a partition in the middle of the agent's walking space.

4.2 Simulation results and analysis

Fig. 5 shows the simulation results. With a one-way flow, some cases exceeded the danger value in area 2 ($\alpha = 2.0$, $\beta = 0$), but all the other cases were below the danger threshold. These results clearly show that Asagiri Pedestrian Overpass satisfied an evacuation plan standard of 1.5.

In the case of a two-way flow, an increase of density can be seen compared with a one-way flow. In particular, in the case of $\alpha = 1.5$ or more, this tendency is very noticeable. In the case of $\alpha = 1.5$, $\beta = 0.5$, some areas exceeded the danger value. In the case of $\alpha = 1.5$ or more, the density of area 2 is higher than that of area 2 or 3. It can also be seen that the increase of density in area 2 ripples out and through to area 1 and 3.

Next, we focus on the number of stoppers rows. The stoppers differ depending on the scale of the flow coefficients, where both flow coefficients are small (giving a combined total of 2 or less), the increase of density in area 3 is more marked than in area 1 or 2. This indicates that stoppers are responsible for the increase in density in area 3. When both flow coefficients α and β are large, the reverse is seen, the density in area 1 or 2 becomes higher than in area 3. The density increase in area 3 appears to cause the density increase in area 1 and 2.

When we introduced a partition to regulate the flow of traffic, the number of cases showing danger values was reduced. For example, in the case of $\alpha = 1.5$, $\beta = 0.5$, the density of area 2 became 25% of the baseline case with no regulation. This demonstrates that the congestion mechanism that caused the spread from area 2 was eliminated by the introduction of traffic regulation. However, with traffic regulation, when the flow coefficients of ascent and descent flow are small, the path width for agents is set and naturally the density tended to be higher compared to no traffic regulation.

5. Conclusion

In this research we have reported the development of the ASPF incorporating information from both the accident report and spatial research. The ASPF has explored measures to prevent an accident by focusing on the domino risk rather than a reconstruction of crowd collapse as in the overpass accident. The simulation results show that a two-way flow, combined with stationary people can trigger an accident even on an overpass that satisfies present design standards. Moreover, we have confirmed that even simple traffic regulations such as partitions can be an effective measure to prevent a pedestrian accident. The results of our simulation underline the highly practical application of ASPF.

References

Akashi City Summer Festival Accident Investigation Committee (January 2002), Accident Investigation Report on the Firework Festival at the 32nd Akashi City Summer Festival

Architectural Institute of Japan (2003), Compilation Data for Architectural Design (Human Being), Maruzen Co., Ltd.

Blue, V. J and Adler, J. L. (2001), Cellular automata microsimulation for modeling bi-directional pedestrian walkways, Transportation Research B, 35, 293/312.

Burstedde, C., Klauck, K., Schadschneider, A. and Zittarz, J. (2001), Simulation of pedestrian dynamics using a two-dimensional cellular automaton, Physica A, 295, 507/525.

Fukui, M. and Ishibashi, Y.(1999), Self-Organized Phase Transitions in Cellular Automaton Models for Pedestrians, Journal of the Physical Society of Japan, 65-8, 2861/2863.

Institute for Fire Safety & Disaster Preparedness (1987), Comprehensive List for Local Disaster Preparations Data (Local Evacuation)

Japan Road Association (January 1979), Three-dimensional Crossing Technical Standards

Kaneda, T, Yano, H, Misaka, T, Suzuki, T and Yamada,T (2002), A Study on Pedestrian Flow by Using an Agent Model—A Simulation Analysis on Asagiri Overpass Accident 2001, T. Terano, H. Deguchi, K. Takadama (Eds) SPRINGER, Meeting the Challenge of Social Problems via Agent-Base Simulation

Muramatsu, M., Irie T., and Nagatani, T.(1999), Jamming Transition in Pedestrian Counter flow, Physica A, 267, 487/498.

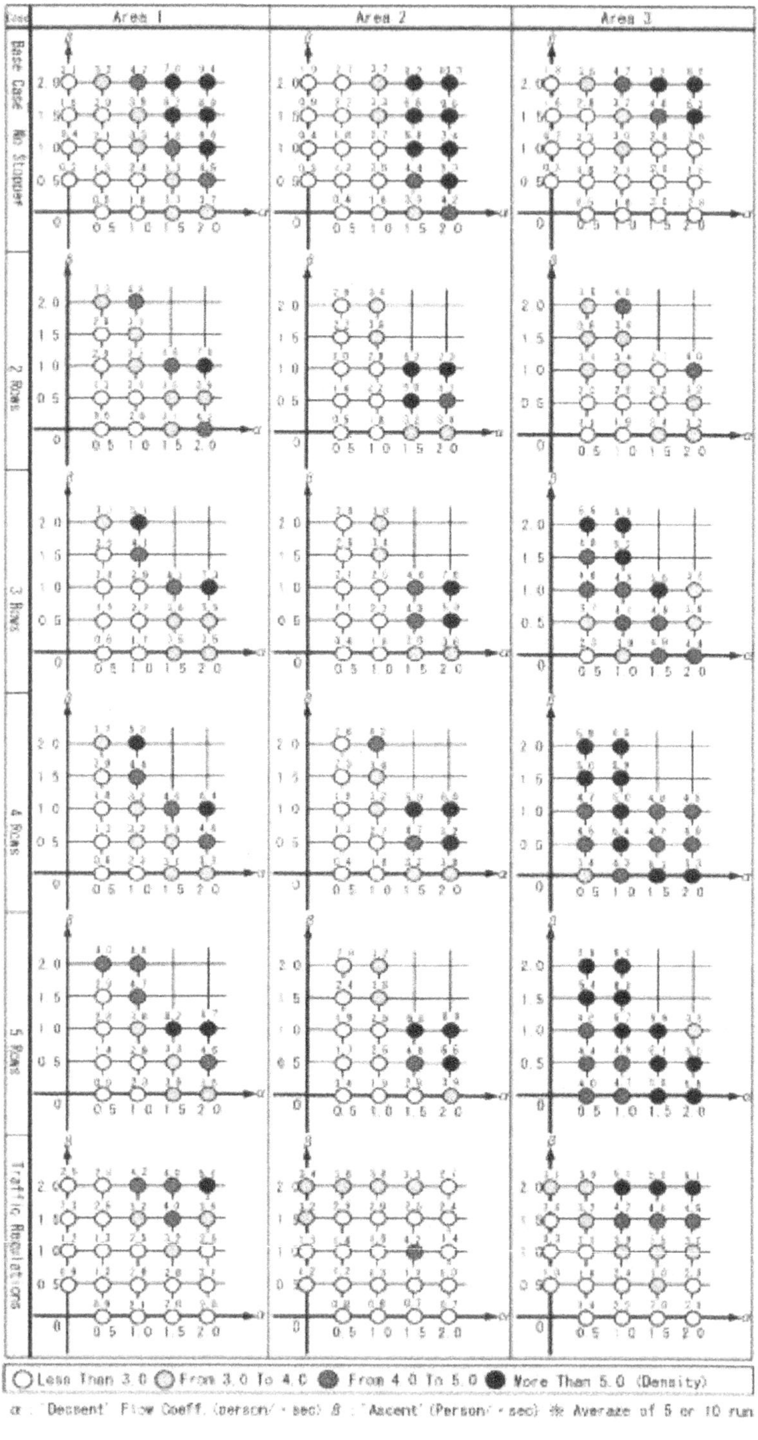

Fig. 5. Simulation results

Appendix .

	Accident Report	Page	Additional Explanations
A. Asagiri Pedestrian Overpass: structure and dimensions	①Overpass: 6m wide, stairs: 3m wide → a bottleneck creating congestion.	4-7 29	Arch action: data from a bearing experiment gives a figure of 6 diameters for the width of an exit, → allowing 35cm for a human being gives a figure of 2.1m for the width.
	②Designed based on a maximum estimate of 14,400 pedestrians per day.	29	
	③ Peak time pedestrian traffic volume is calculated at 50% of the daily maximum i.e. 7,200.	Reference 236	7,200 person/hour = 120 person/minute = 2 person/second 2 person/sec ÷ 6m = 0.33 person/m·sec
	④On the stairs a pedestrian flow of 1.3 person/m·sec is possible. 1.3 person/m·sec × 3,600sec × 3m = 14,040 = about 14,000 →as congestion increases, the flow slows and numbers decrease.	29	The flow coefficient limit at the stairs are ascent: 1.1 - 1.2 person/m·sec descent: 1.4 - 1.5 person/m·sec Evacuation plan: 1.3 person/m·sec【B】: p. 129】
	⑤Usable area: 750m^2	85	Model area: 386.56m^2
B. The number of visitors	① Plans were made for an estimated 120,000 to 150,000. The actual number at peak time was 83,000.	84	The number of visitors were counted from photographs of the event, estimates were made for children who would not have been visible because of their height.
	②The night stalls covered an area of 2,700m^2 with a density of 7 person/m^2 (classified as an area of restricted movement).	84 85	
C. The number of people on the overpass	①By calculating a) the difference between inflow and outflow, b) the pedestrian walking speed and c) the relation between crowd density and the degree of crowding an estimated 6,400 to 6,500 people stayed on the overpass.	86-94	Maximum number of stationary people: 2,438 in the model + 3,337 in the virtual space = 5,775 ≒6,000 At least 6,400 stayed on the overpass and this is taken as the maximum number present on the overpass.
	② With 6,400 staying, this gives an average density of 9 - 10 person/m^2 and at the south side a high density of 13 - 15 person/m^2	94	The limit of crowd density is 17 person/m^2 on the diagram, but no allowance has been made for a planning density greater than 10 person/m^2. 【B】:p. 135】
D. Inflow and outflow	① Pedestrian inflow at peak time (173 person/min between 19:00 and 19:30 → 173 ÷ 60 ÷ 6 = 0.48 person/m·sec) The maximum passing capacity of the overpass is 540 person/min (width 6m × the flow coefficient of the horizontal part 1.5 person/m·sec × 60sec) Even at this peak time the value is around one thirds of the capacity limit and visitors enter easily.	88	With a pedestrian flow density of 0.5 - 4 person/m^2 the maximum flow coefficient of 1 person/m sec does not allow people to overtake.【B】:p. 128】 With about 4 person/m^2 flow becomes congested and planners would allow for the flow to stop and pedestrians to become stationary.【B】:p. 128】
	②The stairs have a capacity of 3m (270 person/min) 3 m × 1.5 person/m sec × 60 sec = 270 person/min With only 173 person/min, pedestrian flow should be good. The southernmost area of the overpass and the south side of the stairs have a good view of the fireworks. →People stopped walking and congestion occurred in the area of the night stalls. →A restriction in the number of people who could use the stairs, gradually decreasing from 120 person/min at peak time.	89	The flow coefficient limit at the exit for the evacuation plan is 1.5 person/m·sec【B】:p. 129】 The flow coefficient limit at the stairs are: ascent: 1.1 - 1.2 person/m·sec, descent: 1.4 - 1.5 person/m·sec. Evacuation plan: 1.3 person/m·sec【B】: p. 129】 3 m×1.3 person/m·sec × 60sec = 234 person/min
E. Crowd classification and density	Data from a crowd pressure experiment 3 - 5 person/m^2 Pedestrians can walk at a normal speed. 7 - 7.5 person/m^2 Pedestrians have contact with their shoulders and elbows, but they can move between each other and still raise and lower their hands. 10 - 11 person/m^2 Pedestrians at the front are pushed by those at the back and the walking speed decreases to a 1/2 or a 1/3 12 ± person/m^2 Pedestrians are pushed and start to stack up and cannot move forward. 12 - 13 person/m^2 No free movement, pressure from all sides 13 - 16 person/m^2 Intense painful pressure and distress	93	Service standard of horizontal pass and stairs【B】: p. 129】 Level of crowd density【B】:p. 135】 The limit of crowd density is 17 person/m^2 on the diagram, but no allowance has been made for a planning density greater than 10 person/m^2【B】:p. 135】 The relation between crowd density and pressure【B】:p. 135】 The walking speed limit for a crowd is 1.1 - 1.2 m/sec, when the crowd density exceeds 1.5 person/m^2, free walking is restricted.【C】:p. 94】
F. The mechanism of a pedestrian accident	①Dominoes: falling down in a line from the back to the front Dominoes: falling down in one direction	107	Dominoes' density: 3 - 5 person/m^2
	②Crowd collapse: falling down from the front to the back Crowd collapse: falling down in clusters in all directions	107	Crowd collapse density: 10 or more person/m^2

Table.1 Description on the accident report

F. The mechanism of a pedestrian accident	③Key features of crowd collapse: 1) an arch formation 2) a people-free void 3) strong crowd pressure from the back	107-108	When congestion first occurs in a crowd with an initial high walking speed, the front is pushed by the back and crushed resulting in a domino effect, an arch formation and finally crowd collapse. 【C) : p. 91】
	④A cause of crowd collapse: tangling of counter flows The flow from the venue to the station conflicted with the flow from the station to the venue when moving round from the stairs to the east side of the overpass. The flow from the station to the venue was pushed to the west side and compressed. Both flows experienced friction on the north-east diagonal line from the corner between the overpass and the stairs.	108	Crowd walking speed (m/sec): counter flow 1.1 (m/sec), crossing flow 1.0 (m/sec), interflow 0.7 (m/sec)【C) : p. 97～98】 The flow from the venue to the station met the flow from the station to the venue causing compression and further increasing the crowd density in the area the crowd collapse occurred. Crowd jostling, shoving and pushing at the point of conflict triggered a pressure wave through the crowd.
	⑤A cause of crowd collapse: a wave of crowd pressure This wave of crowd pressure was repeated several times with the weight of many people being added, until the wave pressure was strong enough to destroy the arch formation and the crowd collapse occurred.	108-109	
	⑥A cause of crowd collapse: small clusters of pedestrians falling down Several clusters of pedestrians fell down in a series of accidents. Several cluster incidents, both large and small occurred in this overcrowded situation.	109	
G. The place and area where the accident occurred	to the station and 6m wide from the east to the west of the overpass, with a concentration in the area from the southernmost part to 23m north. Firstly the collapse occurred in the southwestern most area and then spread on a north-eastern diagonal to a point about 5m from the southernmost side of the overpass. Small scale crowd falling down accidents occurred at two points 30m and 50m from the southernmost side of the overpass.	110-111	The southwestern most part→model measurement area 2
H. The number of people involved in the accident	According to calculations for the central area 20 to 30m² × 13 to 15 person/m², about 300 to 400 people were involved in the accident.	112	
I. Speculation on possible causes	The crowd collapse was caused by a high crowd density that exceeded safety limits and the creation of a space within the crowd triggered the crowd collapse. The formation of counter flows and waves of crowd pressure contributed to the crowd collapse.		
J. Over-crowding	Ⅰ) A bottleneck was created around the stairs at the southernmost part of the overpass. Ⅱ) Effective crowd control measures such as a divided entrance were not put in place.	112	In particular, for I, the following causes are given: the 3m wide stairs were very narrow compared to the 6m wide overpass; the spectators occupied the space on the overpass and stairs to view the fireworks display; and the night stalls were arranged in close proximity to the stairs and their customers blocked the free passage of visitors coming down the stairs. The placement of the night stalls created a potential bottleneck, which then led to the crowd congestion.
K. Creation of a space	①Falling down or crouching, particularly children ②Stepping back and drawing back by the crowd. ③Destruction of the fence at the west end.	112-113	
L. Structure	The ratio of the number of children of elementary age or less was 26%.	Reference 251	

※A) B) C) is 2) 3) 4) in the references

Table.1 Description on the accident report (cont.)

Effects of structural and behavioral strategies toward the environmentally conscious society: agent-based approach

Keiko Zaima[1]

[1]College of Commerce, Senshu University, 2-1-1, Higashimita, Tama-ku, Kawasaki, Kanagawa, 214-8580, Japan

Summary. This paper is intended as an investigation of effects of two kinds of environmental strategies using agent-based simulation. One is structural strategy to firms such as negative sanction to environmentally non-improving firms and positive sanction to improving firms. The other is behavioral strategy to consumers such as communication to modify ways of action. The results showed that behavioral strategy was also very important for the environmental policy design.

Key words. Environmental strategy, Social dilemma, Agent-based model

1. Introduction

The white paper, *Quality of the Environment in Japan 2003*, points out that an increase in environmental burdens is partly caused by piling individual action. For example, the emission of carbon dioxide is increasing in the household sector.

There are even a lot of people who understand the importance of the environment when he or she doesn't take any action for the environmental preservation. Such a phenomenon is called the gap between attitude and action. This is caused by the profit structure of social dilemmas. If all individuals choose cooperative behavior, every individual acquires larger profit. For individuals, however, environmental defective behavior brings larger profit than environmental cooperative action. As a result, individuals tend to choose defective behavior.

To solve social dilemmas, there are two types of strategies. One is structural strategy and the other is psychological or behavioral strategy (Dawes (1980)). The former involves punishment to defective behavior and reward to cooperative behavior. The latter involves communication to improve knowledge, trust and moral, through working upon internal factors of individuals.

Most of environmental policies are categorized in structural strategies and economic theoretical analyses on environmental policies have also focused on them. Its main reason is that economic theoretical models exclude internal or psychological factors of individuals.

The purposes of this paper are to introduce psychological factors into economic models, to construct an agent-based model based on it, and to examine the effects of environmental structural strategies to firms and behavioral strategies to consumers. Our model is based on Zaima (2003, 2005), which examines effects of environmental policies for the diffusion of environmental conscious products.

The plan of this paper is following. In the next section, we introduce a scheme shown by Hirose (1995) on environmental conscious behavior and construct a conceptual model of agent. In section 3, we apply it into economic model. In section 4 we show simulation results of the basic model. Section 5 examines the effects of structural strategies to firms and section 6 examines the effects of behavioral strategies to consumers. Section 7 concludes the paper.

2. Outlines of agent model

2.1 Hirose scheme

Hirose (1995) presents a psychological scheme of attitude and action concerning environmental consideration. Figure 1 shows Hirose scheme.

Hirose scheme involves two processes. One is a stage until an individual forms the attitude of environmental consideration. Another one is a stage until the individual forms the action of environmental consideration.

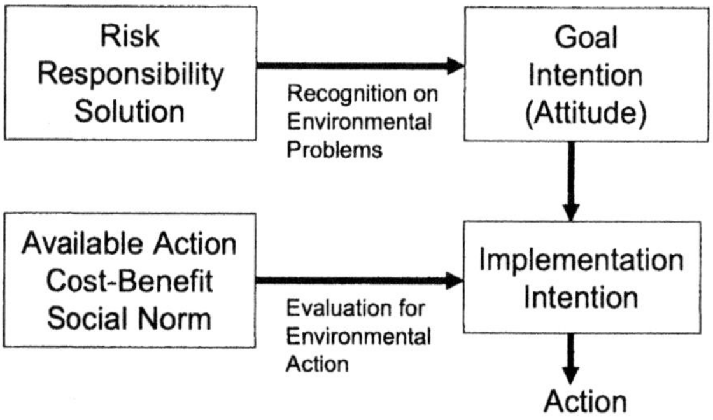

Fig. 1. Hirose scheme on attitude and action for environmental conservation.

In the process of attitude formation, it is necessary of an individual to recognize three factors on environmental problems. They are "risk," "responsibility," and "solution". The recognition of risk means that an individual knows how serious the environmental problems are. The recognition of responsibility means that an individual knows who caused environmental destruction. The recognition of solution means that an individual knows that certain actions can solve the problems.

In the process of action formation, it is necessary of an individual to evaluate three factors on the environmental conscious action. They are "available action," "cost-benefit," and "social norm". The evaluation of available action means that an individual understands which action can be available and practicable to solve the environmental problem. The evaluation of cost-benefit means that an individual considers whether the benefit of an action exceeds the cost of the action. The evaluation of social norm means that an individual considers whether others in the society take the same action or not.

2.2 Conceptual model of agent

From Hirose scheme, we can schematize a conceptual model of agent as a goal-seeking open system, as shown in Fig. 2.

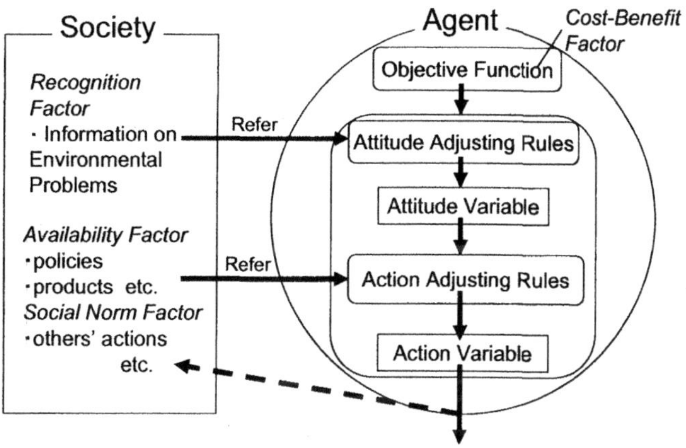

Fig. 2. Conceptual model of agent based on Hirose scheme.

Agent has an internal model consisting of two processes. One process is attitude formation and the other is action formation. In each process, agent refers the society and decide attitude or action variable by its own rules. Agent evaluates its action using objective function. In our model, we introduce a learning process among agents. Agents refer internal models each other and learn more profitable rules.

3. The basic model

In this section we apply the conceptual model shown in Fig. 2 into the economic model concerning the diffusion of environmental conscious products. Our basic model is an extension of Zaima (2003, 2005).

3.1 Society and market

Consider a society, consisting of two classes of autonomous agents. One class is consumers' and the other is firms'. The populations are n and m, respectively. Subscripts "*ci*" and "*fj*" represent the *i*-th consumer and the *j*-th firm, respectively.

In this society, there exists a market of one kind of products. The products can be differentiated on environmental aspects. The environmental quality of products is called "environmental quality level" or "quality level". The quality level of a product is represented as q. The value of q is zero or positive integer not exceeding q^*, that is, $0 \leq q \leq q^*$.

The price of the product with environmental quality level q is given by the equation (1).

$$p(q) = p_0(1 + p_1 q) \tag{1}$$

In the equation, p_0 and p_1 are parameters of positive real number. By the above definition, the price is assumed to increase as the environmental quality level is improved.

3.2 Social macro index of the environmental conservation

In this model, we define the macro value to capture the environmental conservation of the society at any time t as the following (2), considering that the consumption of higher quality products are better for the environmental conservation.

$$E(t) = \sum_q qX_q(t) \tag{2}$$

Here, $X_q(t)$ is aggregated demand of products with environmental quality level q at time t. The maximum value E^* of the environmental conservation in the society is determined by the equation (3).

$$E^* = q^* X_{q^*,n} \tag{3}$$

$X_{q^*,n}$ is the aggregated demand where all consumers in the society demand products with highest quality level q^*.

We define the macro index of the environmental conservation of the society as the equation (4).

$$\varepsilon(t) = E(t)/E^* \tag{4}$$

3.3 Firm's behavior

At any time each firm adjusts the quality level to supply the market, considering market information. The quality level of products supplied by the j-th firm at time t is $q_{fj}(t)$. Any firm should invest in environmental facilities when the environmental quality of products is upgraded. The environmental quality can be graded down or be kept the same level without any cost. The cost function $C_{fj}(t)$ of the j-th firm is defined as follows.

$$C_{fj}(t)=D_{fj}(t)c_0(1-r_{fG}(t))(1-\varepsilon(t-1))+c_1(1-\varepsilon(t-1)q_{fj}(t))y_{fj}(t) \tag{5}$$

The first term is the fixed cost of environmental investment. The parameter c_0 is a base cost of investment and positive real value. The variable $D_{fj}(t)$ is a dummy variable. The dummy variable is set to 1 when the firm upgrades the quality and is set to 0 for other cases. The variable $r_{fG}(t)$ is the green firm rate at time t, which is the rate of green firms whose quality levels to supply are higher than the certain level $q^\wedge$. The green firm rate is defined as follows.

$$r_{fG}(t)=M(t)_{q\geq q^\wedge}/m \tag{6}$$

Here, $M(t)_{q\geq q^\wedge}$ is the number of firms who supply the products with not less than the level $q^\wedge$.

The first term of the equation (5) means that the environmental investment cost becomes lower as green firms increase and the macro level of environmental conservation is higher.

The second term of the equation (5) is the variable cost of production. The parameter c_1 is a unit cost of production and positive real number. The variable $y_{fj}(t)$ represents the production volume of the j-th firm at time t. The second term means that the variable cost becomes lower as the environmental quality improves and the macro level of environmental conservation is higher. We assume that c_0 is enough larger than c_1. This means that improvement of the environmental performance needs large initial costs but it is possible that high quality firms need less cost than low quality firms for long run.

Each firm refers two kinds of market information and adjusts the quality level. This adjusting process is the same as Zaima (2003, 2005). For details, see them.

One is the information concerning consumers' needs. The consumers' needs is represented as the average level of environmental consciousness of the consumer, $S_{avr}(t)$, defined in the next section. The other is the information concerning other firms' behavior in the society. It is assumed that firms know the average level of environmental quality of the firm, $Q_{avr}(t)$, defined as equation (7).

$$Q_{avr}(t)=\sum q_{fj}(t)/m \tag{7}$$

Each firm takes the differences of $\Delta_{1,fj}(t)$ and $\Delta_{2,fj}(t)$, defined by the equations (8) and (9), into account.

$$\Delta_{1,fj}(t) = q_{fj}(t) - S_{avr}(t) \tag{8}$$

$$\Delta_{2,fj}(t) = q_{fj}(t) - Q_{avr}(t) \tag{9}$$

At any time, each firm finds the situation that it faces in the market, according to those values.

Each firm decides the way to adjust its environmental quality level, considering the situation. There are three ways to adjust quality levels, i.e. to upgrade by 1 level, to keep the same level, and to grade down by 1 level. Each firm has a set of rules, called "gene," which determines one adjusting way to each one of situations.

At any time each firm decides the adjusting value $d_{fj}(t)$ according to its own gene and adjusts its quality level of products.

$$q_{fj}(t+1) = q_{fj}(t) + d_{fj}(t) \tag{10}$$

The volume of products supplied by the j-th firm, $y_{fj}(t)$, whose quality level $q_{fj}(t)$ is q, is determined as the equation (11).

$$y_{fj}(t) = X_q(t)/M_q(t) \tag{11}$$

The variable $X_q(t)$ is the aggregated demand of products with level q, and the variable $M_q(t)$ is the number of firms who supply the products of level q.

The profit $\pi_{fj}(t)$ is defined by the equation (12).

$$\pi_{fj}(t) = p(q_{fj}(t))y_{fj}(t) - C_{fj}(t) \tag{12}$$

Every v turn, each firm refers each other, learns more profitable gene and selects a new gene. The fitness function of the learning is aggregated profit given as (13). This learning process of gene selection is described as genetic algorithms.

$$\Pi_{jf}(t) = \sum \pi_{fj}(t) \tag{13}$$

The outline of firm's behavior is schematized in the previous version of this paper (Zaima (2004)).

3.4 Consumer's behavior

Each consumer has its own environmental consciousness. The intensity of environmental consciousness is called "environmental conscious level" or "conscious level" and is written as $s_{ci}(t)$ at time t. The range of conscious levels is the same as that of quality levels of products. Each consumer takes action for the environment according to its conscious level. When a consumer has no concern about the environmental problems, the conscious level is the lowest level 0 and the consumer takes no action for the environment..

The environmental action cost of the i-th consumer $A_{ci}(t)$ is given as follows.

$$A_{ci}(t) = a_0 s_{ci}(t)(1 - r_{cG}(t))(1 - \varepsilon(t-1)) \tag{14}$$

Here the parameter a_0 is a unit cost and positive real number. The variable $r_{cG}(t)$ is the green consumer rate at time t, which is the rate of green consumers whose environmental conscious levels are higher than the certain level $q^\wedge$. The green consumer rate is defined by the following (15).

$$r_{cG}(t) = N_{s \geq q^\wedge}(t)/n \tag{15}$$

$N_{s \geq q^\wedge}(t)$ is the number of consumer whose conscious level is not less than $q^\wedge$.

The equation (14) means that environmental action cost becomes larger as the environmental conscious level is higher, but that the cost can be reduced as the green consumer rate increases and the macro level of the environmental conservation is improved.

It is assumed that consumers are eager to buy products according to their environmental conscious levels. They choose the maximum quality level of the products not exceeding their conscious levels. If they find no products with such levels in the market, they select the minimum quality level of products above their conscious levels. The level of the product selected by the i-th consumer is $q_{ci}(t)$.

The demand of the i-th consumer, $x_{ci}(t)$, is calculated as the equation (16).

$$x_{ci}(t) = (I - A_{ci}(t))/p(q_{ci}(t)) \tag{16}$$

The parameter I represents income and it is a constant, for simplicity.

The utility function of the i-th consumer, $u_{ci}(t)$, is defined as (17).

$$u_{ci}(t) = w_0(1 + w_1 q_{ci}(t))x_{ci}(t) \tag{17}$$

Here, the parameters w_0 and w_1 are positive real numbers. This equation means that utility of consumers becomes larger as the volume of consumption is larger and the environmental quality level of products is higher. The above utility function has a structure of social dilemmas, as explained by Zaima (2005).

Each consumer refers other consumers' behavior in the society and adjusts the quality level. Consumers know the average of environmental conscious levels of the consumer, $S_{avr}(t)$, which is defined as follows.

$$S_{avr}(t) = \sum s_{ci}(t)/n \tag{18}$$

Each consumer takes the differences of $\Delta_{1,ci}(t)$ and $\Delta_{2,ci}(t)$, defined by the equations (19) and (20) into account.

$$\Delta_{1,ci}(t) = s_{ci}(t) - q_{ci}(t) \tag{19}$$

$$\Delta_{2,ci}(t) = s_{ci}(t) - S_{avr}(t) \tag{20}$$

The adjusting process and learning process is the same as firms' behavior. The fitness function $U_{ci}(t)$ of the learning process is given as the following (21).

$$U_{ci}(t) = \sum u_{ci}(t) \tag{21}$$

The outline of consumer's behavior is schematized in the previous version of this paper (Zaima (2004)).

4 Simulation results of the basic model

The set of parameters used in the simulation are shown in Table 1.

Table 1. Values of parameters used in the simulations.

Population	Consumer n=1000, Firm m=100
Production Function	c_0=100, c_1=1.0
Price Function	p_0 =2.0, p_1=0.1
Green Agent Level	q^=10
Environmental Action Cost Function	a_0=0.5
Income of Consumer	I =30
Utility Function	w_0=1.0, w_1=0.05
Cycles of Learning	v=5 Iteration Times 200
Maximum Level	q*=19
t=0, maximum quality value =3, (random given)	

Fig. 3 shows the changes of the consumer's average conscious level and the firm's average quality level. We carried out five times per each simulation, and every simulation result shown in this paper is the average of five runs.

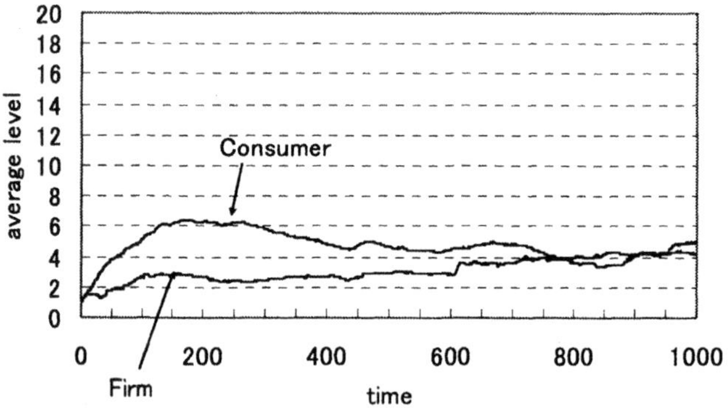

Fig. 3. Simulation result of the basic model with the parameters shown in Table 1.

The firms' average of quality level increases gradually but it doesn't reach high level. The consumer's average of conscious level gains at first, but it declines gradually at around t=200. We call this case "blank case". In the following two sections we simulate several strategies. We compare those results with this blank case to examine the effects of strategies.

5 Effects of structural strategies

As a structural strategy, we consider the external audit of environmental management systems, according to Zaima (2003, 2005).

We consider the following two situations. One is the case that auditors give negative reputation to non-improving firms publicly. And the other is the case that auditors give positive reputation to improving firms publicly.

5.1 Negative sanction to non-improving firms

Negative reputation by auditors means like penalty to the reputed firms. In the extended model, when any firm has no improvement of quality level in continuous three periods, the firm is given negative sanctions τ at the next period.

We examined three cases of τ =-40, -80 and -160. The results were similar for all cases.

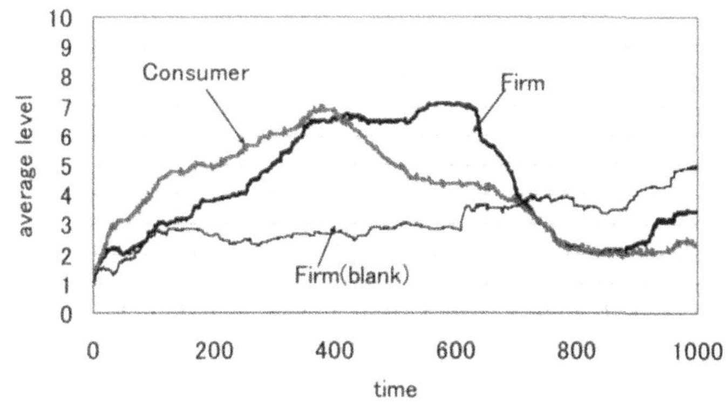

Fig. 4. Structural strategy. Case of negative sanction to non-improving firms (τ= - 80).

Fig. 4 is a case of τ = - 80. The firm's average level gains rapidly at first. But it begins to decline at around t=600, after the consumer's average decreases at around t=400. And both averages reach lower levels than the blank case. This result shows that penalty doesn't have much effect on the change of agents' behavior.

5.2 Positive sanction to improving firms

Positive reputation by auditors means like reward to the reputed firms. In the extended model, when any firm has improvement of environmental quality level in continuous three periods, the firm is given positive sanctions τ at the next period.

We examined two values of τ = +80 and +160. The results were very similar.

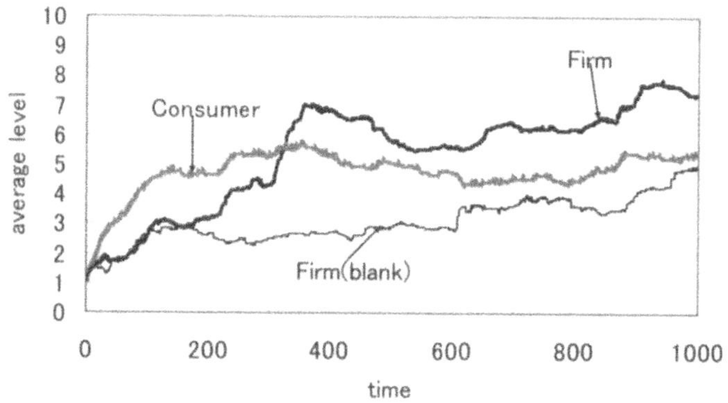

Fig. 5. Structural strategy. Case of positive sanction to improving firms (τ= + 80).

Fig.5 is a case of τ = + 80. The firm's average level gains rapidly until t=400, and then it declines. But it begins to gain at around t=600. The consumer's average also increases gradually at around t=600 according to the firm's change. This result shows that reward has effect on the change of agents' behavior.

Compared Figs. 4 and 5, we can say that positive reputation to environmentally improving firms has a certain effect as a role of external environmental audit.

6 effects of behavioral strategies

As a behavioral strategy, we consider activities of communication by environmental citizens' organizations.

In this section, we consider three situations. The first is the case that green consumers of environmental citizens' organizations give negative opinion to non-green consumers. The second is the case that green consumers give positive opinion to other green consumers. And the third is the case that green consumers persuade non-green consumers to reconsider their ways of action.

6.1 Negative opinion to non-green consumers

Consider the situation that non-green consumers who buy non-green products continuously are blamed by a part of green consumers. Negative opinion means dissatisfaction to the blamed consumers.

In the extended model, the utility of non-green consumer who buys products with the lowest level 0 in continuous 5 times is reduced according to the increase of the rate of green consumers, as the following equation.

$$u^{*}_{ci}(t) = u_{ci}(t) - u_0 r_{cG}(t) \tag{22}$$

Fig. 6 is the case of $u_0 = 10$. The consumer's average level of this case gains at around t=800, though the average of blank case doesn't gain. And the firm's average level increases according to the consumer's change. This result shows that negative opinion has effect on the change of agents' behavior.

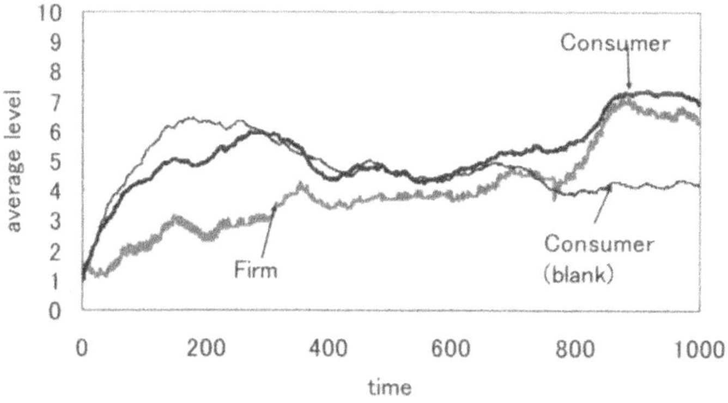

Fig. 6. Behavioral strategy. Case of negative opinion to non-green consumers.

6.2 Positive opinion to green consumers

Consider the situation that green consumers who buy green products continuously are appreciated by a part of green consumers. Positive opinion means satisfaction to the appreciated consumers.

In the extended model, the utility of green consumer who buys products with not less than 10 level in continuous 5 times is gained according to the increase of the rate of green consumers, as the following equation.

$$u_{ci}^{*}(t) = u_{ci}(t) + u_0 r_{cG}(t) \tag{23}$$

Fig. 7 is the case of $u_0 = 10$. The firm's average level rapidly increases at first, but it gradually decreases at around t=500. The consumer's average level of this case rapidly declines at around t=700 according to the firm's change. This result shows that positive opinion doesn't have effect on the change agents' behavior.

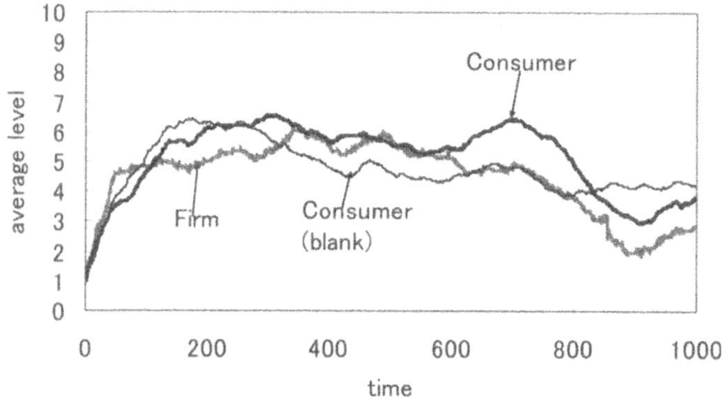

Fig. 7. Behavioral strategy. Case of positive opinion to green consumers

Compared figs.6 and 7, we can say that negative opinion to non-green consumers has a certain effect as a role of environmental citizens' organizations.

6.4 Persuasion to reconsider ways of action

Consider the situation that a part of green consumers persuades non-green consumers to reconsider ways of action.

In the extended model, a slight rate z of green consumers persuades other consumers to reconsider ways of action and to improve environmental consciousness. The rate of persuading green consumers equals $zr_{cG}(t)$. The probability with which persuaded consumers reconsider and modify their ways of action is assumed to equal $zr_{cG}(t)$. Any consumer who reconsiders by persuasion modifies its gene.

We examined three values of z= 0.01, 0.03 and 0.05. Those values mean that the percentages of green consumers who persuade other consumers are 1%, 3% and 5%, respectively.

Fig.8 shows the three cases. The consumer's average level reaches higher level as the rate of persuading green consumer increases. As a result, the firm's average reaches higher level according to the consumer's change. These results show that persuasion to change ways of action has large effect on the change of agents' behavior but that it is available only when the rate of persuading green consumers is enough large.

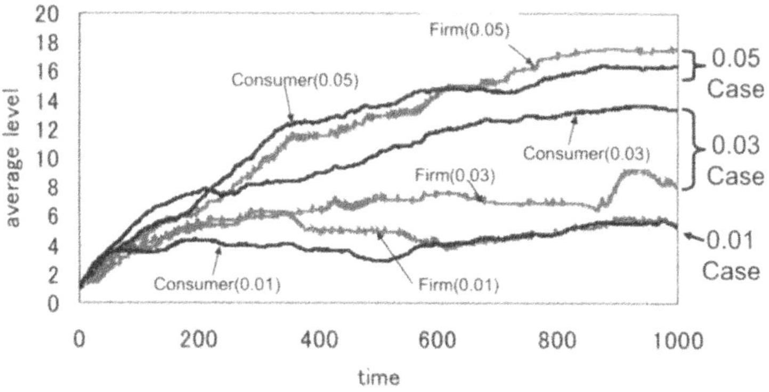

Fig. 8. Behavioral strategy. Case of persuasion in order to make non-green consumers reconsider ways of action. The values of 0.01, 0.03 and 0.05 in the figure mean that the percentages of green consumers who persuade other consumers are 1%, 3% and 5%, respectively.

7 Conclusion

In this paper, we investigated the effects of two kinds of environmental strategies using agent-based simulation. One is structural strategy to firms and the other is behavioral strategy to consumers. We developed agent-based models based on social psychological aspects and acquired the following results.

As for structural strategies, the reward effect to environmentally improving firms was larger than the penalty effect to non-improving firms. Thus we can say that positive reputation to environmentally improving firms has a certain effect as a role of external environmental audit.

As for behavioral strategies, the blame effect to non-green consumers was larger than the appreciate effect to green consumers. Thus we can say that negative opinion to non-green consumers has a certain effect as a role of environmental citizens' organizations.

We also find that persuasion to reconsider ways of action has a large effect on the change of agents' behavior when the rate of persuading green consumer is enough large.

From these results, we can conclude that not only structural strategies to firms but also behavioral strategies to consumers are really significant for the environmental policy design.

As further researches, we mention the following two problems. One is to extend our agent-based models to macroeconomic model. The other is to confirm our results with gaming simulation based on social psychological researches.

Acknowledgement

I would like to thank Prof. Hiroshi Deguchi for helpful comments on an earlier draft of this paper.

References

Dawes R. M. (1980) Social Dilemmas, Annual Review of Psychology, 31:169-193

Hirose Y (1995) Social Psychology on the Environment and Consumption (Kankyou to Shouhi no Shakai-Shinrigaku), Nagoya University Press.

Ministry of the Environment (2003) Quality of the Environment in Japan 2003,

Zaima K (2003), An Simulating Approach on R&D of Environmentally Sound Products: GS for real world grounding of ABM, International Simulation and Gaming Association (ISAGA2003), the 34th Annual Conference, August 25-29, 2003.

Zaima K (2004), Effects of Structural and Behavioral Strategies toward the Environmentally Conscious Society: Agent-Based Approach, Proceedings of The Third International Workshop on Agent-based Approaches in Economic and Social Complex Systems (AESCS'04), pp. 277-284, Pacific Asian Association for Agent Based Social Sciences, May 27-29, Kyoto University, Kyoto, 2004.

Zaima K (2005), Agent-Based Simulation on the Diffusion of R&D for Environmentally Conscious Products, Agent-Based Modeling Meets Gaming Simulation, ISAGA2003, Springer-Verlag, forthcoming.

Author Index

Keyword Index

GPSR Compliance

The European Union's (EU) General Product Safety Regulation (GPSR) is a set of rules that requires consumer products to be safe and our obligations to ensure this.

If you have any concerns about our products, you can contact us on ProductSafety@springernature.com

In case Publisher is established outside the EU, the EU authorized representative is:

Springer Nature Customer Service Center GmbH
Europaplatz 3
69115 Heidelberg, Germany

Batch number: 10755292

Printed by Printforce, the Netherlands